BY REASON OF DOUBT

BY
REASON OF DOUBT:
THE BELSHAW CASE

Ellen Godfrey

Clarke, Irwin & Company Limited, Toronto/Vancouver

Canadian Cataloguing in Publication Data

Godfrey, Ellen, 1942-
  By reason of doubt

ISBN 0-7720-1354-3

1. Belshaw, Cyril S., 1928-
2. Murder – Switzerland – Case studies.
3. Trials (Murder) — Switzerland. I. Title.

HV6535.S93G62   345.494'02523'0924   C81-094718-8

© 1981 by Ellen Godfrey
ISBN 0-7720-1354-3

1 2 3 4 5 JD 85 84 83 82 81

Printed in Canada

To Dave, Jon, Rebecca and Sam

without whose loving support I could never have written this book

Acknowledgements

I would like to thank Beryl Young, who gave me the idea for this book, and who was the first to see the potential of the mysterious disappearance in Paris.

There are a great many other people—too many to mention in fact—whose support and encouragement deserve acknowledgement. Lucinda Vardey, my agent, has backed me every inch of the way; David Cobb, Malcolm Lester and Louise Dennys made possible my trip to Switzerland and Paris. David Cobb's encouragement was the special spark which made this crucial journey possible. And without Sharon Sterling back in Canada, who kept my spirits up and did my work there, none of this would have been possible.

In Vancouver my research was greatly assisted by many friends and colleagues of the Belshaws, and by Professor Belshaw's lawyer, Harry McLaughlin. Officers of Division 1, RCMP and Mark de Weerdt in the Department of Justice, Vancouver, helped me to verify facts, and to understand the intricacies of police and judicial practices when two different countries are involved. Mike Bocking of the Vancouver *Sun* also shared his knowledge of the case with me in a very generous way.

Special thanks to Michael Wyler in Geneva, and to my brother Robert Swartz, for finding me an entrée in Switzerland at the very beginning. Also to Linda Diebel of the Vancouver *Sun* whose generosity and journalistic professionalism made my job so much easier.

Everyone in Vaud was extraordinarily kind, patient and helpful. Maître Jean-Félix Paschoud, Maître Eric Stoudmann, *Procureur-générale* Willy Heim and Inspector Nicholas Margot were most generous either in checking the manuscript for accuracy or explaining the proceedings and helping me to understand the ins and outs of the Vaudois judicial system. A special word of thanks, too, to the president of the criminal tribunal of Aigle, Jean-Pierre Guignard, who was so helpful in explaining Vaudois procedures to a Canadian more familiar with the common law.

In Paris my researches were greatly aided by my friends Geneviève and Michel Fabre and by Maître Robert Badinter.

It should be noted that a great deal of the information regarding the *instruction*, or preliminary inquiry, came from the trial itself. Also, it is important for the reader to keep in mind that the conversations quoted in the book, except where otherwise indicated, came from testimony given at the trial. This has produced the anomaly that English depositions, letters and conversations, translated into French for the trial, have here been put back into English. It follows that what is quoted will no longer be identical to the English original. A notable exception to this is the statement by Harry McLaughlin read aloud at the trial. Although a French translation was read at the trial, Mr. McLaughlin has kindly provided me with the English original, which is reproduced here.

Except where expressly mentioned in the text, the entire trial was in French. There was no transcript kept, nor written record provided. Only the judgement was later made available in writing. I took verbatim notes during the trial and later submitted the relevant portions of the manuscript to the defence and prosecution lawyers, to verify my account of what took place in court. Every attempt has been made to be as accurate as possible. In the case of the woman referred to in the text as Margery Wilson, I have used a pseudonym, and changed a few minor details which would have identified her.

I gathered a great deal more information during the course of my research than I was able to use in the book. A serious attempt has been made to recount only those things which could be verified and independently corroborated. Undoubtedly there are certain facts given and ideas expressed with which each of the various parties will disagree. But I can only assure all parties involved in the Belshaw case that I have done everything I could to be scrupulously fair.

Victoria, British Columbia
July 1981

PART ONE
MYSTERIOUS DISAPPEARANCE

1

On December 3rd, 1980, Cyril Shirley Belshaw, world-renowned anthropologist, stood at the dock in Aigle, Switzerland on trial for murder. His misfortunes were followed avidly by a hostile and sensation-hungry press in Canada, Switzerland, France and the United States.

The Belshaw case was characterized by the authorities in Switzerland as the most difficult they had seen in thirty years, and certainly it is a mystery as extraordinary as any ever dreamed up by a writer of fiction.

For Belshaw it is an ordeal which has not yet ended; there are still many unanswered questions.

What happened to Betty Belshaw? How did she die? How did she vanish completely in 200 metres on a crowded Paris street, at ten o'clock in the morning, never to be seen alive again?

Paris, like all great cities, is a maze of neighbourhoods. There are the districts brimming with history and the elegance bestowed by beautiful buildings and centuries of literature: the sixteenth district; le marais, where one sees the grand monuments of the nineteenth century; the graceful, well-proportioned streetscapes of the eighteenth district. And, like all living cities, Paris contains its seedy

neighbourhoods: the nineteenth district; the back of Montmartre—
industrial areas without distinction or grace, cluttered with little
smokeshops, dry cleaners and small snack-bistros.

There are, too, areas of Paris—particularly those near the
périphérique—strangled by great highways whose strong fingers
have throttled the breath from entire districts, leaving them lifeless
and inert.

In such a *quartier*, the twentieth, stands the Novotel Bagnolet.
The hotels of the Novotel chain are sometimes described as the
Holiday Inns of Europe. They are good, reliable, clean, and con-
veniently located to transportation—a haven for the business person,
or for those who travel for reasons other than the adventure of the
new or the delight of the senses.

It was just such a purpose which caused Cyril Belshaw, on January
7th, 1979, to telephone the Novotel Bagnolet to reserve a room for
himself and his wife for the 14th. Belshaw, an anthropology professor from the University of British Columbia (UBC), was spending
the last half of his sabbatical year with his wife in the ski resort of
Montana-Vermala in Switzerland. Betty Belshaw, herself an English
instructor at UBC, was working on a biography of Katherine Mansfield who had spent some time in Montana-Vermala in the twenties.

Their plan was to spend a week or so in Paris after the Christmas
holidays. Betty wanted to pursue her research at the Bibliothèque
Nationale. Cyril had some of his own work to attend to, and he
enjoyed travelling for its own sake. They intended to drive from
Montana-Vermala in Cyril's Citröen-Maserati, leaving on the morning of January 13th, stopping the night at a motel, the Relais PLM
Beaune, and arriving the next evening at the Novotel in Paris. The
trip was an unexceptional event in the life of this couple, to whom
Europe was a second home.

Cyril Belshaw was later to tell the story of that Paris trip many
many times. As he told it, everything began normally; there were
no indications whatsoever of what was to follow.

The Novotel Bagnolet stands like a bastard Miës Van der Rohe,
towering over a giant intricate cloverleaf at the Porte Bagnolet.
One's car leaves the A3 and is suddenly whirling about in a tracery
of concrete with twelve under- and overpasses. With skill and strong
nerves a driver can debouch practically on the ramp of the Novotel
and recover in the efficient anonymity of a first-class business hotel.

Looking back, Belshaw could remember entering the enormous characterless lobby. To his right, islands of white plastic Saarinen-imitation tables, with a little pot of daisies in the centre of each, surrounded by banquettes of orange and brown chairs, sitting on orange and brown patterned rugs. Beyond, the last diners could be seen through the glass walls, finishing a late meal in the restaurant, the Oeuf au Poule.

To his left was a fifteen-metre expanse of reception desk, set well back from the centre of the lobby. He signed his name: *Belshaw, Cyril*, on the registration form. Then, remembering a remark of Betty's about how unfair it was that it should be only the man's name, always, on the form, he added: *and Betty*. The long drive had been exhausting and the couple went immediately to their room.

The next morning the waiter brought up their two breakfasts, as is the custom in Continental hotels. Cyril explained to the waiter that Betty was in the bathroom, and told him where to set out the two breakfasts. Belshaw's French was fluent; travelling in France presented no problems for him. The leisurely breakfast was finished soon after nine, and it was time to put the day's plans into effect.

The Belshaws were people who liked to arrange things in advance; spontaneity was not their style. Betty wanted to get right to work. She was a conscientious person, liable to worry unnecessarily, and her book had been occupying her mind for some time. For the last few weeks she had been thinking about her job at the university as an English instructor. Lacking any advanced degrees, she could not rise in the University hierarchy, and by taking the year off to ac-company her husband on his sabbatical she had been obliged to abandon her largely administrative position as secretary-co-ordinator to the freshman English course. This last job had become a great burden to her, and she was glad to have a rest from its endless pressures and complications, but giving it up had caused her some regrets under the circumstances. Now her book took the place of these other, older worries. She wanted to get on with it. She wanted to obtain her reader's card and settle down to work at the Bib-liothèque Nationale, with its antiquated cataloguing system and total lack of cross-referencing.

The holidays just past had left her a little tired. She had enjoyed herself, but her nerves were frayed. Their son Adrian and his girl-friend had come from Canada to spend Christmas at the apartment in Montana-Vermala, but now the young people had gone home and she was feeling the inevitable post-holiday let-down.

At the hotel, Betty had to make sure that she had the identification necessary to get her reader's card. She checked that she had the necessary papers, her passport, and enough French francs.

As Cyril Belshaw was later to explain, there was absolutely nothing unusual in Betty's manner that morning. She seemed a little tired perhaps, a little anxious. But they discussed the day's plans in a perfectly ordinary way.

Cyril Belshaw intended to do some shopping at one of Paris' big department stores, the Galeries Lafayette. They could travel together on the same subway line. They decided that at one o'clock they would meet for an aperitif before lunch, at the pub in the Galleries Lafayette. It was the kind of companionable synthesizing of plans which their friends often remarked upon, a happy outcome of thirty-seven years of harmonious marriage. Although they were frequently separated for long periods due to the exigencies of Cyril's profession, at other times they worked side by side, dovetailing their plans.

The walk from the Novotel to the Bagnolet Métro stop was very short and extraordinarily ugly. Filthy streets and cracked sidewalks, light industry, some of it derelict, construction and tasteless new buildings blocking views. Heavy traffic, shopping plazas with no storefronts, billboards and a labyrinth of pedestrian overpasses. Dirty little squares walled with soiled concrete, rubbish everywhere, pointless graffiti. People passed each other without raising their eyes, faces closed to the ugliness, the dirt, the cold raw wind of January, the flying soot.

The Métro was a little better, brightened by huge signs in loud colours: *Nicolas le grand Champagne* and *Banque Populaire—ma banque est solide*. The white tiles were cracked and broken in places and very grimy. At Bagnolet several tracks converge and fork. One puts one's ticket in a slot and it slowly re-emerges, stamped. The subway train itself was not too bad—not nearly as noisy as London or Chicago, though not as quiet as Toronto or Montreal. The train headed downtown, its stops signalled by two dissonant tones. At Parmentier the stations began to show their age, and the posters, in a sixties' graphic style of harsh colours and static shapes seemed bright and cruel in the white artificial light. Past République, Temple, Arts et Métiers, Réamur Sebastopol. The gay colours of the Dubonnet rainbow posters glimmered and flashed by, and then—the Bourse station.

It was here, Cyril Belshaw was to explain later, at approximately 10:00 a.m., that Betty left the subway. Here she parted from her husband and came up onto the Rue Vivienne, under the grey wintry skies and into the cold wind. Perhaps she stood, for a moment, hesitating. On her right was the enormous nineteenth-century Bourse, built in the style of the temple of Vespasian at Rome: ten-metre-high Corinthian columns surrounded by black iron railings and guarded by a gendarme at the gate. From the Rue Vivienne exit it is no more than 200 metres to the front door of the Bibliothèque Nationale. The shortest route is southwest along the Rue Vivienne, right on the Rue Colbert, and then left again to the Rue Richelieu and the entrance to the Library. Or Betty might have chosen to walk northwest, along Rue du 4 Septembre, turning into the Rue des Filles St. Thomas and then to the Rue Richelieu. But whatever route she took on that January morning, she would have been surrounded by throngs of pedestrians and traffic, walking through a *quartier* teeming with life.

There are no reports of anything extraordinary happening on those particular Paris streets on January 15th, 1979. No attacks, no muggings, no robberies, no car accidents. No incidents of any kind. And yet, there, on those peaceful, very ordinary streets, in the space of 200 metres, Betty Belshaw vanished. She never arrived at the Bibliothèque Nationale; she simply disappeared.

No novelist could imagine a more bizarre opening scene than this: an ordinary middle-aged woman parts from her husband on the subway in Paris, on a winter's morning—and vanishes into thin air.

2

The disappearance of Betty Belshaw from a busy Paris street in broad daylight caused a sensation in Vancouver, the home of the Belshaws. Even before the details were known it seemed obvious that the usual explanations would not do. If Betty had been the victim of foul play it was hard to see how her attackers could have taken her, against her will, in full view of the passers-by.

And that the disappearance might have been wilful seemed equally impossible to anyone who knew Betty Belshaw. In fact, the most incomprehensible part of it all was, in a way, that *anything* mysterious or untoward should happen to her.

Betty Joy Belshaw, née Sweetman, was born in Hamilton, New Zealand, in 1921. At the age of 22 she married Cyril Shirley Belshaw, 21, from Christchurch. Thus the two began their married life in 1943, in the middle of the war. Things were easier for them than for many others during those years because Belshaw was a commissioned officer in the New Zealand defence force. He served as a District Officer and Deputy Commissioner for the Western Pacific, British Solomon Islands, for the remainder of the war.

At the end of the war Betty accompanied her husband first to the University of New Zealand and then, in 1947, to London, where he continued his studies at the London School of Economics. Betty played the traditional supporting role while Cyril studied, eventually achieving his doctorate in social anthropology in 1949. In that year their first child, Diana, was born. Cyril's thesis director was Dr. Raymond Firth, an anthropologist who was to remain a life-long friend of both Betty and Cyril and whose name would surface in the investigation that followed Betty's disappearance.

After Cyril finished his studies he took up a post as a Research Fellow at the Australian National University. During that period Cyril did field work in New Guinea, which was to be the foundation of some of his later writings.

And again, when Cyril took up a post as an assistant professor at the University of British Columbia in Vancouver, in 1953, Betty was loyally at his side. Their second child, a son, Adrian, was born that same year.

During the fifties and early sixties Cyril did a great deal of travelling. Some of this was consulting work for governments, in which case Betty stayed home, alone, with the small children. But most of it was field work in Melanesia, the South Pacific region which encompasses New Guinea, and during these periods, which could be more than a year in length, Betty accompanied Cyril.

On one such occasion, in 1958, Betty went with Cyril to the island of Viti Levu in Fiji. They had with them their two children, Diana, then 9, and Adrian, 5. For the children, of course, it must have been an adventure: travel by horseback, coconut palms, sandy beaches and coral reefs. For Betty it was a new and burdensome kind of housekeeping, dealing in an unknown language with the vicissitudes of a primitive rural life-style, strange food, thatched roofs filled with vermin, no modern sanitary conveniences, and the total lack of privacy which is the usual lot of an anthropologist and family doing field-work. Yet she rose to the occasion and later, in the dedication to *Under the Ivi Tree: Society and Economic Growth in Rural Fiji* (1964), the book which came out of this work, her husband paid tribute to her: "my wife, whose interest in people is the greatest asset a field worker could have, who knew more of many things than I could ever hope to discover, and whose arts of improvisation covered everything from teaching our children to designing thatch kitchens ...." The quotation reveals a great deal—and underlines the traditional role that Betty played in her marriage, and the value her husband gave to it.

Until 1966, when she joined the English department at UBC, Betty devoted herself to her husband, to being a support to him in his profession, and to raising her family. Her character, an understanding of which was to play so great a part in the events which followed, seemed to produce upon those who knew her an almost unanimous impression. Unlike so many of us, who, if we were to be described by friends, colleagues, students, children, spouse, acquaintances, would appear to be many different people, Betty Belshaw was a woman who gave the same impression to everyone who knew her.

She was rather stout, 145 lbs. and 5'6" at the time of disappearance, with well-groomed reddish hair and brown-rimmed glasses. Always impeccably dressed and made-up, conscious of her position as the wife of an eminent scholar and with a colonial's exaggerated respect for class and status, she drove herself to perfection in all she attempted. Her house, large and well situated on the University Endowment lands, one of the most desirable and expensive areas in Vancouver, was an appropriate setting for the large parties she felt it her duty to give—and Cyril's publications were prominently displayed where guests would not miss them. When her secretary once said to her, "Oh, do call me Rosemary," she was told, "*I* prefer to be called Mrs. Belshaw."

Her colleagues found her conscientious to a fault, liable to worry over small details, to make mountains out of molehills and serious issues out of minor ones. Some went so far as to call her stubborn and narrow-minded. But even they stressed her enthusiasm for her teaching, and her students honoured her as a devoted and committed teacher who inspired their respect and affection. Betty drove herself ceaselessly, both in her job as an English instructor and as the co-ordinator of the freshman English programme. She worked equally hard fulfilling her responsibilities as the wife of a man who was on friendly terms with the *haut monde* of Vancouver and with some of his most distinguished colleagues, and on distant yet cordial terms with the more lowly of the faculty.

People who knew Betty also spoke of her other side, her kind and loving nature. A colleague's wife, worrying over her children at a faculty dinner, would find Betty taking her aside and giving her sympathy, comfort, and solid advice. She had warmth and feeling in her. Her strivings towards perfection in all things, and towards a smooth surface and lady-like appearance were one side of her nature; her moods, her temper, and her fears and affections were the other.

Betty was also admired for her acceptance of the periods of solitude she endured when her husband's profession obliged him to travel—and in fact they spent a great deal of time apart. As well, she earned respect for taking on heavy administrative loads at work when she might easily have filled her time with more leisurely, less pressured pursuits.

Like so many women of her generation who have seized their roles and played them fully to the best of their abilities, she was prey to anxieties, insecurities and the imbalances which seem inevitable when so much of life has been structured to fit the convenience and well-being of others. The descriptions of Betty's personality suggest angers and resentments unformulated, damped down, but simmering and occasionally breaking out in irrationalities: fears of cancer, of the unknown, slight hypochondria, outbursts of temper, difficulties in sleeping. For although she had achieved more than most women of her generation, class and background, she shared their bitterness and frustrations—those which flow from a life shaped by the priorities of others.

When, in his summing up at the trial so many months after her disappearance, the prosecutor called her "this good wife and mother" there was a click of recognition. For Betty Belshaw really was, in so far as she came to be known in the most exhaustive of investigations, a good wife and mother. As a wife she was totally loyal and faithful; as a mother, absolutely committed to her responsibilities in raising her children.

No discordant note was sounded in the months of investigation which followed her disappearance. She was moody, possibly even manic-depressive, at times forgetful, at times snobbish, at times slavishly deferential to authority, possibly too rigid. But—and about this there really could be no doubt—she was loyal, faithful, virtuous, devoted. It is impossible to find, even in the worst criticisms by those who disliked her, a dissenting opinion about these qualities. Betty Belshaw *was* a good wife and mother.

There was, in her life, no one who had reason to hate her; no one whose pleasure or advancement she prevented, no one who would benefit by her death. She left no fortune, no opening to be seized, no freedom which she had not already granted, openly or tacitly. She left at her disappearance, it seemed, only a bereaved and bewildered husband who had suddenly lost a life-time companion and helpmeet, two grieving children, and colleagues who were personally saddened and professionally a bit more burdened.

That is why the disappearance of Betty Belshaw caused such a stir in Vancouver. Speculation ran rife in the university community. But it was, by necessity, empty of content.

The consensus of rumour at the time was that Cyril was distracted, almost hysterical. Friends told one another over coffee how he was combing the streets of Paris, inconsolable, for three months looking for her; how he feared she had wandered away, perhaps in a period of forgetfulness, and slipped on the icy banks of the Seine. His children, it was said, tried to comfort him, to calm him, with no success. Eventually they convinced him to return to Canada where, shattered, he tried to pick up the pieces of a life with a great mystery hanging over it. Where was Betty, friends in Vancouver asked one another? What could have happened to a woman who had never left home, even for a night? She would never have run away, everyone was certain of that: why, she had never even stormed out of the house for more than half an hour. And although normally such an event might start a storm of gossip about the motives of the person who disappeared, this did not happen in Betty's case. Her friends and colleagues were absolutely certain she had not left of her own free will.

And, after all, there are only two possible explanations if someone disappears. The most obvious—wilful disappearance—was discounted by those who knew her. She had not a single reason. It was not in her nature, she was in good spirits, leading a life she enjoyed, with nothing to fear or to hide. And the second possibility—foul play—seemed equally unlikely, because of the circumstances of her disappearance.

Beyond this there was a profound moral incongruity. Most of us sense some contradiction in our lives, some secret, some hidden side, which may draw upon us the untoward event. Apart from this, we are immune. We have paid the price and in return we are safe—safe on the busy sidewalks of our cities, and in the quiet rooms of a placid marriage. Of course there is always the chance mugging, the accident, the illness. But as for the mysterious, the bizarre, the entrance of evil into our lives? Impossible—if we ourselves have not already opened the door.

Look into the victim's life, runs the truism of detective fiction, and you will find the cause of the disaster which has fallen upon him. But the book of Betty Belshaw's life was open ... and it seemed there was nothing to read there. Nothing, that is, that could explain how this woman, respected by colleagues, loved by her students and honoured by husband and children, could suddenly vanish, be swallowed up by a mystery without a single clue.

3

The gossips of Vancouver had got it all wrong—as they were to do consistently as the Belshaw story unrolled before their astonished attention.

Cyril Belshaw had not walked the streets of Paris despairing, searching for the beloved face in every street, Métro station and restaurant. He had, in fact, followed a more logical procedure. And this, if they had stopped to think about it, was exactly what his colleagues and friends would have expected of him. He had always conducted his affairs thoughtfully, logically, rationally and meticulously. He had always shown a painstaking grasp of detail in his profession, where he had won a world-wide reputation for his significant contributions to anthropology.

Cyril Belshaw's father, Horace Belshaw, was an important influence on his son. Horace Belshaw's career as an economist and scholar, his books upon the agricultural economies of New Guinea and his work as a professor in New Zealand suggested to Cyril the direction that his own work would take.

Cyril Belshaw's role in anthropology has been even more important than his father's. He has come to be considered one of the top seven or eight anthropologists in Canada, and an influential thinker in the field on an international level.

Belshaw's foremost contribution is in the field of economic anthropology. His thesis advisor, mentor, and long-time friend, Raymond Firth, was one of the first to see the importance of economic analysis as performed by an anthropologist in illuminating the structures and functioning of traditional societies. Belshaw carried on and elaborated Firth's work. He interested himself in the relationships between the traditional culture and economic patterns of a society and the role played by administrators during periods of social and economic change.

His early books, *Changing Melanesia: Social Economics of Cultural Contact* and *The Great Village: the economic and social welfare of Hanuabada, an urban community*, and studies such as "Island

administration in the South West Pacific; government and reconstruction in New Caledonia, the New Hebrides, and the British
Solomon Islands'' were competent and thorough, important scholarly contributions to anthropological knowledge. They also proved
useful to the local authorities. Belshaw followed these works in the
sixties with *Traditional Exchange and Modern Markets*, which was
to become a classic text in the area of which he was the leading
exponent.

The effect of these books, along with Belshaw's own experience
as a colonial administrator, was to attract requests by governments,
societies, and international agencies for help in understanding the
traditional structures where economic change was or would be taking
place. As a result of this work, Belshaw grew more interested in
the relationship between the values implicit in the anthropologist's
world-view, and the ethics and morality of administration itself.

As the years passed Belshaw's interests developed from this central concern. He is interested in administration because it is through
administrators that money and power flow to effect change. As well,
his writing is formed by a broad view of the social responsibility
anthropologists must bear, if their work is to help preserve the values
of the cultures they study and contribute to the practical problems
that face administrators. Although there is today much debate about
the social responsibilities of the social sciences, Cyril Belshaw was
always concerned about such questions, and his work from the
earliest days contained a breadth of view and a social conscience
relatively unusual in his field.

In the seventies he wrote *The Sorcerer's Apprentice*, where he
dealt with these social questions, and also *Anatomy of a University*,
a study which used the anthropologist's tools to look at university
administrative structure.

At the same time, he was moving steadily up the hierarchy at the
University of British Columbia. When he first went there in 1953
UBC was a much smaller school than it is today. There were only
eleven people teaching in the area of anthropology-sociology, and
the entire university had only 5500 students. In the fifties and sixties
the university grew rapidly until in the seventies it attained its position as the second largest university in Canada (after the University
of Toronto) with a student population of more than 20,000. Situated
on a beautiful wooded parcel of land on Point Grey, just outside

of Vancouver, its contemporary buildings in varying, not particularly distinguished, architectural styles sprawl about the campus, separated by curving drives and areas of gardens and walkways.

In 1968 Belshaw was appointed head of the by then much enlarged Anthropology and Sociology Department. He became extremely active in university politics, and memos from Professor Belshaw were a common sight when any issue or controversy was exercising the faculty.

To a certain extent his interest in university politics was a natural outgrowth of his scholarly pursuits. But there was a faction at UBC which saw his activities in this area as a result of ambition, an ambition to climb the university hierarchy towards the presidency itself. There were those who felt that his 1974 book, *Towers Besieged: the Dilemma of the Creative University*, showed this ambition too nakedly, and finished off whatever chance he may have had to achieve his goals.

Just before he wrote *Towers Besieged*, Belshaw's academic career had received its first setback. In 1971 and 1972 a controversy over tenure surfaced in the department of which he was now Chairman. To deal with it, Belshaw employed the logical analytical tools he had used for problem-solving in the past. But logic, meticulous planning, the well-written memo, and power politics were unable to stem the tide of nationalism and academic revisionism which were, even in their ebb, still strongly buffeting UBC in the early seventies. His failure to understand the depth of the passions unleashed during those times turned the issue into one of the minor *causes célèbres* which overturned many a well-qualified chairman in those days. When the dust had settled, the memos had been filed, and the heat generated by the dispute had died down, he resigned his chairmanship of the department.

Belshaw now concentrated his attention on the international politics of anthropology and succeeded better on the larger stage. So well, in fact, that when the troubles which followed upon Betty's disappearance descended upon him, testimonials from distinguished anthropologists around the world, including the great Claude Lévi-Strauss, were put forward on his behalf. And he could point to the prestigious and powerful position he had achieved in the world of anthropology, to positions and honours which included amongst many others membership in: the Royal Economic Society, the North

American Liaison Committee of the Royal Anthropological Institute, the American Ethnological Society, the Society for Applied Anthropology, the Canadian Sociology and Anthropology Association, the Society for International Development, the International Social Science Council, the Canadian National Commission for UNESCO and a social science working party of the Organization for Economic Co-operation and Development in Paris. He had served on the executive and been an officer of many of these organizations. At the time of Betty's disappearance he was president of the International Union of Anthropological and Ethnological Sciences and the editor of the prestigious journal, *Current Anthropology*, positions which put him at or near the pinnacle of international academic politics and which testified, as well, to his intellect, his professional standing and his intellectual integrity.

As a teacher, Belshaw was not so highly regarded as he was as a scholar. His students found him uninspiring, although extremely thorough, rigorous and demanding. Even so, his ideas and approach were enough to draw some of them into anthropology, and induce them to make a life work of this discipline. Although they called him dry and unsympathetic, they remembered him and remembered his books, and years after would speak of him with respect. On the other hand, perhaps his detachment helps explain why he produced no distinguished graduate students who went on to make a significant mark in anthropology.

At the time of his wife's disappearance, Cyril Belshaw looked the part of the consummate academic; the exacting, painstaking intellectual, the stereotype of the college professor—except perhaps for his size. He was very small, with thick brown hair, greying sideburns, yellowish salt-and-pepper moustache, and he wore gold-rimmed glasses. Small dark eyes looked out from under thick brows, and his chin was plump, giving him a slightly jowly appearance. His mouth was small, narrow, and prim. Slightly overweight, he held himself erect, and was always well dressed and neat. He looked younger than his fifty-eight years, perhaps because of his creamy white skin, but his neck was beginning to show his age, starting to settle into crêpey folds. Like many small men, he could show a disarming sweetness, with a gentle smile or an unexpected politeness. On the other hand, the strength of character which comes from having to make one's presence felt in a larger world would come out when he was crossed. Then he rarely, if ever, lost his temper; rather he grew more accurate, pedantic and fixed in his purpose. He had done his research, he knew the facts, he stood by his interpretation. That was the stance he took when he met opposition.

So it was completely in character that Cyril Belshaw behaved with common sense, *savoir-faire* and intelligence when his wife disappeared in Paris. When she failed to appear at the Galleries Lafayette for the one o'clock rendezvous, he eventually gave her up and returned to the Novotel. There he found no news of her; there was no message from her at the desk, and no one remembered seeing her pass through the lobby. When the afternoon passed without word from her, he reported her disappearance to the Bagnolet commissariat of police. There he was advised to wait out the night, and if she still had not returned by morning to come back with a detailed description of her and of her effects to aid the police in their search. Belshaw was distressed by the fact that the police did not seem to take the matter of a disappearing wife very seriously, but he could see the sense of their suggestion.

As for preparing a description of Betty, this was a task which Belshaw felt capable of doing properly. Both by training and nature he was a man who noticed and remembered small details. As a cultural anthropologist, he had learned to assimilate small details of dress and gesture in order to induce cultural patterns. When the morning brought no news of Betty he presented himself to the police. His sleepless night had yielded an extremely detailed list of Betty's effects, which included the following:

> green wool suit
> beige blouse
> chestnut-coloured shoes
> travelling bag in green imitation leather and wallet
> emerald engagement ring
> platinum wedding band
> gold Longines watch with worked band
> beige Burberry raincoat
> bifocal glasses with brown frames

He even included such details as the brand name of Betty's brassière. Belshaw felt he had done his part, but he was not satisfied with the attitude of the police who still seemed to believe that Betty had probably left of her own free will. After all, they explained, women do that all the time. Big city police deal with a great number of missing-persons reports, most of which are solved in the obvious ways. But Belshaw did not agree, he was certain Betty had not run away. He arranged to go to the Canadian Embassy to see what more could be done.

He had telephoned for an appointment, but when he arrived there the building was cordoned off, due to a demonstration. Eventually he found what he believed to be the right door, and rang and rang, struggling to maintain his calm. Finally a Mr. Nasrallah, the consul, appeared, to demand harshly what he wanted.

"But I am the man who telephoned your secretary about my wife, who has disappeared. Don't you remember?"

Mr. Nasrallah did remember, and admitted Belshaw. The interview which followed was thorough, and Belshaw gave the Canadian official all the particulars. There was always the possibility that Betty would turn up back home in Canada, or in England where she had friends. Cyril gave relevant details of their connections in these countries to Mr. Nasrallah. Then, increasingly distraught, he returned to his hotel and telephoned his daughter Diana. Diana, an actress, was performing in Calgary. There she found the message to call her father urgently, and this she did.

The Belshaws' two children, Diana and Adrian, now 30 and 26, were both out on their own. Diana was not a well-known actress. As a young woman working her way up in her profession she had played frequently in small theatres across Canada, as well as performed on CBC radio and television. Her directors remember her as hardworking, professional and competent. Adrian at this time was finishing up his doctorate in zoology. Regarded as a brilliant student by his professors and thesis director, he had completed much of his post-graduate work with the aid of scholarships.

The relationship between the Belshaws and their children was good, and the family was a close one; they were known to draw together in times of outside pressure. Adrian, the younger son, had always been closest to his mother. Diana's relationship with her mother was more stormy, as is often the case between mothers and daughters, but she got along well with her father, to whom she was devoted. The man who always appeared to his colleagues to be cool and dominated by the English concept of the stiff upper lip felt free to reveal his true feelings in the confines of his family.

So when Diana returned the call and heard that her mother had vanished, she talked with a Cyril Belshaw who showed feelings which had been strikingly lacking when he reported the disappearance to the police and to the embassy. Cyril was distracted with anxiety, he wept on the phone. Diana did her best to comfort him, and they canvassed the possibilities of what might have happened, with no success.

Two days passed. During that time Belshaw phoned and wrote to various friends. These letters and telephone calls were later examined with great care. To his close friends Cyril showed himself to be tearful, worried, sick at heart. To acquaintances and fellow-scholars he was cold, almost flip, writing such phrases as "Betty has taken off" which seemed to suggest a lamentable lack of feeling, or perhaps a desire to protect himself from the embarrassment and humiliation of the increasingly bizarre situation in which he found himself.

It was the third day with no news of Betty. Both the Paris police and the embassy assured him that there was nothing more he could do in Paris. They would set the wheels in motion—they would keep in touch with him. So, telling them where he could be reached in future, Cyril Belshaw loaded his own and Betty's suitcases into the car, and on January 18th, three days after Betty's disappearance, set off for the drive back to Montana-Vermala.

4

Cyril Belshaw enjoyed driving his still rather new Citröen-Maserati (he had picked it up on his arrival in Europe at the beginning of the sabbatical year.) He was an enthusiast who drove with zest—frequently too fast. Driving back from Paris to Montana, he spent the night in Bex, Switzerland, having covered almost 600 kilometres. He continued the drive to Montana-Vermala the next day. Stopping in Bex seemed curious to some later. Geographically it was the nearest city of any size with a decent hotel between Aigle and Montana-Vermala. A city of light industry and little distinction, it was perhaps simply a coincidence that Belshaw grew tired and stopped the night there rather than continuing the hour or two that it might take him to reach his apartment in Montana-Vermala.

Four kilometres after Bex, at St. Maurice, the highway enters the Rhône Valley, and the mountainous beauty of the Valais begins to make itself felt. The road begins to climb, and the light industry of the Rhône corridor becomes less obstrusive. As the alluvial plain narrows, there is an impression of the mountains moving in on the road; then it widens and the mountains appear to retreat, their shoulders often hidden in mist, rivulets of it running down their folds and crevasses. Below the mist one sees sparse patches of trees, grey-green in winter, and below them the terraced vineyards. Occasionally a shepherd and his flock move across the foothills. These mountains, the Dents du Midi to the west, and the Dent du Morcles to the east, dominate the entire region. Their high peaks provide the ski resorts that attract tourists from all over the world, and their lower slopes are terraced, cultivated and laboriously irrigated with an ancient system of narrow canals which bring the glacial waters of the peaks down to the vineyards. For this part of the Rhône Valley, sheltered by mountains, receives very little moisture.

In addition to undistinguished patches of light industry and periodic neat, five-metre-high piles of stacked firewood, the countryside provides glimpses of medieval castles, sand-coloured, walled and castellated, perched on seemingly inaccessible cliffs high above their former domains. At St. Maurice a magnificent seventeenth-century church and abbey built on an easily defensible ridge dominate the village. There are times when the traveller passing along this route can forget all immediate pressures and feel himself part of the timeless continuum of a countryside where medieval remnants are as familiar and as real as the infrequent refrigeration plant or glass factory.

At Saxon the mountains again retreat as the plain widens and the orchards begin. Gnarled apricot and peach trees, covered with snow in winter, alternate with plowed fields whose dark rich earth, filled in the summer with asparagus and corn, are in winter barren and edged in white.

But it is the vineyards which are the most noticeable feature of this landscape. Cut out of the mountainside, narrow steep terraces climb upward wherever possible. These *tablards* provide the livelihood for the isolated villages along the road Belshaw followed when he left the autoroute and began the slow upward climb towards Montana-Vermala. Sharp hairpin turns on roads barely wide enough for cars to pass and frequently unprotected by any railing mount steeply between the vineyards. The rows of staked vines, decorated in winter with withered ochre-brown leaves, support a life whose poverty can be seen in the unrenovated and bleak eighteenth-century houses and medieval villages such as Ollon and Lens. But as one climbs towards Montana-Vermala these small villages give way to the unremarkable cottages of the middle-class vacationer; twentieth-century contractor's versions of traditional ski chalets soon dominate the landscape. As the air grows colder and thinner, the snow heavier, the twisting road more and more dangerous, the homes of the Valaisian peasants disappear entirely from view, and are replaced by these chalets and by stands of spruce covered with snow and looking like Christmas cards.

And Montana-Vermala itself? It is hard to believe Katherine Mansfield chose this village to write "The Garden Party" and "The Doll's House". Whatever attracted her to it in 1921 is surely gone. It is *tout touriste* now. The narrow, snow-covered streets are full of young skiers. The stores, pubs, and hotel-restaurants lack charm or character.

The fine thin air at a height of 1700 metres is, of course, refreshing. Perhaps it was this which drew the ailing Katherine Mansfield. Nowadays the views of the Valaisian Alps, of the Weisshorn, the Zinalrothorn, and the Cervin, of a horizon of ragged snow-capped peaks, are often blocked at street level by fifteen-storey apartment blocks, many complete with underground garages, which line the twisting closed-in roads. Only from the windows of these balconied structures of concrete with their imitation-Swiss-style balcony railings can the famous views be enjoyed. From this height the mountains give the illusion of being very close; the Rhône Valley which separates them from Montana is invisible and the viewer feels part of a vast expanse of snowy crests.

But surely it could not have been the views alone which drew the Belshaws to this spot full of young ski enthusiasts and old men, millionaires so they say, who walk carefully along the snowy roads, well dressed and breathing with difficulty. Neither were serious skiers. The couple had been there before in the early seventies. Perhaps, looking for a retreat when Belshaw needed time off to write *Towers Besieged* and *The Sorcerer's Apprentice*, they had stumbled upon Montana-Vermala when it was relatively unspoiled and, having enjoyed a pleasant stay in 1972-3, now returned to it in 1979 because it was familiar.

The village itself is very much like ski resorts around the world: real-estate offices, tourist shops, cafés, hotels, camera stores. Montana-Vermala boasts over a hundred ski lifts.

On the outskirts of the village is the Jolilac—in an area where the apartment buildings are more spread out and the Alps more visible. The lake—the Joli Lac itself—is in winter completely covered with snow. Around this artificial feature of the landscape are the curved roads which developers believe give spontaneity to their arrangements, and situated with their backs to the mountains, facing the lake, are two chalet-style apartment buildings, the Bellevue and the Jolilac.

Cyril Belshaw had rented a two-bedroom apartment for himself and Betty as their temporary European home for the last half of his sabbatical year. And although Switzerland is generally a very expensive place to live, the monthly rent for the Jolilac apartment was only 950 Swiss francs (then approximately $665 Canadian)—very reasonable by Vancouver standards.

On January 19th, then, Cyril Belshaw arrived in Montana-Vermala to take up his life alone in the apartment and to wait for news of Betty. Later his actions during this period would be thoroughly

investigated and analysed by the Vaudois authorities. And his behaviour during this time would form the basis on which, two years
after his car journey from Paris, he would be tried for murder.

5

When Cyril Belshaw arrived, the Jolilac and the neighbouring Bellevue apartment building were three-quarters empty. He tried to occupy himself, but was distracted by anxiety. He talked to Diana
frequently by telephone, and Diana, aware of his deepening distress,
made up her mind to come to Montana-Vermala. On January 21st
Belshaw left the apartment to make the long drive to Geneva along
the snowy roads which had become so familiar. That night he slept
at the Hotel Grand Pré and the next morning was there to meet
Diana at the airport.

There was great rapport between father and daughter, and sincere
devotion. They greeted one another with tears. Diana tried to re-
assure him. "No guilt, none of that," she told him. "Let's remember the happy things." At the back of her mind, unsaid, was the
fear that her father would blame himself for having done something
which might have driven her mother to some desperate expedient.
Of all the unlikely possibilities that they were obliged to think of,
suicide was certainly one that had to be faced.

On the drive back to Montana-Vermala and in the days that
followed, they canvassed every possibility. Sometimes they took
turns blaming themselves for things they had done; harsh words
spoken unthinkingly now returned to reproach them. On January
31st Adrian joined them. They phoned frequently to Paris only to
be told that there was no news, and that there was nothing they
could do. They phoned friends to tell them of Betty's disappearance.

No one could offer any rational explanation or suggestion. There was no clue, no lead ... only one agonizing day after another, punctuated by nights filled with nightmares.

On February 5th Diana returned to Canada. As an actress she had professional responsibilities and dared not stay away too long. On February 6th Adrian returned to Vancouver. The children had done what they could for their father. Now there was only the waiting ... alone.

Belshaw was finding it wearing. On February 8th he visited his doctor, complaining about not being able to sleep. But he said nothing of Betty's disappearance, or his anxieties. His deeper feelings were opened only to those closest to him.

Belshaw decided he had to do something. He couldn't sit distracted, day after day, in the half-empty resort community, worrying. He made arrangements to attend a conference in England, and on March 30th he left for London, and then for a conference at York. While there, he had two experiences which shook him deeply.

He had heard that the Salvation Army in London were experts at finding missing persons and that they had extensive files on missing persons in their offices all over Europe. On April 2nd, he paid them a visit. He spent several hours talking with a Major Smith, the officer at the Salvation Army who concerned himself with such matters, and the conversation made a profound impression upon him. He was later to recount how Major Smith took him back through Betty's life, examining her psychological state, her medical state, drawing out and dredging up incidents from the past which would have been painful to remember under any circumstances: a serious depression Betty had had in the sixties; all the things that had worried her. It was a gruelling conversation, poignantly recalling all that was most worrisome and unhappy in Betty's past. Major Smith also told Belshaw that there were many cases of suicides when no one had had any inkling that the person involved was depressed or suicidal. This shocked Belshaw, who had believed up until that time that he would surely have known if Betty had been troubled enough to consider taking her own life. Of course, he had thought of the possibility of suicide before, but it had had no reality for him. Major Smith now brought him face to face with it. Smith asked for every hint of suicide, of depression ... under Smith's probing Belshaw remembered incidents long since forgotten. After the interview, Belshaw walked the streets of London and wept.

Then, when his spirits were at a low ebb, while at York, he received a message from the Canadian High Commission that the Paris police wanted to speak with him. Suddenly there was hope again. The message came towards the end of the week. The following Monday found him in Paris. There he learned it was a false hope; there was in fact no news at all. It was just a question of revising the dossier. He returned to Montana-Vermala exhausted. The past two months had taken their toll, and his emotional state was very fragile. His book, which he had laboured so hard to finish—a comparison of Canadian and Swiss federalism—had been sent off to the typist in Canada. He had nothing to do except worry and imagine dreadful possibilities. Day followed day. And still there was no news.

Then on April 13th, two Swiss police investigators called upon him at the apartment in Montana-Vermala. These were Inspectors Reichen and Guignard (by coincidence one Inspector bore the same name as the man who was to direct Belshaw's trial). They told Belshaw that they were aware of the circumstances of the disappearance of his wife, said, according to their testimony at the trial, they had a body which they were trying to identify, and asked if they could get Betty's dental x-rays and charts.

Belshaw explained that because of Betty's fear of cancer, there were probably no x-rays. But there would certainly be dental charts. After some discussion Belshaw agreed to write the dentist for these. He also provided the police with a colour photograph of Betty. The conversation was perfectly amicable. It seemed to Belshaw that the Swiss police were finally doing *something* and, as he later wrote to Diana, he was glad of it.

He preferred to write for the dental charts himself. If the matter were handled discreetly, the whole dental clinic need not know of the request. After all, he knew about the gossip in Vancouver. Hints of some of the more fantastic stories circulating had reached him. Betty had now been missing for three months. With nothing concrete to go on, people were saying that the two had been international spies, and that Betty had run afoul of some powerful spy organization. They were saying that the two had been mixed up in something unsavoury ... they were even saying that Betty had been involved in black magic and had been 'whisked away'. Some talked of the rash of disappearances that had occurred lately, and wondered if extra-terrestrials were involved. It was all too ridiculous and depressing for a man of Cyril Belshaw's temperament. To be a target for gossip was painful enough, to be involved in such stories was humiliating. He wanted as little of it as possible. He wrote to Dr. Nishiguchi, who was in fact a friend, asking him to handle the matter personally. "Keep it confidential," he wrote, asking the doctor to get the records himself and not to trust the matter to someone in the clinic. On May 7th the records arrived, and on May 9th he took them to Inspector Reichen in Sierre, the nearest town with an office of the Valaisian *police de sûreté*.

Still there was no news. Belshaw, lonely, restless, far from family and friends had had enough. He decided to return to Canada, where at least he could bear the uncertainty, the terrible imaginings, the nightmares, nearer to family, in his own country. And perhaps he could face out the gossip and put an end to some of the more bizarre surmises. By mid-June, after a three-week stop in London, he was home again. And still there was no news of Betty.

PART TWO
THE LE SEPEY CORPSE

6

In March, while Cyril Belshaw was still in Montana-Vermala and before he left for England for the conference at York and the meeting with Major Smith, a macabre discovery took place. This event was to become the centre-point in a web of circumstance which would eventually entangle Belshaw in disaster.

In order to grasp the full significance of the events which followed it is necessary to bear in mind the geography of the region. The map on p. 26 shows a triangle of towns to the east of Lac Léman, each of which play a part in the Belshaw drama. High in the Valaisian Alps is Montana-Vermala. Approximately sixty kilometres from Montana-Vermala lies Aigle. Montana is in the canton of Valais; Aigle is in Vaud. (The cantons now federated into the Swiss nation were once separate states, or city-states. Each has its own history, its own distinctive 'national' character, and its own code of penal procedure.)

Northeast from Aigle a highway mounts precipitously towards Le Sépey, and the col des Mosses—the third point in this triangle. On March 28th, a crew of *cantonniers*, local roadworkers, were clearing from the sides of this road rocks which the spring thaw had thrust to the surface and which were now in danger of tumbling down.

Close to Le Sépey, near the Larrevoin bridge, they made their

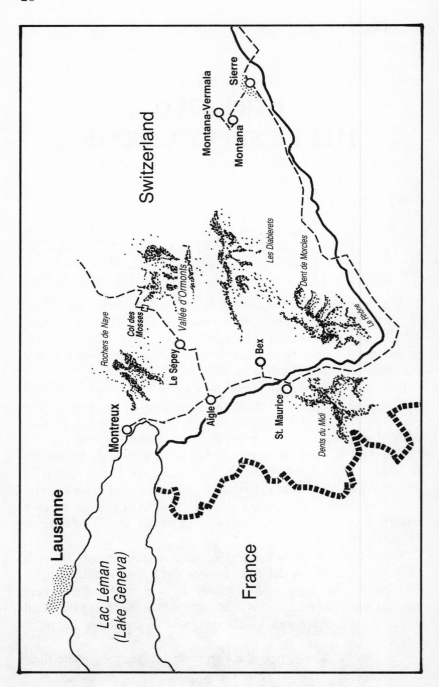

gruesome discovery. Just past the bridge there is a lay-by where drivers can pull off the road, stop, and enjoy the view. Below the lay-by the roadworkers began to clear away garbage which had been jettisoned from above. Something which looked like the carcase of an animal had been thrown down from the road. Its descent down the slope had been stopped by a tree seven metres below the road.

The farmers of the region sometimes dispose of dead livestock this way, particularly in winter, and as it is illegal, the roadworkers called the local Vaudois police. It was on their arrival that the grisly truth became apparent: the object the *cantonniers* had found, head and limbs partially wrapped in torn garbage bags tied with twine, was barely recognizable, but it *was* a human body.

The road which climbs from Aigle towards Le Sépey passes very few houses, and the majority of these are shuttered and closed in winter. Its narrow hairpin bends and turns are, in most places, guarded by a steel fence or railing. However, a few spots have nothing more than orange-tipped stakes to mark the verges. Shortly after Aigle, vineyards give way to thin alpine forest. Here and there can be seen spruce and larch in small copses approaching the road. It is not easy to find a place with a clear descent, no barrier, and the certainty that no unexpected terrace of vines, small plateau, or patch of underbrush would break the fall. High on both sides of the road, when from time to time the snowfall thins, can be seen forbidding peaks: Les Diablerets and Les Mosses.

The Larrevoin bridge is itself very narrow, and on three corners an object thrown from it would fall, without impediment, down the steep incline and into the underbrush lining the impassible crevices. But on the fourth corner, the far right-hand corner as one mounts towards Le Sépey, where the lay-by is, the land slopes away more gently from the bridge. The lay-by itself is surrounded by large boulders, with spaces in between.

The Vaudois criminal police, the *police de sûreté*, were called in as soon as the local police realized that there was a human body involved. They assumed at once that the body had been jettisoned at night, when darkness hid the exact nature of the slope. And it seemed clear, too, that it must have been done by a stranger to the locale, who would naturally pick a place where he could safely leave his car, not realizing, at night, that at this spot he risked discovery of the body. And yet, the body's descent was stopped by only one tree. It was pure chance, even dropped from the far-right corner of the bridge, that it did not slide smoothly over the snow, wrapped as it was in plastic, to disappear forever among the rocks and brush of the mountainside.

It was thought then, and said later by police investigators and Vaudois authorities, that the discovery of the Le Sépey Corpse (as the newspapers were always to refer to it afterwards) was a pure fluke. The area was very thinly populated, the slopes on both sides of the road were for the most part inaccessible, and the chance of a large object thrown from the road being recovered was minute.

The condition of the body served only to deepen the mystery. It was reported in Vancouver, later, that the body was in pieces; one newspaper report even claimed it had been decapitated. This was not true.

But the truth was sinister enough. For every effort had been made to hide the identity of the Le Sépey Corpse. It had been entirely stripped of its clothes and jewellery. It had been wrapped in three strong dark grey sixty-litre plastic garbage bags and tied with strong white twine. Because it had been thrown into the bush animals had discovered it, and their assaults, along with the natural decomposition, had so mutilated it that they had destroyed any chance of identifying it by its appearance. In fact, this body thrown into the underbrush had become a horrifying and grisly sight—the pictures of it alone were later to completely unnerve a Canadian doctor who was obliged to look at them. Only the teeth and jaw were intact. The throat had been completely eaten away by wild animals, as had the breasts and part of the right thigh. The muscles of the throat area were entirely gone.

The discovery of the Le Sépey Corpse caused a sensation. On March 29th it was announced in headlines on the front page of all the papers of the region, including *24 heures*, the *Tribune de Lausanne*, the *Journal* of Aigle and the *Nouvelliste du Rhône*. The papers also played up the discovery in huge type on the posters they put out daily, which were plastered about local stations and kiosks. The Vaudois police set out at once to try to identify the body. They checked out all local reports of missing persons and subjected the remains to a thorough forensic examination.

The results were not promising. The body had no obvious fractures. It appeared to be the body of a middle-aged woman with lightish-coloured hair and well-cared-for teeth which had been fitted with four gold crowns. The cause of death was difficult to determine, and while more tests were being conducted the *police de sûreté* widened their inquiries: after they had checked out local disappearances, they sifted through cantonal disappearances, then nationwide reports. They examined numerous reports of missing persons, and still they could not identify the body. It appeared that whoever had gone to all the trouble of stripping the body of everything which could identify it and disposing of it on a slope on a deserted alpine road had succeeded in his obvious aims. For although one unlikely event had occurred—the discovery of the body—it seemed at this stage that the body would never be identified.

The body had been found by the roadworkers on March 28th. By the middle of April the police were no nearer to identifying it than they had been at the moment of discovery. Almost two hundred missing-persons reports had been examined to no avail. A thorough forensic examination had yielded no clues. The police were frustrated, but there was no question of their abandoning their investigation.

7

Because the body had been discovered in the canton of Vaud, the investigation fell under the jurisdiction of the local magistrate, the Aigle *juge informateur*, Daniel Bournoud. His role was to direct the inquiries of the *police de sûreté*. The officer put in charge directly after the discovery of the Le Sépey Corpse was Inspector Wyss, who at thirty had been with the *sûreté* for only five years. Perhaps the authorities erred in putting such a young and relatively inexperienced officer in charge of the case. But it is likely that in the early stages no one in Vaud realized that the discovery of the Le Sépey Corpse would mark the beginning of one of their most difficult, controversial and sensational cases.

There is, after all, not a very high crime rate in the Suisse Romande. In Vaud, with its population of 530,000, in a bad year there may be ten murders. Some years there are only one or two. A certain proportion of the violence starts out as fights in bars between migratory labourers from Southern Europe who come to work as labourers in Switzerland. In any case, there is an almost 100 per cent conviction rate. At the time of the discovery of the Le Sépey Corpse, Vaudois authorities could remember only one unsolved murder, that of a French prostitute.

It is impossible to ascertain exactly what part Cyril Belshaw's failure to get in touch personally with the Valaisian police played in slowing down this investigation. In any case, it was not until the Valaisian police received a telex, direct from Berne, about a woman missing in Paris whose husband was living in Montana-Vermala, that they were able to suggest a possible link to the body which their Vaudois colleagues were trying to identify. Upon receipt of this telex, apparently sent in response to an enquiry from the Canadian Consulate in Berne direct to the head of Interpol there, the Valaisian police telephoned their counterparts in neighbouring Vaud. It was decided to make a routine check.

It was in carrying out this check that the two police officers, Inspector Reichen from Sierre, and Inspector Guignard, a Vaudois, paid their visit of April 13th to Cyril Belshaw. They interviewed him in his apartment at the Jolilac, and returned with a photograph of Betty and a promise of dental records which had to be sent from Canada. On May 9th Cyril Belshaw brought the dental charts to Inspector Reichen in Sierre. They were forwarded to Lausanne, and compared with the teeth of the Le Sépey Corpse. They did not match.

So the *police de sûreté* continued to check the records of missing persons not only in Vaud, in the Suisse Romande and in all of Switzerland, but now in the rest of Europe, and even from further afield. Hundreds of missing-persons reports were examined. And still the body remained unidentified.

Exactly what happened next may never be clear. Different people involved in the investigation give different accounts. It seems likely, however, that it was Inspector Wyss, working with a colleague, Inspector Jan of the Vaud police forensic science laboratory, who decided to request further dental records, direct from Canada. Later the two officers could give no real reason for this decision. "It was just an idea," they would say, "a hunch." *"Le nez du policier"*— perhaps best translated as "a policeman's intuition". The jaws of Mrs. Belshaw and of the Le Sépey Corpse had many similarities, yet the work done on the teeth was completely different. The officers had no x-rays, only a kind of schema designating each tooth and what work had been performed on it. Wyss decided to try to get a more exact record. He discussed the matter with the *juge informateur* who agreed to request new dental records.

On July 20th a telex was sent via Interpol to Canada, demanding new and, if possible, "better" dental records. Moving at a leisurely pace through the coils of red tape the request was sent from Ottawa to Vancouver where eventually, on August 22nd, it fetched up at the University detachment of the RCMP.

The University detachment is a small RCMP branch just on the outskirts of the campus itself, next to a small shopping centre on the Endowment lands. There the Interpol request was processed and treated as a standard missing-persons matter. On August 23rd a member of the RCMP detachment there, Constable Smith, telephoned Belshaw, who was by now back in Vancouver, to ask for the name of his dentist so that better records could be obtained. Belshaw gave it to him.

The next day, August 24th, 1979, Belshaw telephoned the detachment. Later he arrived bearing a written statement:

I wish to make the following statement in order to correct information which I supplied to the Swiss police authorities.

The Swiss police authorities requested me to obtain my wife's dental charts, in connection with the search resulting from her disappearance in January. These did not reach me until later than anticipated, and in fact a few days before I had to leave in May for London and Paris, and ultimately Vancouver.

When they arrived I felt I could not face the psychological trauma of possibly identifying my wife without the presence of family and friends or the delays in returning to my home and family after many months of hope that my wife might be found alive. On impulse I altered the charts during the copying process, before distributing them.

While this has probably not had material consequences for the investigation, it is clear that it might have done so, and it is important for me to express my regrets for a foolish action and to clarify the matter for the authorities.

I understand that the correct dental chart is now being forwarded by the RCMP.

PART THREE
FALSIFICATION OF THE EVIDENCE

8

In both the legal and the moral sense, the falsification of the dental records lies at the heart of the Belshaw case. When the falsification became known it had a profound effect on public opinion. In Vancouver, in Vaud, and in Valais it made newspaper headlines and excited a great deal of comment. Everyone who heard about the falsification was struck by it. In many cases without even knowing Belshaw, they considered the implication of this act and made up their minds about Belshaw's guilt or innocence.

The climate of public opinion affected the case directly; both the gossip in Vancouver and Belshaw's desire to avoid publicity and scandal were to come up in the trial and be discussed in relation to his actions. On a deeper level, the shaping of public opinion was a paradigm of what was to happen at the trial. For Belshaw's trial was to be an elaborate attempt at fairness: a struggle to transcend bias and prejudice and to find the truth. So much of the case would depend upon the interpretation of ambiguous acts and behaviour.

Looking at the Belshaw case one sees with remarkable clarity how difficult it is to know the truth about any act—not in the abstract or philosophical sense, but in the ordinary way. Each actor in the drama had to decide what he understood of Belshaw's behaviour, and whether or not he believed and trusted him. Eventually a tribunal would sit in judgement upon a fellow man; each member of that tribunal would reach a verdict based upon his own experiences of life, his ability to evaluate facts and implied facts and to interpret their significance. Out of these individual decisions would come justice—or lack of it.

Public opinion would judge Belshaw in the same way. The gossip in Vancouver became a court of opinion which weighed Belshaw and his actions.

The effect of this upon Cyril Belshaw can not be ignored. He was a man of great reticence about his personal life, with a strong sense of his own right to privacy and a pronounced distaste for the sensational. He was horrified to see his name in bold headlines in the Vancouver *Sun*, and revolted by the public interest in his wife's disappearance and tragic end.

In this context it is important to remember that Cyril and Betty Belshaw were New Zealanders. They came from a community which is so often described by its own citizens as a backwater. The truth or falsity of this view is irrelevant; the attitude exists independent of reality—it is the colonial state of mind. It co-exists with a kind of smugness and, beneath this, a fear of being compared unfavourably with the *real* best, being revealed as less than "world-class". In fact the word "world-class", and the way it is used so often in colonial societies as a compliment, clearly reveals this state of mind.

In ex-British colonies, and perhaps particularly in New Zealand, the remnants of colonial British snobberies of class, rigid standards of behaviour, and inflexible attitudes tend to live on in ossified form. The Belshaws seemed in this respect to be products of the society where they were born, educated, and spent their formative years. They were attached to their middle-class values. They respected status, titles, good birth and good breeding. They valued intellectual achievement too, but they liked it best when it accompanied a senior person, a person with position and power.

The Belshaw family were—and so described themselves at the trial—very conscious of the image they presented to the world. In this they seemed almost like the familiar stiff-upper-lip caricature of the British. To be vulnerable to the public gaze, to reveal one's inmost self outside one's family, these things were insupportable to Cyril and Betty Belshaw. It may be that these attitudes were part of what made Belshaw's behaviour and actions so incomprehensible outside his family circle.

Most of us, when we consider the implications of some act or another, try to imagine ourselves in a similar position. This is a useful exercise, as far as it goes. The results may provide some degree of empathy. But while they will in some cases approach startlingly close to the truth of the matter, in other cases they will be totally irrelevant.

Police officers who have learned from experience how various is the human heart and its motives rarely, if ever, use this method to understand the motives of suspects or the probability of a certain act being likely for a certain person under certain circumstances. They will not generalize about whether such-and-such is sufficient motive for an act of violence or for murder. The limits of this kind of knowledge have become apparent to them, and they distrust it. But in the end our justice is based on empathy. Juries sit in judgement, they listen to the facts and the interpretations and they look at the accused and they think … What would he do if? What would I do, if? For when all the experts have finished testifying, when the judge has explained the law, when the evidence is in, it is against these questions that everything is weighed.

So, later in his trial, Belshaw would be asked over and over about the falsification. How could you, how *could* you do such a thing? What the questioners meant was, *I* can't imagine doing this, except under the most despairing necessity. Therefore …

So it was in Vancouver. Faced with the evidence of those altered dental records most Swiss and Canadian observers reacted in the same way: they decided only a guilty man could do such a thing. They were capable neither of an extraordinary act of imagination which would reveal to them a state of mind that might drive someone to such an extreme; nor were they capable of understanding a temperament that would judge such an act the lesser of the evils which pressed upon it.

Of course, they did not know Cyril Belshaw; they could not imagine themselves in his skin. And in this light it is important to note that Cyril Belshaw's son and daughter and his very closest friends *could* imagine it. They were absolutely certain that his motive was not the obvious one. They knew with an unshakeable certainty that he had not been involved in the death of Betty.

But it was at this point that public opinion judged Cyril Belshaw and found him guilty. Gossip condemned him; newspaper headlines were harsh with innuendo. People justified Cyril Belshaw's fear of their inability to understand, and revealed that unfortunate glee that so many feel in believing the worst of others. After all, the worst is more titillating, more fun to talk about.

But Cyril Belshaw deserved to have his point of view judged less glibly, and an effort of imagination can open more of it to us. It is helpful to try to recreate the scene as he waited for news of Betty in Montana-Vermala.

He himself described his state later, when he struggled in court to communicate all he had suffered. Day followed day with no news. He knew that Vancouver was rife with rumour. That sickened him. Worse, he lived daily in the uncertainty of not knowing what had become of her—an uncertainty much accentuated by his conversation with Major Smith in England.

As a beginning towards understanding Belshaw's psychological state, as he was to describe it later, imagine how the spouse of a suicide must feel: the guilt, the self-hatred, the constant analysis of the past. All the failures in his relationship with the one he loved are more than reproaches, they have become accusations which press upon him night and day and from which he cannot escape. But if, on top of this, he is uncertain, not knowing her fate ... if he waits day after day for news and hears nothing ... if he tells himself, one day, that he must learn to resign himself to the fact that his lifetime companion has killed herself, and yet the next day an idea, a wild theory, gives him a glimmer of hope, he would surely soon be reduced to a pitiable state of nerves, where reason and irrationality battle with no objective points to mark battlefields won or lost. Imagine, on top of this, being oppressed by the shame and humiliation of lurid newspaper headlines and gossip from those from whom you had always wished to keep your affairs private. More difficult still, imagine that during this time you live alone, day after day, in a foreign country, far from everything which has enriched your life: friends, intellectual stimulation, work, warmth, support, love. Imagine yourself a native of warm and temperate climates enduring all this in a cold wintry landscape, under low grey skies, where every day brings no news, only the fall of the fine, white deadening snow. Alone, frightened, and worst of all uncertain ... it is a prescription, surely, to go a bit mad.

There is evidence that Belshaw was in such a state just about the time the dental charts arrived in Montana. For this man who had all his life been dominated by reason, forethought and logical analysis tried to reach a psychic to find Betty.

A friend mentioned to him the name of a Mr. Croisé in Holland. Belshaw checked him out and heard good things about him. He discussed the matter by phone with Adrian and then, on April 20th, wrote to Croisé. In the end nothing came of it; ironically Croisé had suffered a nervous breakdown and was out of business. But here we have factual evidence that the Cyril Belshaw of this period was not the calm rational man of his public persona.

As he described his mental state during this time, it is possible to imagine that he simply could not face the moral implications of his wife's suicide, nor the horror of her having met with a kind of violence which would bring him further into the public eye.

He had already, since Betty's disappearance, learned of the public's lively interest in him, its hunger for the salacious and sensational. Irrational dreads tormented him; he longed desperately for Betty alive. Indeed that was the way it still might be, if she were not proved irrevocably dead. Alone, silent day after silent day, with nothing to do, logic, reason, fantasy, hope, dread, mix and become indistinguishable. The truth becomes what you will it to be.

After all, when we hear that someone we love has died we always say first: "No, it isn't true! No, I don't believe it!" This reaction of denial is fundamental before one can come to accept the death of a loved one. Even under ordinary circumstances death is the hardest fact to accept.

Belshaw, looking at those cold technical dental schemas, marked in black and white, gold crown on such-and-such a tooth ... what did they have to do with the living and breathing Betty who might, just might, if she were not dead, walk in the door this very night, and apologize for putting him to so much grief? Those technical charts must have to do only with a dead woman and he could not allow that to be Betty. He wanted to hope—it was the endurable mental state. The alternative was grief, guilt, and unbearable public humiliation.

This complex psychological state is what Belshaw would later attempt to communicate, with varying degrees of success. This irrational and tormented state of denial was not comprehensible to the watching bar of public opinion in the stolid community of Vancouver. And if we ourselves try to understand it, most of us are unable to.

Yet, our own actions and behaviour and motives often surprise us and we are totally daunted in unravelling their significance, so it may be just too glib to use tests of understanding which fail upon ourselves, in passing judgement upon others.

9

Unfortunately for Cyril Belshaw there was no way for him to *prove* the validity of his explanations of the falsification. They were subjective, and the Swiss wanted facts in order to assess the significance of this falsification.

First, from their point of view, was the incontrovertible fact of the falsification itself. Of this there could be no doubt. Belshaw had written out an admission of his action when he realized that his falsification would be discovered, and not before.

As soon as they received Belshaw's statement, the Vaudois authorities moved quickly. New records were obtained from Dr. Nishiguchi in Vancouver—copies of the same dental charts which had been sent to Belshaw in Montana, as well as x-rays. A comparison was made of these records with the teeth and jaw of the Le Sépey Corpse. On September 20th, 1979, nine months after Betty Belshaw had been reported missing in Paris, and six months after the body had been discovered by the side of the road, the Le Sépey Corpse was identified as Betty Joy Belshaw.

Now all the fears of accident, of suicide, of amnesia had been overtaken by a more dreadful reality. This woman to whom appearance, propriety and dignity were paramount had, after death, been stripped of her clothes, her human dignity, her identity, jettisoned down a slope, and left to rot. No one who had seen the photographs of her remains, or the garbage-strewn mountain slope where she was recovered could remain unmoved by the horror of what had happened to her.

The long period during which the body of Betty Belshaw lay undiscovered under the cold snows of the alpine winter had done more than deprive her of a decent resting place. It had made things very difficult indeed for the Vaudois investigators. By the time the body was discovered it was in such an advanced state of decomposition that the forensic experts could not tell how long it had lain under the snows and thaws of the mountain. Nor, due to the depredations of animals, could cause of death be accurately determined.

There were, in the final forensic report filed in August, some slight indications which the *police de sûreté* found suggestive. A faint pinkish cast to the roots of the teeth was noted, and some experts considered this to be a sign of strangulation.

In itself, this was not enough. But combined with the attempts which had been made to prevent the discovery of the body and to hide its identity, as well as the husband's falsification of the only reliable means of identification, there was, in the minds of the Vaudois authorities, no more room for doubt. This was no longer a question of a missing person, Vaud was convinced: a violent crime had been committed. To complicate matters the most important witness, the husband, was deeply involved, yet they were unable to question him. This man was a foreigner and a renowned scholar. His home was a country under the common law, which did not have clearly defined extradition procedures or reciprocal judicial conventions with Switzerland.

The first step was taken by the senior *juge d'instruction* of Vaud, Roland Chatelain. As was his prerogative, he took the case out of the hands of the Aigle *juge informateur*, Daniel Bournoud, and directly into his own. Then representations were made to the Canadian authorities.

But as far as Canada was concerned there was no material evidence linking Belshaw to any crime. The Canadian government told the Swiss that an attempt at extradition under the circumstances would probably not be successful. In order to extradite Switzerland would have to make a *prima facie* case, and Canada did not believe they could do so with the evidence they had so far presented. When the suggestion was made that Canada might investigate, and if necessary indict, Belshaw—an arrangement Switzerland had sometimes used with other countries and which it employs for its own nationals whom it does not extradite—it was made clear to the Swiss that Canada had no jurisdiction in the matter. Belshaw had committed no crime in Canada. Therefore it would not be possible to begin legal proceedings against him. The Canadian consulate in Berne interested itself in the matter, and Ottawa was kept informed.

The Swiss, now realizing that they could not draw on Canadian legal procedures for help, set out to conduct their investigation according to their own laws, as best they could. The first step, Chatelain decided, was to question Belshaw. On September 21st, 1979 he declared a *commission rogatoire*. Two Vaudois police officers, Inspectors Fischlin and Wyss, were instructed to set off at once to Vancouver. They were to carry out an investigation of Belshaw and, acting with the co-operation of the Canadian authorities, to do whatever else they deemed necessary to investigate the matter, "formal proof having been brought that the death of Mrs. Betty Belshaw was caused by violent means".

Two good policemen would find out what was behind the falsification. A solid investigation would move the matter out of the realm of gossip and speculation. And it would fill in the answers to other questions too, such as whether anyone else in Canada might have been involved in the death of Betty Belshaw. So the Swiss authorities believed, on September 21st, when Judge Chatelain charged Inspectors Fischlin and Wyss to go to Vancouver.

10

From the point of view of the RCMP there was a bit of the Inspector Clouseau in Fischlin and Wyss. Part of it was, inevitably, the language problem. Neither Fischlin nor Wyss spoke much English. Fischlin could make himself understood, but was certainly not fluent; Wyss could frequently get the gist of what was being said, but could not speak English. So they were obliged to turn to the French-speaking officer detailed to them, Sergeant Langois, in order to have their questions put properly into English.

Fischlin, the senior of the two, was an identification man. His area of expertise was in scene-of-the-crime work, fingerprints and related matters. He did not have a great deal of experience in interrogation. Wyss had even less. His inexperience frequently caused him to over-react, and more than once his interjections would derail a line of questioning that Fischlin or the RCMP were developing. Wyss was just thirty, short, blond, with a thick moustache and dark-rimmed glasses. Fischlin also appeared to be small, perhaps because he was quite slender. He had thinning hair and a slightly nervous manner. Wyss with his low forehead looked rather like a Schnauzer, and Fischlin like a ferret. They made quite a contrast to the RCMP officers with whom they worked, who with a few exceptions were all big men close to six feet tall.

Fischlin and Wyss arrived in Vancouver at 4:30 p.m. on the evening of September 23rd. The next morning they attended a meeting held at the Serious Crimes Office, E Division, District 1 Headquarters. The office is housed in a huge, expensive, rather isolated office tower just past the Arthur Lang Bridge in Vancouver. Things did not go well.

The Swiss officers, of course, intended to question Belshaw and then to do a thorough investigation among his friends, colleagues and enemies. Standard operating procedure. In Switzerland, they would have been able to arrest him, bring him up before a magistrate, put him in preventive detention and question him until they were satisfied. In Switzerland, Belshaw would have been obliged to answer their questions.

Now, at the meeting at the Serious Crimes Office, the Swiss were brought face to face with one of the most serious difficulties they encountered in the early stages of the investigation, and one that would affect all subsequent events, up to and including the trial itself.

The Swiss officers were told by their Canadian counterparts that Professor Belshaw did not have to answer their questions if he did not wish to; that in Canada, the suspect has the right to remain silent.

Fischlin and Wyss could not believe it. It seemed impossible to them that police work could be conducted in this fashion. In Switzerland, refusal to co-operate with the police, refusal to answer questions—no matter how often asked or how tedious or how incriminating or how irrelevant—is seen as a sign of guilt. The RCMP officers who joined in that first conversation remembered it long afterwards. It certainly could not have been only jet-lag which rendered Fischlin and Wyss so uncomprehending, so incredulous. Constable Terry Smith, the officer who worked most closely with them, and later a more superior officer in the Division found great difficulty in getting their points across. Many of the RCMP officers would remember the frustrations and difficulties of those early conversations. But it can not have been easy for Fischlin and Wyss, after a long flight, in a foreign language, trying to grasp a system of investigation entirely different from their own, in which many of the methods they were accustomed to using to solve crimes would be useless.

In Vaud, after the police arrest a suspect they have to bring him before a magistrate within twenty-four hours. During that period— or before the arrest for that matter—they can question the suspect without informing him of any rights; he does not have the right to remain silent, anything he says can later be used against him, and if the police do not wish to allow him to contact his lawyer, they are not obliged to do so.

After the suspect is brought before a magistrate, the penal code of Vaud comes into effect. The behaviour of the police is strictly regulated. Everything they do is written down and becomes part of the dossier on the case.

A key point of difference between the civil and the common law is the difference in the roles of the *juge d'instruction* and the judge who hears the preliminary hearing in common-law countries. For under the civil law it is always part of the *juge d'instruction*'s role to examine the suspect about himself, about his work, his health, his background, his attitudes, his previous brushes with the law and his ambitions for his future. The judge and police officers try to form a picture of him first, before seeing how his actions relate to the crime. Other witnesses will be quizzed on the same subjects, asked *their* opinion of the accused. All this information will enter the dossier. In common-law countries, this kind of information is for the most part inadmissible. It is considered prejudicial and, particularly at the preliminary hearing, the judge will not allow mention of it.

Under the civil law, the defence will also have a chance to suggest additional questions to be asked of suspect and witnesses, and it can request further investigations be made. The information accumulated by the State on its own and at the request of the defence will all become part of the dossier.

Fischlin and Wyss were acting under the direction of the *juge d'instruction*: "to interview Cyril Belshaw, to conduct a search of his residence, to carry out all other operations useful or necessary, and to act in conjunction with local authorities." Their instructions suggested that they should be present when such actions were carried out, but that their own activities should fall short of active participation.

Belshaw's Swiss defence counsel would later attack the activities of these two officers bitterly—a thing which is unusual in Vaud where the police, as an arm of the judiciary, are usually sacrosanct. The suggestion would be made that they were over-zealous in their pursuit of Belshaw, and that they investigated no other possible leads into the cause of Betty's death. Canadians who were either interviewed or present at some of their interviews were surprised by some of the questions they put, which seemed more designed to embarrass and harass than to reveal the truth of the Belshaw mystery. But at this time so many facts were not known in Canada, facts which, when they later became clear, explained the line of some of those early questions.

Fischlin and Wyss spent part of their first day paying a visit to Mark de Weerdt, an officer from the Department of Justice whom they expected would authorize their commission and assure that it was operating within a legal framework.

Here again they were surprised. From their point of view they were a duly authorized *commission rogatoire* established by a judge. But from the Canadian point of view these officers had no official standing. There had been no judicial hearing before a magistrate in Canada to authorize their letters rogatory—in fact, no such document was ever presented in Canada. The Swiss officers simply identified themselves to De Weerdt. A discussion followed between De Weerdt and the RCMP officers to which Fischlin and Wyss listened.

De Weerdt explained again the rights of Canadian citizens with regard to their not having to answer questions. Fischlin and Wyss found the information just as unlikely coming from De Weerdt as they had from the RCMP. From their point of view the short interview was not particularly satisfactory. They were finding the Canadians distinctly unhelpful.

From the RCMP's side, however, it had become more important than ever that the Swiss policemen be accompanied everywhere by one of their officers—partly as a courtesy which they would have extended to any foreign police officer, and partly to be certain that the Swiss operated by the rules in Canada.

So it was that at 5:00 p.m. on that first day, when Fischlin and Wyss began their first interview with Belshaw, several RCMP officers were present. The bilingual Sergeant Langois was there to help with translation. Constable Smith, as the officer who had been involved with the case, was there too. And later they were joined by still more officers.

And Cyril Belshaw—who still believed that the last that was known of his wife was that she was missing, vanished in Paris, who could still imagine her in his mind's eye as alive—now found himself summoned to the police station on the Endowment lands of UBC and confronted by several policemen. The interview which followed lasted over two hours. It was extraordinarily harsh, even by the admission, later, of the prosecution.

Belshaw was told baldly for the first time of the discovery of his wife's remains and their positive identification. Belshaw was shocked. His mouth grew dry, and his tongue stuck to the roof of his mouth. His expressions of horror and dismay struck some of the police as those of a man who was acting, and Constable Smith told Belshaw that he did not seem particularly upset.

Then the interrogation really began. Before Belshaw had a chance to recover himself, he was assaulted by questions. ''Why did you kill your wife? We know you did it,'' the Swiss officers insisted. Question followed question without let-up. Questions were interjected suddenly, dropped, and then repeated later. Fischlin took some garbage bags from his briefcase and told Belshaw that Betty had been found in such bags, available only in Montana, so how could he contend that she had disappeared in Paris?

When Belshaw, struggling to control himself, managed to stay calm, the officers asked him whether he was a Christian. "No, I'm an atheist," he replied. The officers responded that perhaps that was the reason that he was so callous, so lacking in feelings of remorse and guilt which would have been prompted by a Christian conscience.

Constable Smith asked Belshaw if there was another woman in his life. No, of course not, Belshaw told him. I am a happily married man. "I urge you to be frank with us," Smith said.

Belshaw, however, persisted in his denials. Smith told him they would be obliged to investigate thoroughly. Wouldn't it be easier, Smith suggested, for Belshaw to simply tell the truth?

From Smith's point of view, this was just a simple statement of fact. But Belshaw saw it as a threat. The Swiss police were growing exasperated by Belshaw's self-control. "If you were in Switzerland you would not be getting such easy treatment," one told him. To Belshaw, it was another threat, and one that was to come clearly to mind later.

What Belshaw did not know was that this entire interview was being taped. An RCMP officer had concealed a tape recorder microphone in his clothes, and the tape recorder was running under the table. This is neither illegal under Canadian law, nor particularly uncommon. The tape was later transcribed in two parts; the English section was transcribed by stenographers at the University detachment, and the French part was sent out to a French-speaking stenographer and transcribed later. Both transcriptions, along with a copy of the tape, were sent to Switzerland. Edited versions were to enter the dossier, and to cause a lot of trouble.

Later the public prosecutor of Vaud was to speak of Belshaw's demeanour under questioning—and particularly during this interview—with admiration. "A very, very tough man," he would comment. A man who could keep in mind accurately a myriad of tiny details. A man who almost never contradicted himself, who after a hard day of work, after being confronted by the shocking news of his wife's death and the horrifying description of the disposal of her body, held his own under the fiercest of questioning. Eventually even turning to French to communicate directly with Fischlin and Wyss, Belshaw handled himself extraordinarily well, the prosecutor thought. He did not make any significant damaging admissions; he did not contradict himself; he explained everything in a way that must satisfy the logic of his inquisitors. And at all times he was calm and under control.

Although the interview ended officially at 7:10 p.m., the Swiss police then asked Belshaw if they could see his wife's jewelry. Belshaw agreed and everyone drove over to his house. Belshaw did not feel he could drive, so a constable drove him; this officer then stayed with Belshaw during the search which followed. Several RCMP officers and the Swiss police now entered the large half-timbered Tudor-style house which faced busy Chancellor Boulevard. As Belshaw watched, the "look at the jewelry" escalated into a full-scale search. The police were looking through his wife's clothing and papers, and he was becoming more and more distressed.

First he phoned his daughter Diana and talked with her, then at 8:30 p.m. he phoned his Vancouver lawyer, and the two discussed the matter for some time. By a quarter to nine he had made up his mind.

"Leave the house," he told the police. "You don't have a search warrant."

The officers protested, "But you gave us permission."

"Yes," Belshaw agreed, "but now I want you to leave."

Permission had been revoked, and all the officers left the house, Fischlin and Wyss more unhappy than ever with Canadian procedures. As the officers were leaving, Belshaw saw Constable Smith, who was just coming up the walk. Smith had not been present during the search, and he was arriving only as the others were on their way out. Suddenly, Belshaw broke down and wept on Smith's shoulder. I can't bear it, that they would suspect me of such a thing, he told Smith.

The next day Fischlin and Wyss wanted to question Belshaw further. But by this time he had consulted with his lawyer, Harry McLaughlin, and had an opportunity to think the matter over. McLaughlin suggested that Fischlin and Wyss submit their questions

in writing. This the Swiss were unwilling to do. It was not a procedure they were accustomed to. They had difficulty accepting the
idea that they had to negotiate before questioning a suspect, and
then arrange to do so under terms agreeable to his lawyer and
himself. Eventually, when they realized that they had no other
choice, they did submit a list of questions to McLaughlin. But as
there was nothing in them which they had not already asked Belshaw
and which he had not already answered, McLaughlin advised them
that such an interview would be pointless. From the Swiss point of
view then, no more co-operation of any kind was forthcoming from
Belshaw. They could only regard this as a very suspicious circumstance.

Fischlin and Wyss now began moving through the community
questioning the Belshaws' family and friends, colleagues and neighbours. They were thorough. They talked to members of the Anthropology and Sociology department who knew Cyril, and members
of the English department who had worked with Betty. They talked
to secretaries, professors and instructors. They were trying to de-
velop a picture of both Belshaws, of their life together, of their
working life and their private life, of their public personae and their
more secret private selves. They even talked to the Belshaws' doctors. Very quickly the Swiss officers, with the help of the RCMP
who also conducted interviews, formed a composite picture of the
two. This picture would later enter the dossier in the form of a
written character-sketch of each, studded with quotations excerpted
from these interviews. The *juge d'instruction* would study them,
as they would become an important consideration in his later rulings.
As well, they would become a major part of the trial when—for the
first time—they would be made public.

The two Swiss officers may have looked into Betty's past for
other leads as to what might have happened to her—other, that is,
than Cyril having been the cause of her death. No such evidence,
however, appeared in the dossier. It seemed that whatever they did
find led to dead ends.

In any case, Fischlin and Wyss learned a great deal. But they
suffered from the difficulty that those most loyal to the Belshaws,
most convinced of Cyril's innocence and probity, were the most
reticent. Whereas the Belshaws' enemies, or those who were not
close to them, generally managed, even when trying to behave with

decency, to drop a spiteful remark, or to make an innuendo. So no concrete evidence of Betty's brief lapses of memory, which might have suggested the truth of Belshaw's statements about them, surfaced during this investigation. However, information of another kind did come their way.

It is a commonplace that no one's life is without blemish. In fact, one sometimes gets the impression that we have only to hear of a blameless life, a totally upright person, to direct towards such a person all our suspicions of hidden corruption and secrets squirrelled away. In the case of Betty Belshaw, however, such suspicions had been shown to be totally unfounded. No secrets lurked in her past which might have led to her death.

If the solution to Betty's murder lay in her past, then it seemed her death would forever remain mysterious. If, on the other hand, it lay in her character, then Fischlin and Wyss might have had some justification for being pleased with the results of their investigation. For to their eyes a picture began to emerge of a woman of uncomfortable rigidity in certain areas. Although friends, and even those who did not like her, cited evidence of Betty's generosity, warmth and kindness, and students remembered her with love and admiration, all but the most loyal also talked of another side to her. A judgemental side, proud and unforgiving. They described a narrow-minded woman who did not want to teach Alice Munro's *Lives of Girls and Women* because of its masturbation scene. "Proper and formal," they called her.

A colleague of Betty in her department confided, "She was hard to work with, nervous, narrow-minded and very stubborn. She was a perfectionist who made mountains out of molehills, who worried herself sick over unimportant details. It was probably fortunate that Cyril travelled so much, and that they were apart a lot. He could be overbearing, and she was hard to live with. He left for the sabbatical early and she had so much to do. She had to get English 100 all organized for her successor. She had to wind up all her and Cyril's private affairs, and get the house ready for the tenants who would be in while they were away. Why, as I remember it, she was frantic that last month before she left. She was doing some wall-papering for her tenants, buying new bedspreads, having a dinner party, she never had time to stop and chat. We all said she really needed a rest; she seemed close to a nervous breakdown.''

Another remembered a conversation with Betty before her departure. ''She was tired, almost frantic ... I was having trouble with my marriage, and thinking about divorce. Betty said, 'I don't know how you can consider it. I don't know what I'd do if Cyril left me.' She seemed so anxious. I thought the year away would do her a great deal of good.''

Betty had been tired and overworked, everyone agreed. There were suggestions that she may have been taking medication, possibly tranquillizers or sleeping pills. Even suggestions that these medications might have caused lapses of memory or brief periods of confusion. But these last were not verified by the investigators and so nothing more was heard of them, and later neither prosecution nor defence ever suggested that Betty might have become confused and wandered away of her own accord.

If Betty's life was blameless, and if a picture of a victim who might provoke only through her personality alone was being drawn by the Swiss authorities, more concrete evidence had surfaced in the case of Cyril. Evidence of a secret and less blameless side to *his* life, a side they felt, that Betty would not have understood.

Preliminary investigation in Switzerland had suggested to the Swiss police that there had been other women in Belshaw's life— but they found it difficult to verify these stories. Belshaw himself denied during his first interview that he had been unfaithful. And now Betty's close friends told the police that there was no other woman. They were certain that Cyril and Betty were devoted to one another and that it was impossible that Cyril had been unfaithful to Betty in Vancouver. Cyril's friends merely looked blank.

But Fischlin and Wyss persisted. Investigation in Montana-Vermala had turned up evidence of a female friend, a blonde, and they believed they could find her identity in Vancouver. They had doubts about the picture of a happily married man losing his wife in Paris. A man, it was now obvious, who had falsified her dental records and who was, from their point of view, refusing to co-operate with the police. And here is where luck deserted Belshaw entirely, and appeared on the side of his worst opponents. Fischlin and Wyss found the woman they were looking for. And they did so in the most unfortunate manner possible for Cyril Belshaw.

PART FOUR
DISCOVERY OF THE SECRET LOVE AFFAIR

11

Belshaw had a way with women. Or that was one way of putting the facts which slowly emerged from the police investigation. He had not been a faithful husband, and this fact was known to some of his friends and colleagues. A university community is, after all, a relatively small and inbred society, where over the years it is impossible to be totally discreet. Fischlin and Wyss learned that Belshaw had been seen from time to time with different women. But it was very hard to get information. People just did not want to tell them things. Then they had a stroke of luck.

A police report from the RCMP was communicated to them. No matter that this incident had taken place after all the events they were investigating—after the disappearance of Betty and after Cyril's return to Vancouver. It was just the lead they were looking for.

According to the report, on July 19th, 1979 Constable Fleet of the RCMP was performing a routine patrol of the university campus. At 11:00 p.m. he was driving down the south campus road, approaching a semi-secluded circular turn-around, with an island covered with bush in the centre. There was a car parked on the far side, invisible until one circled the turn-around. Constable Fleet approached the car, which appeared to him to be empty. As he approached, a man, as he said in his report, "climbed off a woman". His clothes were in disarray. Her skirt was partly undone and her underpants were visible.

The car was a red sportscar, a two-seater with a gear shift in the middle. Constable Fleet questioned both parties. The woman gave her name as Margery Wilson. She could not find her driver's licence so she showed her social insurance card. The man showed his licence to Fleet. He was Cyril Belshaw. "Why don't you do this somewhere else?" Fleet said to them, and left, recording the incident in his notebook.

Both Wilson and Belshaw later, separately, denied this account. And it is indeed possible that the circumstances were not as Fleet described, that the two were merely talking over an examination paper in the car, as they claimed. But in any case, the police now had the name of a woman—a woman with whom Belshaw had been seen, alone, late at night, in a car. This was a lead they could follow up, and they did.

Mrs. Wilson's address was in the files of the RCMP and this information was given to Fischlin and Wyss. They did not wish to question Wilson immediately, in case she were not the woman who had been seen in Montana-Vermala, so it was agreed that they would check first on this, and that the RCMP would then follow up if necessary. Later, two RCMP officers visited Wilson to discuss her part in the case. They called upon her, at her house, which was not far from Belshaw's, where she lived with her husband and children. She was, of course, deeply distressed by their visit, and they had only begun to talk to her when her husband came home unexpectedly. The officers left, and Mrs. Wilson promised to call them again the next day. However she failed to do so, and when they called her she told them that her lawyer had advised her not to talk to them.

Wilson was an attractive woman in her early forties, her hair a rather light brown, approaching blonde. She was married to a well-off professional man. Twenty-five years earlier she had met Belshaw when she was a student of nursing and he a young professor. They had become friends then, and both worked on the Canadian University Service Overseas programme, CUSO, which, just in its formative stages at this time, was to become a popular, broad-based organization, sending Canadians to work in developing countries;

Belshaw was one of its directors. Eventually Wilson had married and moved away.

Later she returned to Vancouver, and she and her husband bought a house on the Endowment lands. So it came about that she and Cyril Belshaw renewed their acquaintance. Mrs. Wilson had two young children. Her friendship with Belshaw had been a support to her in a difficult marriage. Now she had returned to UBC to continue her studies, and would frequently talk over her academic problems with Belshaw. That, she told the officers, was what they had been doing in the car that evening.

Even though they had not talked directly to Wilson, Fischlin and Wyss had found out a great deal. They had a good picture—from their own point of view—of Cyril and Betty. They had talked to their friends, colleagues and family. They had, they believed, discovered the identity of the woman in Cyril's life—the woman they had been looking for when they came to Canada. But at the same time they had been frustrated at every turn. First by the attitude of Belshaw himself. It was absolutely inconceivable to them that Belshaw could just decide to refuse to talk to them. It was hard to see how a police officer could do his job under such circumstances. Then there was the matter of Wilson. Here too they had met with a stone wall. They had identified her—but they couldn't get any solid information about her relationship with Belshaw. Later she would, at first, refuse to sign a statement: when the Swiss asked the Vancouver RCMP to write up their visit with Mrs. Wilson, the RCMP were reluctant to do so because Mrs. Wilson was not prepared to read over the report, and sign it. Fischlin and Wyss decided to return to Switzerland, and consult with their superiors and the *juge d'instruction*. It was really, it seemed to them, impossible to investigate in Canada.

Certainly this view was clearly expressed by the Swiss newspapers. Pierre Pittet, writing in *24 heures*, said, "The Vaudois investigators thought that M. Belshaw would want to participate in the enquiry to facilitate the eventual discovery or location of the murderers. But, on the contrary, M. Belshaw learning from the press that Swiss justice was more and more anxious for his testimony, hired a lawyer in Vancouver and hid behind Canadian law.

He remained in the shadows, refusing all comment.'' Speaking of Belshaw's explanation for falsifying the dental records, the noted crime reporter, Pierrette Blanc, writing in the *Tribune de Lausanne* said, ''The *juge d'instruction* of Vaud, Roland Chatelain, is ready to believe him. But he wants him to come and explain matters in Lausanne. Belshaw has systematically refused. What is he afraid of?

''Then the Vaudois inspectors went to Canada. But Belshaw is no more talkative. He hides behind Canadian law using it to explain a silence which renders him more and more suspect in the eyes of the Swiss.''

The Swiss were tempted to believe that the RCMP knew perfectly well how to induce a suspect and witnesses to talk, but just weren't prepared to do it. There was a wall of misunderstanding and mistrust between the Swiss and the Canadians—as wide a wall as that between the civil code and the common law. Certainly Fischlin and Wyss didn't think they were the ones to break it down. They had done all they could.

12

When Fischlin and Wyss returned to Lausanne, they consulted with the *juge d'instruction*, Roland Chatelain. They reviewed the whole situation. Clearly a suggestive picture had been built up. But was it correct? A lot of police work needed to be done.

First Belshaw's story had to be checked. Was there any evidence that Betty had indeed made the trip with him to Paris? When was she last seen alive by someone else? Had there been any fights or quarrels between the couple while they were in Europe? Was there a financial motive—that is, would anyone benefit financially by

Betty's death? Had the neighbours at the Jolilac seen or heard anything? Had anyone in Paris?

Then Chatelain felt more was needed, if possible, from Canada. By the second week of October, just a little over two weeks after Fischlin and Wyss returned from Vancouver, Chatelain was requesting help, through the press and the Vancouver RCMP, from those who knew Belshaw. He issued a call for anyone who had any information about Cyril or Betty Belshaw, either in Canada or in Europe, to make it available to the RCMP. The RCMP themselves, as part of the reciprocal arrangement operating between national police forces, continued to check out leads for the Swiss.

In Lausanne, the capital of Vaud, the police set to work. They began collecting records of every financial transaction. They visited Montana-Vermala; Beaune, where, according to Belshaw's account, the couple had stopped on their journey to Paris; Inspector Wyss visited the Hotel Bagnolet in Paris, and the Bibliothèque Nationale. They worked on the provenance of the garbage bags and twine. In the months that followed a mountainous dossier was produced.

Meanwhile, the affair was proving a sensation in the Suisse Romande. The story had everything necessary to make it a *cause célèbre*: the renown of Belshaw himself; the glamorous life-style— or so it appeared—of the couple who travelled freely between Canada, London, Paris and Switzerland; the grande luxe address of the Montana-Vermala resort (at that time the press was mistakenly quoting the price of $2,200 per month for the apartment rented by the couple); the fact that the case was now being handled by Roland Chatelain himself. The story was inherently dramatic and romantic. *L'affaire Belshaw* made headlines. The press played it up, and they did so with a great deal of licence. They speculated on Belshaw's guilt, they called his behaviour suspicious, and they condemned the Canadian judicial system. Certainly they were still, at this early stage of the matter, referring to the Belshaws as Mme. Betty B. and Professor Cyril B. But it is hard to see what good this did. The Vancouver papers had made contact with Lausanne journalists, and were exchanging tidbits. They were reading and digesting the Swiss copy, and the Swiss attitude towards the case was filtering into the press in Vancouver.

Then the Swiss newspapers got hold of what seemed at first a really good angle. The Jugoslav concièrge of the Jolilac apartment building, Zdravko Vrgovic, began giving interviews. He stated categorically that he had seen Betty alive weeks after Cyril reported her missing. He was certain, he told reporters (and he was quite pleased to talk to them as long as they would listen) that he had seen Betty, and talked to her between January 20th and February 6th—school holidays in Jugoslavia, when his mother and children were visiting him. Betty alive and walking around, shopping in Montana-Vermala a week after Cyril had reported her missing? The newspapers loved it. It conjured up visions of a fight in Paris, Betty going home on her own, Cyril following her ... and then what? The newspaper reporters tried to shake the concièrge, but he was insistent. He remembered Betty, she had been carrying a red purse.

This story reached Vancouver too, where it was instantly discounted by all of Betty's own friends. "Never," they declared to one another and to anyone who would listen, "would Betty carry a red purse. Out of the question. The concièrge must be making it up." The story was later to be abandoned, as it could not be corroborated. But when it first came out, it heightened the sensationalism surrounding the case.

The *juge d'instruction* and the Lausanne *police de sûreté* wanted all the more to talk to Belshaw. In Vancouver he refused to comment on the Vrgovic story—or so the judge told the Swiss press. The police began to set certain wheels in motion, so that if Belshaw presented himself in Europe they could talk to him. It was not their experience or habit to be baulked of an important witness—perhaps by now a suspect.

As their investigations continued, more and more small but significant clues were unearthed. Or, in many cases, no clues were found where, if Belshaw's story were true, there ought to be some. Some of the witnesses, long-time friends of the Belshaws', made serious allegations against Belshaw. The police had to check these out. The forensic evidence was examined and re-examined. Foreign experts were called in for second opinions on time and cause of death.

As the dossier lengthened, the Wilson love affair grew in importance. A picture of Wilson had now been identified by witnesses in Montana-Vermala, who had seen the two there. The police went on to discover that Belshaw and Wilson had been together in Europe the summer before the sabbatical began. In June, while Betty was frantically getting the house ready for the year away and finishing off her administrative responsibilities for English 100, Cyril Belshaw and Margery Wilson were enjoying an idyllic holiday together. They lived together in a little apartment in Montana-Vermala. They travelled to Ferney, home of Voltaire, and to Paris, where they spent three days together. They had not been discreet, it was very easy to find traces of them.

What did it all mean? Was this a serious love affair that could threaten a thirty-seven-year marriage? Or was it an insignificant adventure between a man to whom sexual fidelity was not important and a younger woman, an adventure which merely added a little spice to both their lives without endangering their serious relationships or their family responsibilities? It could have been insignificant, or it could have been a passionate romance which might provide a motive for murder. Wilson would not talk, nor would Belshaw.

But the Swiss had put out their lines and were watching the bait. They were prepared to wait.

PART FIVE
UNEXPECTED ARREST AT ROISSY

13

Although Belshaw had been told officially that his wife was dead during the first few minutes of his interview with Fischlin and Wyss on September 24th, Vancouver first heard the news in the press on October 2nd.

On October 3rd a memorial ceremony was held at the Frederic Wood theatre at UBC. It lasted half an hour and was written up under ironic headlines in the Vancouver newspapers.

Over two hundred friends, colleagues and sensation-seekers attended the simple service. In Betty's honour members of the English department read Milton and quoted from the Psalms. A student paid tribute with Thomas Hood's "Ode to Autumn". Taped music by Mozart was played. Cyril, Adrian and Diana were there. People looked at them curiously, trying to read some sign of their feelings in their faces. But the Belshaws held themselves under control, as was their custom.

The ceremony was muted; Betty had been missing a long time, and now this service was taking place in isolation—distant from the time and place of her death. It was not a funeral and it provided no opportunity for catharsis.

Betty's friends and colleagues wanted desperately to dignify her passing. As they listened to the music and the poems of the brief tribute they thought that no end they could have imagined could have been more horrible to Betty. A woman whose pride and sense of decorum ruled her life—to end naked and decomposing on a Swiss mountainside, her final tribute a blare of sensational newspaper headlines and the lurid curiosity of sensation-seekers. What worse indignity could be imagined for such a woman? Even the details: the garbage bags, the twine ... the months unrecognized and unmourned. Mourners are soothed when they can imagine that the death of a loved one has happened the way that person would have wished, quickly perhaps, or with family and friends at the bedside. What had happened to Betty was a desecration so profound, in relation to the person that she had been, that it was almost unbearable. All the odes of Milton and the poetry of the Psalms could never wash away the horror of Betty's ignominious and revolting end.

People were watching Cyril too, and afterwards they talked about his demeanour at the service. One friend remarked with surprise about an ambiguous remark Cyril had made: "We haven't heard the last of this, not by a long chalk." This was not the first of the many suggestions that there was a great deal more to Betty's death than met the eye but that Cyril was just not free to reveal the details. Yet another friend said that she had been near Cyril, that he had turned to her, had clutched her hands and said, with tears streaming down his face, "We must carry on somehow."

Possibly there had been an idea that the memorial service would not only pay tribute to Betty, but would give the university community a chance to rally around Cyril, to show their loyalty to one of their own, who now, during a time of bereavement, seemed to be increasingly under a cloud.

Yet somehow this did not seem to be the final effect. Cyril's demeanour, even in Vancouver, struck people unpleasantly. The tears he had shed at the memorial ceremony somehow failed to erase the over-all impression of indifference. Perhaps people were determined to believe the worst, despite evidence to the contrary. For Cyril's coldness was much talked about. His characteristic reticence separated him from the majority of his peers; its effects reverberated throughout the whole of his ordeal, even to the final judgement itself. But to his closest friends, during this time Cyril certainly did not appear cold or indifferent. He was still grieving—and he was very worried. He had an important UNESCO conference coming up in Paris. Professionally, he felt obliged to be there. Yet he could not help but remember the veiled threats of Fischlin and Wyss. Knowing how anxious the Swiss were to talk to him he wondered if he would be wise to attend. Still, he had his professional life to lead, and it involved a great deal of travelling. Sooner or later he would have to take the bit in his teeth or he would become a prisoner of the Swiss in his own country, fearing always to travel.

So he made plans to go to the conference.

Several weeks before he was due in Paris there was a tug on one of the lines the Swiss *police de sûreté* had out in that city. Their patience had paid off, for they now learned that Belshaw was to arrive there for the UNESCO conference.

On November 7th Roland Chatelain issued a warrant of arrest. Now Belshaw was a wanted man in Switzerland, with an official charge against him.

In Vancouver, Belshaw was still vacillating. Though he did not yet know of the warrant, he called a close friend the night before his departure and agonized over the decision to fly to Paris. He knew something of the Swiss legal system. Once in its toils he might find himself trapped, unable to defend himself according to Canadian ideas of what is just. If he were put into preventive detention he would lose all opportunity to find out himself what had happened to Betty. It was a difficult decision. Eventually, however, he decided to go.

And so, at 12:55 on November 11th, when Cyril Belshaw stepped off his Air Canada flight at Roissy airport he was arrested by the airport police, who were waiting for him. He was immediately turned over to the central *police judiciaire* and the prosecutor at Bobigny, a suburb of Paris.

And then, while he awaited his extradition hearing, he was committed to the notorious prison of Fleury-Mérogis.

14

Harry McLaughlin, who had acted for Belshaw in Canada vis-à-vis the Swiss police and their RCMP colleagues, practised, without partners, out of an expensive office tower on Pender West, in downtown Vancouver. From his small office a huge window gave a magnificent view of Vancouver, sparkling in the sun or, more often, grey in the rain and mist. McLaughlin specialized in contested divorces and was not very well known among the fraternity of lawyers who practise at the criminal bar. And his advice to Belshaw, up to this time, though perfectly proper in Canadian terms, had helped to contribute to the misunderstandings and suspicion with which Belshaw was now regarded in Switzerland.

McLaughlin was a middle-aged man with thick dark curly hair, and a face that gave nothing away. He gave the impression of being a fighter, a hard man, slightly uncomfortable with himself and with an edge of nervousness to his personality that never quite wore off.

In one way McLaughlin served Belshaw magnificently. Because if it were he, as he claimed, who found and retained Belshaw's counsel in Europe, he could not have done better.

At the time of Belshaw's arrest in Paris, Jean-Félix Paschoud, one of the most well-known and well-respected lawyers in the Suisse Romande was in Paris on business. He was consulted, and agreed to visit Belshaw at Fleury-Mérogis prison. Only after talking with Belshaw would Paschoud decide whether or not to take his case.

Paschoud was born near Lausanne in 1918. He was the principal partner in the firm of Carrard and Paschoud. His father and grandfather had both been well-known lawyers in Vaud, and he was the third generation of Paschoud to practise in the firm. Paschoud spoke English fluently, with subtlety, and numbered among his clients many of the international community of celebrities who have chosen the gentle and secure communities of the Suisse Romande for their homes including Graham Greene, Charlie Chaplin, and Coco Chanel.

Paschoud is an unusual man, for a powerful lawyer. Although obviously intelligent, and with a great deal of charm, he is also a man of passionate convictions. His capacity for deep feeling shows in his face, which is worn with a patina like the shivered glaze of antique Chinese porcelain. Of medium height, with thinning dark hair, black-rimmed glasses, and the long upper lip characteristic of the region, he has an attractiveness compounded partly of charm, but more of his sincere and intense nature. When speaking to you, he comes up very close and looks intensely into your eyes, watching your reactions and communicating his own conviction.

Paschoud's first meeting with Belshaw was crucial. If he decided to take on the case Belshaw would have, in his corner, one of the most influential and skilful lawyers in the Suisse Romande. And even more important, he would have, as defender, a man whose integrity and sincerity were beyond question. In this small community, where everyone knew everyone, such things could not be without importance. If he could ally himself with Paschoud, Belshaw would no longer be a stranger, an outsider to a small closed community. He would, by virtue of his lawyer, obtain instant position and respectability.

So Paschoud paid his crucial visit to Belshaw in Fleury-Mérogis. He stayed for half an hour and questioned Belshaw deeply, searchingly. By the end of that visit Paschoud was committed to Belshaw. He had made up his mind, and was never to waver: Belshaw was innocent, absolutely and completely innocent. He was a man trapped in a nightmare and Paschoud intended to free him. Paschoud was certain that he would succeed, and he devoted himself, in the year that followed, to the Belshaw case with the thoroughness and commitment that had carved him such a high place in the legal community.

Then Belshaw had what appeared to be another stroke of good fortune. He was able to retain, to act for him in the case of his extradition from France, the services of Robert Badinter.

Robert Badinter was one of the most renowned lawyers in France. His fame had spread even to Switzerland. When the *police de sûreté* heard that he had been retained, they were dismayed. They thought the fish had slipped the hook and that they would never get Belshaw to Switzerland at all.

Badinter had made his name in several celebrated cases. He had opposed capital punishment in France, taking the battle up to the French Supreme Court. He was known as a fine lawyer and as a fighter for just causes. The public prosecutor of Vaud was to say, later, "Badinter must be one of the best lawyers in the world. We thought Belshaw would never be extradited."

Robert Badinter's office is on the Rue du Faubourg St. Honoré, in one of the most elegant *quartiers* in Paris. A magnificent eighteenth-century building with a courtyard, walls faced with marble, ten-foot-high ceilings, a wide curved staircase. In the office everything is on a large scale—in proportion to the high ceilings. Lush contemporary furniture, desks made of great sheets of plate glass, contemporary prints.

Badinter himself is a small, fine-boned man, dark, elegant, beautifully tailored. Very quick and bright. He was immediately interested in everything about the Belshaw case.

In discussions with his client Badinter explained that relations between Switzerland and France are regulated by an old nineteenth-century treaty of extradition, which is usually honoured. The procedure requires that Switzerland send an original warrant of arrest and an extract of the charges. When this is done, extradition is almost always granted. After all, a lot more French criminals escape to Switzerland than *vice versa*, so the French are more than anxious to co-operate.

The scope for Badinter to exercise his much vaunted legal skills was, in fact, very limited. The defence in an extradition charge has no right to challenge the charges themselves. They can only really argue whether or not the charges fall within the scope of the extradition treaty and whether the proceedings are in accord with the law.

In this case, Belshaw was wanted for murdering his wife, and the evidence produced by the Swiss was the autopsy, and the condition of the body in Switzerland—that it was found naked, wrapped in Swiss garbage bags and so on. Badinter felt the only chance would be to argue the right of the French courts to limit extradition to *serious grounds*. After all, no evidence of murder or violent death had been produced. Nor was there any proof that Betty had met her death in Switzerland. The only evidence was that of the falsification of the dental records, which might be seen as just contempt of court. The Swiss, Badinter could contend, must enlarge the charges if they wanted to extradite Belshaw for murder.

So Belshaw had to make up his mind whether or not to fight extradition. He could accede, go to Switzerland, and there, with

Paschoud behind him, hope that the matter would be cleared up during the *instruction*, the preliminary inquiry, and never brought to trial. Perhaps he wavered, for at one point McLaughlin announced to the Vancouver press that Belshaw intended to go to Switzerland voluntarily. But eventually, after considering Badinter's advice, Belshaw decided to fight his extradition to Switzerland.

This, too, of course, was a sign of guilt to the Swiss. Badinter would explain that Belshaw had made plans to go to China and feared that if he were to go to Switzerland he would be put in preventive detention. And Belshaw himself said that there were things he had to do, some in connection with clearing up Betty's death, which would be impossible if he were in preventive detention.

Badinter was as charmed by Belshaw as Paschoud had been. He found him to be a sweet likeable man, though obviously he was depressed by being in jail. And although the chances of blocking the extradition were slim, Badinter encouraged Belshaw as best he could and, under instructions from his client, began to prepare for the extradition hearing.

The first hearing was held on December 12th. There Belshaw made a statement which caused headlines in the Vaudois newspapers. "Canadian Professor Distrusts the Procedure of Vaud," announced the *Tribune de Lausanne—le matin*.

At the hearing, the paper explained, the president of the court simply asked Professor Belshaw to identify himself. And then when asked by the president if he would willingly go to Switzerland, Belshaw replied that he would not. Belshaw told the court, the *Tribune* went on to say, "that the procedures of the canton of Vaud did not inspire confidence in him, the indicted person being kept in secret without being able to communicate freely with his lawyer. Therefore he opposed extradition. The president told him that the French court would not be considering the facts with which he was accused, but the professor declared that he could find proofs to show that he was not responsible for the death of his wife." The implications were clear. The Swiss papers were telling their readers that the same man who had defied the Vaudois inquiry and from their point of view had refused to co-operate with the Vaudois police, was now showing his disdain for the entire Vaudois legal system.

Belshaw's remarks, of course, had no effect on his extradition hearing. It was continued to January 9th, when his lawyer would present his plea. But they did have an effect in Switzerland. They entered his dossier as one more suspicious circumstance, one more sign of guilt. And they were noted—and remembered later—by the *juge d'instruction*, the public prosecutor, and by the police.

15

Robert Badinter conducted his defence of Belshaw at the extradition hearing on January 9th, 1980 with all the skill and elegance for which he is so justly renowned.

The hearing began with the presiding judge, President Fau, explaining that the *chambre d'accusation* of the Court of Appeal of Paris had only to verify whether or not the demand for extradition was legal. It had no jurisdiction to consider Belshaw's innocence or guilt.

Then, with President Fau listening attentively, Badinter rose to make his plea. He spoke with great intensity of the seriousness of the accusations which weighed upon Cyril Belshaw, and he based his case on the vagueness of the extract of charges accompanying the Vaudois warrant of arrest. He pointed out that the verdict of the Parisian court would be of extreme importance, particularly because this decision could not be appealed.

Growing more analytical, Maître Badinter methodically dissected the charges cited in the warrant. In this document Vaud stated that Belshaw had lied when he said he travelled to Paris with his wife in January 1979. But, Badinter emphasized, the warrant gave no evidence to back up this contention. Then Badinter showed the court a Parisian hotel bill for two people, and two breakfasts, dated January 15th, 1979, the day Betty disappeared, and charged to Cyril Belshaw.

Next Badinter turned to the question of the falsified dental records.

The warrant of arrest accused Belshaw of having tried to deceive the Vaudois investigators by supplying a falsified dental chart. But, Badinter explained, at that time Belshaw had been in the grip of a kind of neurotic anxiety caused by the disappearance of his wife. He simply refused to believe that she could be dead in Switzerland. And, Badinter stated, it was Belshaw himself who after having sent the falsified dental charts to the Vaudois authorities in a moment of madness, confessed to what he had done. Then, as one Frenchman speaking to another, Badinter told the president, "The period of neurosis was over ... But the Swiss rationalists refuse to recognize the existence of neurosis."

The president expressed surprise that Belshaw had not willingly surrendered himself to the Vaudois authorities, as he would doubtless do if he were innocent.

It must be understood, Badinter explained, that Belshaw "was stupefied by the behaviour of the Vaudois detectives in Canada, by their searches, their questions, their sarcastic remarks ...." And then too, Badinter was careful to point out, an Anglo-Saxon could not help but be shocked by Swiss penal procedure, and particularly by the secrecy of the *instruction* (abandoned in France since the Dreyfus case, in the nineteenth century). We must admit, Badinter told the court, that Swiss procedure is not particularly advanced in so far as the rights of the defence are concerned.

Finally, bringing all his passion and forensic eloquence to bear, Badinter brought out his last and most weighty argument. He told the court he would read from the truly astonishing concluding statement of the Vaudois autopsy report. After a suitable dramatic pause, and reading with a kind of relish, he then declaimed, "No element permits us to determine the cause of death.... Considering the circumstances in which the demise was produced it can, in reality, only be a violent death, and only the hypothesis of a murder can reasonably be sustained." Then Badinter cried out, "To demand extradition for murder it is at least necessary to prove there has been a murder! Yet there is no such proof! And if Mrs. Belshaw died of natural causes, and if someone, for countless reasons that can easily be imagined, wished to conceal her body ? And if she died in France and was brought to Le Sépey, a dozen kilometres from the frontier? The Swiss have gone too far, too fast."

The French public prosecutor responded to Badinter's arguments by stating simply that the Swiss request was perfectly in order, and expressing, for his own part, his surprise that Belshaw had not voluntarily gone to Switzerland. But he did agree that it would be quite proper for the *chambre d'accusation* to ask for more information from the Swiss authorities before pronouncing on their request.

When the pleas were complete, Belshaw addressed the tribunal. Speaking slowly in English, he spoke of his wife of thirty-six years, remembering that she had disappeared almost exactly a year ago in Paris. "I had nothing to do with her death ... and I have nothing more to say to Swiss justice, with whom I have been in constant contact."

The hearing concluded with a long, smiling conversation between the president and both lawyers. Then the president announced the verdict would be rendered on January 30th. Belshaw returned to Fleury-Mérogis.

On Wednesday afternoon, January 30th, the *chambre d'accusation* of the Court of Appeal of Paris pronounced. The judgement was brief. It ruled that the request for extradition was properly based, that Mrs. Belshaw had indeed met her death in Switzerland as the Swiss authorities contended; that Belshaw had lied when he stated that she had accompanied him to Paris and there disappeared; further that Belshaw had furnished the Swiss police with falsified dental records, thus holding up identification for five months. Therefore the *chambre d'accusation* ordered that Belshaw be extradited to Switzerland.

This ruling may appear at first to be based on the facts and not on whether or not extradition was proper in Belshaw's case. But the matter is not so simple. One of the most important questions the French court had to decide was whether Betty met her death in France or in Switzerland. If the Swiss could bring forward enough evidence to show that a crime had indeed been committed in Switzerland, then the case would belong in their jurisdiction.

If the French court believed Belshaw's statement that Betty had disappeared in Paris, they might have acceded to Badinter's arguments, and ruled that there was no proof a crime had been committed in Switzerland, and therefore no grounds for extraditing Belshaw. However the *chambre d'accusation* decided from the evidence before it that they would accept the Swiss contention that a murder had been committed, and that it had occurred in Switzerland. The concrete evidence for murder may have been slight, but it seemed to have been enough for the French.

Procedure required that the extradition order be signed by the Prime Minister of France. However this was only a formality, and on February 1st Belshaw was handed over to the Swiss authorities at the frontier and immediately committed to the Vaudois prison of Bois-Mermet in the city of Lausanne. He was welcomed with headlines by the Lausanne press, who were quick to point out that he was not being held in secret, that he was allowed to communicate at all times with his Vaudois lawyer, whatever doubts he may have expressed about Vaudois procedure.

As for Belshaw, he had fought and lost. He was now in the grip of Vaudois law.

16

As the author of a serious study of Swiss federalism, Belshaw was familiar with the Swiss political system. His book, however, did not touch on Swiss law or penal procedure, except to note that the procedure varied from canton to canton. However, as soon as the Vaudois authorities began to investigate him, it is to be expected that a man of his temperament—thorough, exacting, and analytical—would have done everything he could to learn as much as possible about it.

The clash between the tradition of common law and the Swiss civil law was crucial to the Belshaw case. So it is important to try to understand as much as possible how the two systems differ.

Since the revolution of 1848 power in Switzerland has been divided between different authorities in a federal system of checks and balances unique to that country. The Swiss have a centuries-old tradition of liberty, the outcome of a long and bloody history, and they guard this tradition jealously. Their attitude towards their legal system is quite different from that of a more unitary state, such as France.

Foreigners often describe the Swiss as smug, but they do not show this attitude towards their legal system. They are well aware that facets of it have been criticized, and they anxiously spring to its defence.

One of the key criticisms was expressed succinctly at the extradition hearing by Badinter when he said that Swiss procedures were not particularly advanced "in their attitude towards the defence". However, the Swiss believe this criticism to be unfounded. The law in Switzerland is generally regarded with respect by both defence and State counsel. The average citizen too seems well satisfied with the system as it has evolved in the last century. In particular the Swiss are quick to point out that the secrecy of the *instruction*, mentioned so slightingly in court by Badinter, and which has frequently been the target of attacks, has been upheld by the European Convention of Human Rights in Strasbourg. Defence lawyers in Vaud were polled in February 1979; they voted that they did not wish the system changed, they did not want to be present at the interrogations of their clients during the *instruction*.

The theory behind the *instruction* is that a suspect only goes to trial when there is a great weight of evidence of guilt. It follows on this that the majority of those accused will be convicted. A well-known English scholar, comparing the civil law with the common once remarked that if he were innocent he would prefer to be tried under the civil law, but if he were guilty he would choose the common law. His belief was that under the civil law the guilty were more likely to be convicted, and the innocent never brought to trial; that is, that the civil law distinguished more accurately between guilt and innocence. This, in any case, is certainly the view the Vaudois have of their own system. Naturally they don't want to see the innocent convicted, but they do not mind seeing them put to a great deal of inconvenience and embarrassment, if that is what it takes to be sure the guilty are tried and convicted. Obviously the system can only function justly if the preliminary stages are rigorously fair.

In Vaud the magistrate who bears the responsibility of directing the *instruction* and ensuring it is carried out properly is either the *juge d'instruction cantonale*, or one of the various district *juges informateurs* who serve under him.

During the investigation the police officer in charge confers with the relevant judge frequently, reports to him, and is directed by him. Between them they must abide scrupulously by the legal procedure for such investigations. This is the *juge*'s responsibility. His handling of the case will be under close scrutiny when the dossier is passed to the *tribunal d'accusation* which must decide if the case is to go to trial. And everything he does is subject to review and appeal by the defence to this same tribunal.

Switzerland is ruled by the Penal Code of 1937 which sets out all the crimes and their penalties. The code is very brief—130 pages long and written in clear precise language that a layman can easily grasp. Questions of interpretation are dealt with by precedent, as under the common law, but the code is the final arbiter in all penal matters. When it comes to the penal procedure, however, the rules and regulations of how an investigation and trial are carried out vary from canton to canton. The Belshaw case fell under the 1967 Code of Penal Procedure of the canton of Vaud.

For certain temperaments it is easy indeed to fall in love with Vaud. Its capital, Lausanne, is a charming city, of approximately 130,000 people, and the canton offers a mixture of magnificent scenery, gentle climate, and a kind of warm civility one does not necessarily expect from a French-speaking people.

There is great variety in the landscape; the place names suggest some of the grace and beauty of the region: in the Vaudois Alps there is the Vallée des Ormonts, and the Pays d'Enhaut, the famous peaks of the Dents du Midi, and Les Diablerets. There is also the area around Montreux at the tip of Lac Léman, frequently called the Vaudois riviera. Mild climate, magnificent bays, sheltered vineyards, and on the banks of the lake, all the sweetness of the Mediterranean climate: fig trees, almonds, mulberry, laurel, cypress, magnolias and palm trees. It was in this region, at Clarens, that Rousseau chose to set *La Nouvelle Héloise*. The castle of Chillon, made famous by Byron, dominates the coast road along the lake between Montreux and Aigle.

The Encyclopaedists blossomed in this region in the eighteenth century. (The rationalists to whom Badinter had referred so ironi-

cally in his plea might be seen as their intellectual descendants.)
Voltaire lived here for a time, as did Benjamin Constant, Mme. de
Stael and many of the other prominent figures of the age of reason.

Perhaps Vaud held the same kind of attraction for these so-rational
thinkers of the past as it did for the New Zealand-Canadian Belshaws. Tense, anxiety-ridden, holding themselves in, pressed on
by their academic ambitions and webbed in by the complexities of
a life lived on so many social and academic levels and in so many
places, they may have found respite in this easy, time-free and
friendly countryside. Its insularity and bourgeois character, its
beauty, its openness and harmony made it the perfect outward rep-
resentation of the setting in which the Belshaws wanted to show
their public face.

And to add to its attractions for the Belshaws, there was the
elegance of its cities and towns. Catering to the rich of Europe, the
cities of the Vaudois riviera bulge with the elegant show windows
of Cartier, Longines, Gérard Péregaux, Rodier, Céline, Hermès,
Christofle, Balenciaga, Rolex and Jaeger-le-Coultre.

Of course, there is another side. The subtle differences that separate one culture from another exist alongside the worldly congru-
ences. There are rules and customs that bind the inhabitants of Vaud,
from which the foreigner, in his ignorance, can be exempt.

This is a society where a policeman or jurist will ask about a
person, who is he? A petit-bourgeois? A peasant? Where a judge
can preface a remark to the courtroom with, ''We Vaudois petit-
bourgeois ....'' A society which functions smoothly because it is
small, relatively homogeneous, and bound by consensus. The
stresses of racial hostilities, sexism and class envy remain muted
by the civil compact, and by pride in a long history of solutions to
problems which still daunt other states.

Yet the face of Vaud does seem to reflect its heart. It is a relatively
unspoiled countryside, a climate without great extremes of cold or
heat. An ancient history of battles for freedom won and stoutly
defended, a Protestant desire to do right and maintain a vigorous
and exacting high-principled justice—all these have shaped the complex penal procedures of Vaud.

Vaud's system is unique. It is not the same as Geneva's to the
west, nor that of Valais to the east; fifty years of evolution have
shaped it and given it its distinctiveness.

The cantonal tribunal consists of fifteen judges, nominated by the cantonal legislature. Above it, above the entire Vaudois system, there is always the Supreme Court of Switzerland, to which a Swiss citizen can appeal if he feels his fundamental liberties have been violated.

Within the system itself, there are basically three stages through which a suspect passes and he has different rights in each of them.

In the first, the suspect is the *prévenu*, the *presumed* (literally forewarned). When the police arrest someone, that person is a *prévenu*. After the arrest, the police, as has been pointed out, must within twenty-four hours bring this person before a magistrate, who will then assure himself of the person's identity and inform him of his rights, under the code, to legal counsel. The magistrate, at this time, may decide to put the *presumed* in preventive detention. Theoretically this can last only fourteen days, but it can be prolonged month by month, if the magistrate so wishes and if his request is approved by the *tribunal d'accusation*, a tribunal which is superior to the one where the case will be tried and serves as a court of appeal and review court for all penal matters.

Here we see the first striking difference between the Vaudois system and the common law. For the *presumed* can be detained, without charge, for a very long time. However, he can at any time make an appeal and be heard personally. He also has the remedy available of later sueing for wrongful detention.

Once the *presumed* is heard by the *juge d'instruction* or one of the seven Vaudois *juges informateurs* (who are usually, but not always, lawyers) the inquiry becomes the *instruction*. The inquiry carried out by the police will be directed by one of these magistrates, and everything which is done becomes part of a strictly regulated written record called the dossier. Every inquiry the police carry out is recorded here, all the testimony and all the evidence. The penal code lays out a detailed description of this *instruction* and all the safeguards to see that it is carried out fairly. And the code states baldly: "the investigation is secret until complete."

The secrecy of the Vaudois *instruction* is a contentious matter. In Belshaw's case his lawyers would later protest, with only limited success, about their access to the dossier. And observers, trying to discover the clues which led the Vaudois investigators to their conclusions, had to grapple constantly with this element. Neither the

Swiss nor the Canadian newspapers were able to discover anything of substance during the *instruction* itself. Even after the trial little, if any, information was officially released.

As soon as the judge believes there is enough evidence that the *presumed* is the author of the crime under investigation he decides to indict him. The *prévenu* now becomes the *inculpé*. At this stage, under ordinary circumstances, where the case has no particular complication, all the parties, including the defendant, can see the dossier. Often, however, the judge decides that some or all of the dossier should be kept secret for a specific period. This decision is appealable, however, and sooner or later the defence must get the opportunity to study the dossier. The defence can ask for more investigation, and can challenge material in the dossier. When this is all complete, a hearing is held before the magistrate, which corresponds roughly to the preliminary hearing in common law.

If the judge decides there is a case which belongs in a criminal tribunal, he sends the file to the public prosecutor. The prosecutor adds his opinion and comments and then sends the matter to the *tribunal d'accusation*.

This court has played no part in the investigation, and has no interest in the guilt or innocence of the suspect. It now makes a decision about whether the *indicted* will be bound over for trial. If the judgement is made to bind over the *indicted* for trial, he then becomes the *accused*. The *tribunal d'accusation* can also hear appeals regarding the propriety and fairness of the *instruction*.

There is a ten-day period allowed for these appeals; when this is over, the entire dossier is sent by the public prosecutor to the president of the appropriate tribunal.

It should be made clear that the idea that under the civil law a person is presumed guilty until proven innocent is discounted by all the Swiss. Certainly their attitude at the trial of Cyril Belshaw and their comments after the verdict would show all those involved in the Vaudois system to be deeply concerned over the rights of the innocent and, even more, over the danger of a miscarriage of justice. Two or three celebrated cases in the past, which are seen as miscarriages of justice, have deeply marked the psyche of Vaud. Everyone who discusses its legal system mentions them sooner or later.

One was the case of a famous Geneva lawyer named Jaccoud. He was condemned for having murdered the father of his mistress, and during the time he served his sentence, and for fifteen years after, he continued to protest his innocence. Although most of the Vaudois authorities are convinced that Jaccoud was indeed guilty, his continual protestations of innocence, and the spectre they raised about a judicial error, made a lasting impression. The case was so equivocal and interesting that Georges Simenon, who lives in Vaud, based a novel on it.

The second case was, in fact, an error. A German citizen named Richter, living in Switzerland, was condemned for theft. Later, after Richter had served his sentence, it was discovered that his wife and her lover had perjured themselves; his innocence was proved retroactively.

The Vaudois deeply fear such cases, for they undermine their justice. Respect for the system is fundamentally important and error erodes it. The conviction of a person who might be innocent represents as deep a horror to the Swiss as it does to anyone living under the common law. And equally horrifying to them is the possibility of the acquittal of the guilty. No glib distinctions of one system being more fair to the innocent than the other can be sustained, but it is important to bear in mind that *any* miscarriage of justice concerns the Vaudois, not just the conviction of the innocent.

In Cyril Belshaw's case, their system would be functioning under the glare of publicity in France, Canada and Switzerland, and eventually the whole western world. It would show its successes and its flaws while the world watched.

Now, on the 1st of February, 1980, the Vaudois *instruction* drew its mantle of secrecy over Belshaw.

17

On the same day that Cyril Belshaw was delivered up to Swiss justice by the French authorities, the case was taken out of the hands of Inspector Wyss and given to a more experienced officer, Nicholas Margot.

Nicholas Margot, *inspecteur principal adjoint, police de sûreté*, Lausanne, was to become a principal player in the Belshaw drama. He is a tall gentle-looking man, with thinning brown hair, forty-three years old. He has the same lean fit look that characterized all the Vaudois involved in the Belshaw case, and which was in marked contrast to the stolid heaviness of both Belshaws.

Margot was well-suited to this investigation. He was born of a Swiss father and an English mother in Bath, and his family lived in London until their return to Switzerland when Margot was nine. Margot had kept up his English, as well as his contact with common-law legal and investigatory procedures. Not long before taking over the Belshaw case, he had spent six months studying the English criminal detection system on a scholarship exchange programme with Scotland Yard in London.

Margot had the impassivity so common to English and Canadian policemen, as well as the more subtle and introspective attitude one might expect from a Vaudois and a denizen of the Suisse Romande. He enjoyed discussing his system in the abstract, something most English policemen would not have found interesting. In his work he was careful, meticulous, exacting, imaginative, flexible, and extraordinarily patient. If necessary, he would go over and over the same ground until a new clue appeared. He was prepared to wait for a long time until the dice fell out right for him. And all his work was marked by sensitivity and intelligence.

Margot could be hard and unsentimental. But he had, at bottom, a basic respect for the suspects he dealt with—both innocent and guilty—and a genuine interest in them. And all this was in the context of a deep belief in the fairness of the Vaudois criminal justice system. When he discussed this system he showed no dis-illusion or cynicism. The guilty were discovered and punished; the innocent, if they co-operated and were open with him, were soon released.

From the time Margot took charge of the case, there were no more accusations of "psychological mistakes" of the kind for which Fischlin and Wyss had been criticized. Although the defence would later attack the interpretations which Margot had drawn from his interviews and placed in the dossier, there were never any suggestions that his investigation was anything less than perfectly correct.

On February 2nd, Belshaw was visited by the *juge d'instruction*, Roland Chatelain, at the prison of Bois-Mermet. The interview lasted fifteen minutes, and directly afterwards Belshaw was indicted for falsifying the dental records and for murder. And bright and early on Monday morning, February 4th, Inspector Margot began taking his statement.

At the same time Paschoud was making every effort to get Belshaw out of preventive detention. By the 7th the *procureur-générale*, Willy Heim, was considering Paschoud's request that Belshaw be freed at once on 50,000-franc bail, his freedom to be assured not only by the bond, but by the promise of both Belshaw and Paschoud himself that Belshaw would not leave the country.

It was a difficult decision for Heim and one he weighed with care. He knew the Canadian government, through its consul in Berne, was watching every move. He knew that Swiss justice had been attacked in the Parisian *chambre d'accusation*. It could be said, in fact, from his viewpoint, that Vaudois justice itself was on trial; and he was in the position of being its guardian.

The office of the *Ministère-Public* is loosely analogous to that of the public prosecutor or district attorney under the common-law system. The public prosecutor himself is the central figure in the development of criminal cases in Vaud. He follows each case, and plays an important role in many of the procedures required by law as the suspect passes through the stages of *presumed, indicted*, and *accused*. Over coffee each morning he discusses cases in progress with the *juge d'instruction*.

The centre of all this activity, the office of the *Ministère-Public*, is in *la cité*, the medieval centre of old Lausanne. To reach the *bâtiment du Grand Conseil*, where the office is situated, one must mount narrow streets, cobbled in exquisite patterns of scallops, past the thirteenth-century cathedral, towards "the château" which was first established by the Bishop and then taken over by a powerful Bernois count during the Bernois period. As one climbs the broad shallow steps towards the *bâtiment du Grand Conseil* one passes a statue of the Vaudois William Tell, Major Davel, who not being as fortunate as Tell, had his head cut off by the Bernois in the struggle for Vaudois independence.

The building itself is entered by giant carved light oak doors, six and a half metres high with brass knockers shaped like lions' heads high in their centres. Inside is a dark, unadorned, unfurnished lobby with unmarked doors leading off in all directions.

In the very early morning, before 8:00 a.m., when Willy Heim is often already in his office, the past seems to weigh heavily in this elegant old building. Small circular staircases mount to and descend from doorways. It is common at this time of day to see two very fresh croissants and the morning newspaper waiting outside an office door.

Further exploration brings the visitor to a plain door marked with gleaming brass letters: *Ministère-Public*.

Passing through this door to the reception area, which is empty at this early hour, and then through two doors padded with white leather fixed with brass studs, one arrives in the office of the public prosecutor himself.

Willy Heim, the incumbent, sits behind a leather-topped Louis XV desk, in the dim, sparsely furnished office. The large room, lit only by a small brass study-lamp on the desk, is austere but elegant, perhaps reflecting the personality of its inhabitant. There are period prints on the walls, and by the door sketches by local cartoonists of some of Heim's best moments in court.

It is from this office that Heim directs the prosecutors who work under him, and trains the legal talent that in many cases goes on to take up important positions in the judicial system of Vaud. Heim also has further responsibilities. Not only does he direct Vaudois justice, he is also the permanent representative of the Swiss Federal Public Prosecutor for the Suisse Romande. Whereas most cases are tried in the cantons, some, particularly those with political implications, are tried at the federal level. Heim acts for francophone Switzerland in such cases.

He is a tall slender man of sixty-three, with a quick intelligent face, lively and full of humour, thick dark arching eyebrows and a brush of dark hair. Heim, like Paschoud, has the Vaudois long upper lip, and he is distinguished as well by the long jaw more often associated with the Norman. He speaks well, and shows himself to be extremely sensitive, always attempting to pitch his statements, his replies, and his humour to the listener, rather than speaking to enhance his own image.

In a community where everyone knows everyone, only a man of unquestioned integrity and fairness can expect to maintain respect in the office of the *Ministère-public*, and this Heim has achieved. His reputation for forensic skill has earned him the high position he holds.

In early February, 1980, this reputation for integrity and breadth of mind was called into play as he made his decision on Paschoud's request for bail.

Heim considered the matter seriously, and discussed it on several occasions with Paschoud. In the end he recommended that bail be refused. In the first place, the Vaudois system does not look kindly upon the idea of bail, because it is believed to work to the benefit of the rich. But even more important in Belshaw's case, Heim later said, he came to the conclusion that Belshaw, who had falsified a dental chart and so gravely hampered the pursuit of justice, who had refused to come to Switzerland to explain himself, and who fought extradition, had shown himself by such actions to be a man who might attempt to leave the country before his trial.

Belshaw's forebodings about preventive detention thus proved justified, and his long stay in the prison of Bois-Mermet began. The prison was a relatively new one, and the Swiss assured concerned friends of Belshaw that he was "comfortable" there. He had a "room" to himself, and all the books he wanted.

Belshaw's behaviour at Bois-Mermet was to impress everyone. He was friendly to all and soon became well liked by the prisoners; he was made prison librarian. In letters home he wrote to friends that he was finding the experience fascinating, meeting a kind of person whom he had never met before. These letters could not help but annoy the Swiss, who felt that at some level Belshaw was mocking them. Yet, at the same time, he earned their respect—the respect of the police, of Margot, of the *juge d'instruction* and of Willy Heim. Perhaps it was respect for Belshaw as a man, perhaps simply respect for a worthy adversary, but all commented on the stoicism and courage with which he endured his imprisonment.

Meanwhile Margot's investigation was continuing. In Canada, a Vancouver *Sun* reporter, Mike Bocking, acting on a tip, went out to visit Wilson. She talked to him on her doorstep in her dressing-gown for half an hour. The next day, realizing that she could no longer hide from the Belshaw case, as it was now obvious the press were on her trail, she phoned RCMP headquarters and arranged to come down and to talk to officer Arnie Nylund. This she did; she told him frankly about her whole situation and she voiced her concerns for the difficulties she feared the press and police would make in her private life. Nylund found her frank and open, and her situation aroused his sympathies. But he felt obliged to warn her that she was mixed up in a case that might come to court. If it did so, she could not expect to avoid unpleasant publicity. In the meantime, the police would do everything possible to keep matters confidential.

Margot's investigation was thorough. To some extent he retraced the steps of Wyss and Fischlin, but he also went further afield. In February he went to London, where he interviewed Major Smith and friends and colleagues of the Belshaws. His enquiries in Switzerland, particularly in Montana-Vermala and Le Sépey, continued.

On March 14th, Heim received an appeal from Belshaw's defence against the refusal of the *juge d'instruction* to let them see the dossier. Three days later he proposed to the *tribunal d'accusation* that the defence be allowed to examine those portions of the dossier which were already complete. They would not be allowed to see those parts of the dossier in progress until April 30th. This recommendation was accepted by the tribunal and so, for the first time, the defence had the opportunity to find out the nature of the evidence so far accumulated against Belshaw.

By the end of April, after two months of investigation, Heim and Margot still felt there were too many unanswered questions. It was decided that the *police de sûreté* must make another trip to Canada. This time Margot would go. Margot, with his fluent English and much more extensive understanding of Anglo-Saxon behaviour and legal systems, would be directing the investigation.

On April 14th, 1980, Margot set off for Vancouver together with Inspector Wyss. Now Margot himself visited the campus of UBC and talked to Belshaw's family and friends. He was more subtle than Fischlin and Wyss, and he had the advantage of not having to work through an interpreter. Of course, the situation differed greatly from that of the previous visit: this time Belshaw was in detention, and the falsification of the dental records was public knowledge.

Margot had Belshaw's permission to search his house, which he did. He also interviewed Wilson. He had, of course, learned a great deal more since Fischlin and Wyss had first discovered her identity. Now, for the first time, he could meet the woman herself.

Wilson spoke frankly and openly to Margot; he found her a credible witness and a very likeable woman. So Margot was finally able to confirm the details about her travels with Belshaw in Switzerland and France and to get a first-hand impression from Wilson about the importance of the relationship and the role it had played in the lives of the two lovers. He compared his own interview to the information received from the RCMP and found that he was in accord with their judgements.

Margot and Wyss also travelled to Toronto and Montreal to interview family and friends. And each interview was meticulously written up and entered into the ever-lengthening dossier. All this information would be kept secret from the public until the trial, when it would be presented as an important and contentious part of the prosecution's case.

Margot returned to Lausanne on April 28th and, with the new information he had gleaned, talked again at length with Belshaw.

By now, under ordinary circumstances, Margot would have had a complete picture of the man under investigation. He had interviewed him in person many times, had talked with him for many hours. He had spoken to his friends, his children, his colleagues and his lover. And yet Margot felt himself up against something very unusual, a barrier he could not pass.

Never, Margot reported to his superiors, in all the suspects I have interrogated in twenty years of police work, have I met one who is capable of what Belshaw has done. He has not once revealed his real self to me. I have seen only the mask. A man who cannot bear to be in error, who doesn't like to be contradicted, who must always be right.

Other suspects had always, sooner or later, opened up to Margot, talked to him almost as a friend. And he had grown to understand them, to feel compassion for them. Later, years later even, acquitted or convicted, they would stop by his office in Lausanne to say hello or go out for a drink. For who knew them better, after so many hours of probing conversation, than Margot?

But not Belshaw. He alone withstood every probe. He kept to himself, cold, dignified and utterly private.

By the time Margot returned from Canada the long summer was beginning and the Vaudois judicial process was starting to slow down as jurists, investigators, experts, and legal counsel took their various holidays.

In June Paschoud decided to ask a colleague to join him in defending the Belshaw case. He chose Eric Stoudmann, a well-known lawyer who had acquired a high reputation in the area of criminal law. Paschoud realized that as his own area of specialization was civil law and international law, he would need the counsel of a man more expert in criminal law. Eric Stoudmann was also a Vaudois. He was forty-six years old, slim, with an attractive Van Dyke beard which had grown white in the centre but was still black at the sides. He had dark hair and wore dark-framed glasses. The two lawyers would, from this time, work together, discuss the various legal points, and share later in the final plea. It was Stoudmann who would occupy himself with the more technical charge, *faux dans les titres*, falsification of the evidence, and in this, as in all other matters relating to criminal law, he showed himself to be thoroughly expert and exceedingly able.

It was also in June that another important event took place. On June 20th the major players in the game all took part in a reconstruction—a reconstruction of the scenario the prosecution was now convinced represented the true events leading up to the death of Betty Belshaw.

18

In summer Vaud presented a different appearance entirely from the grey-skied and snowy countryside that Belshaw remembered from his drive from Paris to Montana-Vermala.

Now Willy Heim, Roland Chatelain and Jean-Félix Paschoud in one car, and the three police officers, Fischlin, Wyss and Margot, and Belshaw himself in another, drove through the green countryside of the Vaudois riviera.

Their route led them out of Lausanne, where tourists revelled in fine weather and filled the narrow streets and sidewalk cafés, along good roads bordered by magnificent views of Lac Léman and the Chablais mountains. The terraced vineyards, now green with tinges of purple in their early leaves, shining in the gentle light, mounted steeply from the autoroute, which curves following the coast of the lake as it approaches Aigle. The two cars passed whitewashed chalets, small villages where villas peeped from behind stone walls, larger towns surrounded by apartment blocks and light industry.

After Aigle, the party passed through the very countryside that Belshaw travelled on his fateful trip to Paris. He was under observation, but remained his usual stoical self. They drove past orchards where the apricot and peach trees unfurled their small green leaves, and, in the fields, tender shoots of asparagus were pale against the earth in their trenches.

Past Sierre, the road begins to climb through the vineyards. The winter before, these had been empty of human figures. Now a peasant could be seen working here and there.

They entered Montana-Vermala itself, drove through the small town past the playing-field in the centre, past the golf course, the police station, along the curving roads to the little lake, now free of its winter cover of snow and living up to its name of *joli lac*, "pretty lake".

The apartment building, the Jolilac, looked different too. The high wall of drifted snow which, banked against a hedge of cedars, had separated it from the Bellevue apartment in winter, was gone. It was now possible to leave the window of the Belshaws' former apartment, on the ground floor, without stepping through metre-high drifts. The roads were no longer lined with high mounds of ploughed snow. There would be problems in reconstructing exactly the events of that second week in January, when Montana-Vermala was wearing its winter dress and seventy centimetres of snow had fallen on an already deep base. Margot had, of course, already talked to the neighbours. But no one had heard or seen anything. One old man, an inhabitant of the neighbouring Bellevue apartment, was the only person living there that week in January whose window overlooked the Belshaws' apartment. He had reported to Margot that the Belshaws' shutters had been closed two or three days before their departure to Paris. But Margot had not put too much faith in this detail which, if it were true, might have suggested to him the grisly possibility that Betty had been dead several days before Cyril left the Jolilac, and that he had been unable, or unwilling, to move her body until the planned trip to Paris. Was it not more likely that the old man had confused the dates and that the shutters had been closed during the time of the Paris trip itself? In any case, now Belshaw could explain himself; now Heim and Chatelain and Paschoud could see the *mise-en-scène* for themselves.

Already Margot and Heim had constructed a possible version of events. In order to test it, a police officer of Belshaw's height and weight had attempted to carry a woman of Betty's height and weight a distance equal to that from the Jolilac apartment to the driveway of the neighbouring Bellevue. The officer had found it difficult, but just possible.

Margot knew that Belshaw's car had only been returned from the garage on the afternoon of January 12th, the day before he left for Paris. So whatever happened in that apartment—if anything did— Betty could not have left it by car before that time. The question now to be answered was, what *could* have happened on the evening of January 12th, 1979?

The Jolilac apartment building faced the artificial lake, so there was no building in front. On arrival, however, Heim and Paschoud could see at once that anyone coming out the front door would be very visible from the street. In fact the entire walk across the lobby of the building, a distance of seven or eight metres, out the front door, along a walkway to the street in front, would be exposed to public view.

When everyone climbed out of the cars, Paschoud was horrified to see that Belshaw was handcuffed, and to learn that he was to remain so throughout the entire reconstruction—a period of six or seven hours. He remonstrated with Chatelain, to no avail. Chatelain simply told him that in his opinion Belshaw was dangerous, and that he might be violent or try to escape; that he, Chatelain, had made up his mind and would not be dissuaded. Paschoud was later to say that this incident ''shocked him to the core''. No doubt it strengthened his growing conviction that the *instruction* was being carried out with a fixed opinion of Belshaw's guilt, and not at all with a mind open to the possibility of his innocence.

Now the group began to look around, their eyes always on Belshaw to watch his demeanour. For a man of Paschoud's nature, this examination of the Jolilac apartment was very distressing. He could not help but feel how painful it would be for Belshaw to go back to this place which must arouse so many memories: happy memories of the weeks he had spent there with Betty and the Christmas the couple had enjoyed with Adrian and his girlfriend, as well as the harrowing memories of the days spent in this very apartment, waiting, alone, for Betty to reappear, suffering the days of loneliness, suspense and disappointment. Now, as they walked over the rooms, Paschoud cringed as the police asked Belshaw questions in a manner he, Paschoud, saw as unconscionably intrusive. ''Where was your bedroom? Where did Adrian and his friend stay when they came to spend Christmas with you? Show us exactly what you did the last evening before you went to Paris! Where did you eat ? What time do you claim you went to bed? ...'' Paschoud could *feel* Belshaw's emotions as he answered these questions, questions which must have brought back such painful sensations.

But to Belshaw, who had endured hours of similar questioning, this was just one more trial of endurance. He bore it as he had borne all the rest, and kept himself under control.

The party looked as well at the ground-floor corner window of the Belshaws' apartment. It was secluded from view at ground level by a hedge of cedars, and to pass from this window to the next-door driveway of the Bellevue apartment without being seen would be relatively easy—if snow were not blocking the way.

With these thoughts in mind, the party examined the Belshaws' apartment. They looked out the windows of the apartment to the Bellevue. They noted that to reach the street from where they were, it was necessary to take the elevator up one flight to the lobby from which the entry led out the front door. They examined and noted the distances from doorways to elevator, from elevator to lobby, from lobby to front door, and from front door to roadway.

Then they drove back along the twisting roads, down the mountainside, all the way back to Aigle, and turned up towards Le Sépey. They stopped at the lay-by just at the far corner of the Larrevoin bridge. They noted the characteristics of each corner of the bridge, and their observations confirmed the earlier conclusion: the body was disposed of at night, by a person unfamiliar with the area.

Again everyone left their cars. They walked carefully down the slope to the patch of brush, about seven metres below the parking place, where the body had been found. The place was marked with a stick. Belshaw was asked to come up to the stick, and to look at it. While the police, *juge* and prosecutor watched his every expression for any tell-tale sign of guilt, he was asked to explain how he had jettisoned the body. But Belshaw was as collected as ever, and if the prosecution had hoped to shake his aplomb they were disappointed. The reconstruction, though suggestive, was, in the end, inconclusive. Except for Paschoud, who had his certainty of Belshaw's innocence confirmed, and his concern about the unfortunate attitude of police and prosecution strengthened.

In the weeks that followed, the *juge d'instruction* interviewed Belshaw three times; on June 26th, July 1st and July 11th. Meanwhile Margot patiently continued his investigation.

On August 1st an appeal against Belshaw's remaining in preventive detention was launched by the defence. Heim, after serious consideration, recommended against it, and on August 5th the *tribunal d'accusation* so ruled.

Then for six weeks the official judicial machine closed down for the long vacation. However, the defence now, for the first time, had been allowed to view the entire dossier and were hard at work digesting it and preparing their response. At their request Inspector Margot went back to France for further investigation. The results of this trip, too, were entered into the record. On September 5th, Chatelain closed the dossier and passed it along to the defence to make counter propositions if they so wished.

There was an interval after the 5th, the period set by law for the defence to consider the dossier. On the morning of September 24th

Heim received the dossier in his office in Lausanne. He spent the day writing out the articles of accusation which were forwarded to the *tribunal d'accusation* that afternoon.

And so, on October 9th, 1980, the *tribunal d'accusation*, charged with deciding whether or not there was enough reason to believe that Belshaw was the author of the crime, handed down its ruling. Belshaw would be tried for *faux dans les titres*, falsification of evidence, and murder. Belshaw was no longer the *indicted*. He had become the *accused*.

On October 15th the dossier reached President Jean-Pierre Guignard of the criminal tribunal of Aigle. In the Vaudois system, as soon as the president of a criminal tribunal receives the dossier he takes over the case. And in the role of the president can be seen most clearly the enormous difference between the common-law and civil-law systems. The president is part of the inquisitorial process which dominates the Vaudois system. He reads the entire dossier which now, it must be remembered, is full of unsubstantiated statements, allegations, counterstatements, police reports, evidence produced by the defence, procedural arguments before *juges d'instruction* and the *tribunal d'accusation*, records of visits to the scene of the crime, etc.—matters which, under the common law, it would in many cases be improper for the judge to know about. If the president feels it necessary, if he feels more is needed, he can send the dossier back and reopen the entire *instruction*.

The president then chooses two "judges" and one substitute "judge" to sit with him on the case. They are usually town notables whose names stand by virtue of political nomination. They are not chosen because of any legal expertise, but rather because of their standing in the community. The president also chooses which witnesses will appear, which experts will be heard, and which evidence will be brought forward. Under the common law, this function is usually performed by the prosecutor. If the president refuses to designate a particular witness, expert, or piece of evidence, the other parties may appeal this decision. The jury of six, plus two substitutes, is chosen by lot with both parties having the right of six peremptory refusals. Thus the complete tribunal consists of the president, two "judges", one substitute judge, six jurors, and two substitute jurors. The jurors in Vaud are chosen from the voters' rolls. When all are chosen the trial date is set.

President Guignard proposed November 23rd as the first available date on his calendar. However, on that date Willy Heim was scheduled to lead in an important political case at the federal level, before the federal criminal court. He was to prosecute two Jurassiens accused of bombing the home of a political opponent. So the first date convenient to all the parties was early December.

By now Belshaw had been in prison for nearly a year. The Vaudois *instruction* had lasted seven months, ending in September. During that time Margot had directed, or carried out himself investigations in Montana-Vermala, at Le Sépey, along the route near where the body had been discovered, in Paris, London, Vancouver, Toronto and Montreal. Through Interpol, the New Zealand police had been alerted, and they had reported back to Switzerland details about the background and education of both Belshaws, and also taken statements from one of Betty's sisters, Mrs. Grey, who was still living there. Margot had taken a picture of Betty along Belshaw's route from Montana to Paris, trying without success to find someone who remembered seeing her. Later Stoudmann, for the defence, had taken a picture of Belshaw to the PLM motel at Beaune, to the restaurants where the couple had eaten on their travels, and to the Novotel in Paris. No one had remembered seeing Belshaw either, although there was no doubt that he had been there.

Margot had correlated statements from scores of friends and colleagues of Belshaw, some of whom he had interviewed himself, and some of whom the RCMP had interviewed for him. He had talked to neighbours in Montana-Vermala and to shopkeepers in the town. He had interviewed the couple's doctors. An extensive examination of the couple's financial affairs had been carried out. Every receipt, cheque, credit-card voucher had been analysed. Margot had searched Belshaw's house and looked through the couple's files and papers.

And Margot had interviewed Belshaw at considerable length. He had used all his skills in interrogation, every method he knew for delving into the mind and psyche of the man under suspicion.

Margot had been in constant discussion with Chatelain, and Chatelain had consulted from time to time with Heim. It had been an exhaustive investigation. At the end of it each of the three men: Chatelain, Margot and Heim had reached a definite conclusion about Belshaw's role in Betty's death.

As for Belshaw himself, since his arrest at Roissy he had been in prison, visited only infrequently by friends passing through and once a week by Paschoud. For eleven months he had endured the frequent interrogations of police and magistrates and the uncertainty of his precarious situation.

Now it was official—he would be tried for murder.

Professor Cyril Belshaw (*photo: courtesy UBC*)

Betty Belshaw (*photo: courtesy UBC*)

Diana Belshaw
(*photo: Charles Crawford*)

The Jolilac apartment (*centre*) at Montana-Vermala (*photo: A.I.R.*)

Inspector Nicholas Margot

Inspector Wyss

Investigation at the Larrevoin lay-by

above: The Larrevoin bridge (*photo: A.I.R.*)

below: The slope where the Le Sépey Corpse was discovered

The prison of Bois-Mermet in Lausanne (*photo: Robert Swartz*)

The City Hall, Aigle, where the trial was held (*photo: A.I.R.*)

above: Maître Jean-Felix Paschoud
(*courtroom sketch by Barrigue*)

left: President Jean-Pierre Guignard
(*courtroom sketch by Barrigue*)

below: Maître Willy Heim (*photo: A.I.R.*)

Cyril Belshaw and Maître Eric Stoudmann (*photo: A.I.R.*)

After the verdict (*left to right*): Professor Burridge (UBC), a gendarme, Cyril Belshaw, Mr. Mooney (Canadian Consul in Switzerland), Diana Belshaw, Adrian Belshaw (*photo: A.I.R.*)

PART SIX
ON TRIAL FOR MURDER

19

The news that Belshaw had been formally accused came as a distinct shock in Vancouver. Until that time Harry McLaughlin had still been contending that the Swiss had absolutely nothing to go on, and that there was very little, if any, likelihood of the case coming to trial.

The story of the falsification of the dental records was now public knowledge, but the details about Belshaw's infidelity had been guarded by the law which provided for the absolute secrecy of the *instruction*. Furthermore, many of the details turned up by the *instruction* which had led the *tribunal d'accusation* and Heim to believe they had a strong enough case to try Belshaw were so small, in themselves, that even if known, they would not have appeared to be grounds for a murder charge.

The charge *faux dans les titres*, falsification of evidence, could not be regarded as a serious one with particularly severe consequences, even if upheld. The maximum sentence is five years, and the time spent in preventive detention is deducted from the sentence. Also, if Belshaw were convicted, any sentence would certainly be mitigated because of his professional status and the many testimonials to his character.

As for the more serious charge, the Swiss penal code distinguishes between *assassinat*, which is described as premeditated murder or a killing which is particularly perverse or dangerous; *murder*, the charge laid against Belshaw, which is simply the act of killing someone; and *murder under the influence of passion*, which is described as "killing while in the prey of violent emotion, and in such circumstances that the circumstances render the act excusable". The sentence for murder is a minimum of five years with *réclusion*. No maximum sentence is laid out by law, and the sentence is frequently as long as twenty years. *Réclusion* is, in theory, a more rigorous kind of imprisonment than the standard *emprisonnement*, the sentence laid out for lesser crimes. But in practice there is little difference between the two.

When the news that Belshaw had been officially charged hit the newspapers in France, England, Canada, the USA, and both German- and French-speaking Switzerland, journalists from all the major European capitals began to make plans to attend, and wire-service stringers were put on alert.

Many of these journalists were surprised, when checking with their Swiss correspondents, to be told that the trial would take place on Wednesday the 3rd of December, Thursday the 4th, and if necessary Friday the 5th, and that the verdict would come down on Monday the 8th at five o'clock. As North American or British murder trials of such importance and celebrity can easily drag on for weeks, if not months, it was astounding to hear that the duration of this trial would be a mere two or three days.

Journalists from countries under the common law, however, were reckoning without the seven-month *instruction*, unaware they were encountering a judicial process in which the trial is only the final act. The procedures under which an *instruction* is carried out allow for many of the arguments about admissibility of evidence which under the common law are not put forward until the trial. Since anything in the dossier is admissible in a Swiss court (although the defence may make objections even during the trial), it is usual for such disputes to centre around the dossier and to be resolved well in advance of the trial.

For example, allegations made by witnesses which might be considered slanderous or prejudicial, and which the prosecution has not been able to substantiate, are usually withdrawn from the dossier before it goes to the president of the criminal tribunal. This may be done by the prosecution—and was done in the Belshaw case—

or it can be done at the request of the defence. If the defence wishes something removed or added, they can request it of the public prosecutor, and if denied, can appeal to the *tribunal d'accusation*. The final form of the dossier is particularly important because the president of the criminal tribunal reads it before the trial. Not everything in the final dossier will necessarily emerge at the trial, but anything in it is admissible should any party choose to introduce it.

The president's reading of the dossier comes after the defence has had its opportunity to read it, study it and, if necessary, protest about anything it contains to the *tribunal d'accusation*. It is unlikely that there will be any surprises. The president also decides, on the basis of the dossier, who is to be heard and for how long, which witnesses are relevant, and which are not. The defence will bring forward their own witnesses and experts at the trial, but again all of this will be known in advance, and scheduled.

For all these reasons, Cyril Belshaw's trial was to be a short one.

Now as foreign journalists began to assemble for the trial, they tried to gauge the significance of what they were to observe. In order to do so, they would need to understand as much as possible about the judges and jurors, the milieu which had shaped them, and their concepts of justice.

20

One of the great concepts of law is expressed in the phrase "trial by a jury of one's peers". The evolution of this concept can be traced from its medieval origins, where it frequently meant exactly what it said, through contested cases in the United States where blacks were tried by juries of whites, up to the present day when in North America and England, at least, it seems to be taken for granted that citizens chosen from the voters' rolls will represent the "peers" of the defendant. In many cases, of course, this is manifestly untrue. The concept of "peers" is often stretched dangerously far when differences of race or radical differences of social class and political orientation are involved.

But whatever the flaws of this system, there is no doubt that it operates most unfairly when citizens sit in judgement upon those from another country and culture, and attempt to understand and interpret their motivations and actions. Surely some of this must have been in the back of Cyril Belshaw's mind when he weighed the dangers of going to Switzerland, of undergoing an *instruction*, and—in the worst case—of being tried under an alien system by a jury of Vaudois.

The mores and standards of Vaud have created a society which is pleasant to live in, so long as one's behaviour conforms to that expected of foreigners, tourists and upright Vaudois citizens. But a different face is turned towards a potential miscreant—and it was easy to imagine that this face might be shown to Belshaw by his jury. For could a petit-bourgeois Vaudois jury deal fairly with Belshaw, born in New Zealand, an intellectual, a Canadian?

As journalists drove from Lausanne towards Aigle in December of 1980, in the gently falling snow, the terraced vineyards could be seen faintly outlined against the mountain slopes, and the peaks of alps were just barely visible in the white mist. To the right of the road which runs through the Rochers de Naye was Lac Léman, often called Lake Geneva by foreigners, wintery blue-green and calm in the snow. On its far side, when the snow thinned, could be seen the Dents du Midi. Even though it was unusually cold and windy, this winter lacked the harshness of the Canadian winter, and recalled instead the same period two years before when the events of Betty Belshaw's disappearance were played out in weather almost exactly similar.

The temperature varied between −1 and −5 degrees Celsius. At times the clouds thinned, the white sky brightened until it became blue, the countryside was brilliant in snow and the mountains suddenly appeared distinct, their folds and peaks decorated with snow, majestic guardians of the countryside.

The houses, two and sometimes three storeys high, with their freshly painted shutters of green or dark orange or blue and their steeply pitched roofs usually more than a storey in height, had neither the appropriateness or perfection of design visible in the parallel countryside in the south of France, nor the pragmatic assertiveness of their Canadian counterparts. On the other hand, this gentle harmonious countryside appeared from the road to be marred by none of the new suburban villas which pimple the landscape of Provence. Such suburbs exist between Lausanne and Montreux, but approaching the winding roadways between Montreux and Aigle, one enters a landscape which shows no signs of time or of change, peaceable and secure, almost empty, in the middle of winter, of human figures. There was just the occasional glimpse of a man dressed in a heavy jacket and cap, face barely visible, walking towards a house along the verge of a vineyard; a woman walking her dog out from the front of the house; a mother wheeling a pram along the roadway below some railroad tracks, waving and smiling to a friend on a departing train. The road, too, was almost empty of traffic. As in most thinly populated countrysides, the houses are scattered, perhaps a kilometre from one another along the roads between the little towns of Villeneuve, Roche, and Ivonne.

Crime is rare here. And when it occurs it is often sudden and violent, with the perpetrator caught in the act. "Student kills girlfriend in bar"—a typical headline from a Vaud newspaper during December 1980.

In the whole district there are less than a hundred lawyers, and not one who can fill a practice by specializing in criminal law alone. This, after all, is a country where you buy your bus ticket from an unattended machine before boarding, and only occasionally are checked to see if you have it; where your hotel asks you how many of the little bottles of drink from your room's bar you have consumed before totting up the bill, and takes your word for it; and where, when you leave your map in the local restaurant, they come to find you the next day to return it.

When considering the character of the citizens who made up the jury in the Belshaw case, it is wise to remember that in Aigle one is in the heart of the Suisse Romande, where the petit-bourgeois— a description by which most Aiglois readily identify themselves— appear to live contentedly without the undue stress and anxiety of their faster-moving urban counterparts. Words such as "stress", "anxiety", "nervousness", which are to play a large role in the trial, seem alien to this countryside and to those towns of friendly and relaxed people who speak so surely of what it is to be "nous Vaudois".

Around Aigle are the vineyards which, together with tourism, provide the economic base for the town, and which were also to provide the professions of most of the jurors at the trial.

On the streets of the city in winter, strangers whose eyes met in passing greeted one another with a *bonjour Madame, Monsieur*, and stepped aside into the snow for the other to pass. Each transaction, each meeting in the street, was signalled by a litany of smiles and thank yous, courtesy and friendliness making graceful the small exchanges of every day.

In early December 1980, the sidewalks were slippery and local inhabitants were commenting to one another about the annoyance of the *verglas* as they strolled into well-heated stores to purchase a few slices of roast beef at $6.00 a pound, a beautiful *bûche de Noël* to give at Christmas or a bottle of the local Dorin or Pinot Noir wine.

In the old city itself, the streets are narrow and cross one another at odd angles. The grey sky is covered with misty wisps of moving clouds, as are the tips of the mountains. Snowflakes fall, all different sizes, petalling lazily down to lie on streets thick with ice and frozen slush. At the railway station a man in an orange slicker swings a pickaxe in a mighty arc, to break up the *verglas* at one end of the platform. Two schoolgirls walk along the street, dressed in bright red snowsuits, chattering about their instructor who gives them too much homework in geometry. They seem easy and happy.

This is the outward appearance of Vaud. It is from the voters' list of this community that the jurors have been chosen who together with the judges will consider the implications of Cyril Belshaw's love affair, his constant travel, his falsification of the dental records. Shaped by their rooted, Protestant community, with its fixed patterns of behaviour, its clear ideas of respectability, its pride in its past and its institutions, they will judge Cyril Belshaw—by a majority vote—innocent or guilty of murder. If he is found guilty every member of the tribunal will have a say in setting his sentence.

21

On Wednesday, December 3rd, 1980, snow is falling in Aigle, the sky is overcast and the air is unusually cold as Cyril Belshaw enters the medieval *Place du Marché*. Here, five of Aigle's main streets debouch onto the square, dominated by the old *Hôtel de Ville*, a building in the classic style of the Bernois period and dated over the lintel 1640, though built a century earlier. Across from it, with no attempt having been made to harmonize the styles, stands the modern *Hôtel de Ville*, the city hall. It is a four-storey building, flat-roofed, contemporary and undistinguished, white with blue trim. There is a long narrow two-storey wing at right angles to the main section which contains the police station, the offices of the president of the tribunal, the clerk's office, court ante-rooms, a waiting area and the courtroom itself.

Stepping carefully over the snow, wrapped in a tightly belted beige Burberry coat and flanked by tall gendarmes, Belshaw runs the gamut of the press, flash-bulbs popping in the dull grey light. He walks down the long corridor, and enters an ante-room to wait.

Journalists from France, Switzerland, Germany, the USA, Canada, and several wire services jostle before the courtroom door, clutching their passes. The clerk of the court, the *greffier*, a young woman who looks conscientious and determined, waits for the signal, and then at 9:00 a.m. opens the door. The journalists stream in, anxious for front-row seats. The members of the tribunal are already seated.

As the journalists settle in their places, the atmosphere is tense. The Swiss press comment among themselves about the president, Jean-Pierre Guignard. He is known to be a man of strong opinions, not averse to letting them show to court and jurors. He is seen as temperamental and strong-willed, and they wonder how he will handle such a celebrated trial. They have seen him before, they know he tends to slide into the prosecutorial role that the president must take in many civil trials where there is no prosecutor, only a plaintiff and a defendant, rather than the more inquisitorial but judicial role required during a criminal trial where the prosecutor acts for the State.

Guignard was born in Geneva and received his law degree there. His parents were from Vaud, however, and he considers himself a Vaudois. He served as a prosecutor before taking up his position as president of the tribunal of Aigle. In fact, he was one of the public prosecutors in the office of the *Ministère-Public*, working under Willy Heim, and it was Heim himself who recommended that Guignard let his name stand when the position of president of the Aigle tribunal came open. In private life a devoted family man with two teen-age children, on the bench he has shown himself to be unpredictable. At times he has been compassionate and sensitive, at other times harsh and opinionated.

It is the president who will actively direct the trial and set its tone. The judges and jurors have not read the dossier, and it is Guignard who has chosen the order of the presentation of evidence and decided which sections of the dossier will be read aloud to form the basis of the prosecution's case.

The room is a long one, perhaps fifteen metres in length, with a wall of windows at each end. Half of the room is taken up with spectators' seats. The other half is like a stage set for the principal players; the backdrop is the windows, through which can be seen the building across the way with its carved shutters, and above, the serried roofs and chimneys of the medieval city. Beyond, when the mists clear, the Alps rise gentle and muted, grey-brown and distant.

At stage left is the high bench where the president, judges, and clerk sit. The bench is of functional dark mahogany, as is all the furniture of the courtroom. At the centre of the bench sits President Guignard. He is a handsome man in his fifties with a strong high nose, a charming smile, and a great shock of white hair which springs up irrepressibly like a cockscomb from his head. He is dressed in a black robe trimmed with wide satin bands down the front and sleeves. Flanking him are the two judges and one substitute judge, stolid burghers in dark suits. Farthest from the spectators sits the clerk.

Directly in front of the judicial bench is placed a long table for the all-male jury. The six jurors and two substitutes look serious as they straighten their papers, make ready their pens. They too seem to be solid, unimaginative citizens, dressed in dark suits, most wearing glasses. Only one stands out as a slight maverick, his suit a light grey, his chair pushed slightly back and apart from the others.

He wears Argyle socks, a departure from the atmosphere of male sartorial conformity.

About two metres across from the tribunal's seats, at stage right, is a long plain table at which sit Paschoud and Eric Stoudmann. Paschoud, looking tired and serious, is dressed in a morning suit, though he has left on his outdoor boots. To his right sits Stoudmann, wearing a black robe and white stock tie.

At the far end of the room, silhouetted against the bright white light which streams in through the windows, sits the *procureur-générale*, the public prosecutor, Willy Heim. He is dressed in a black morning suit and appears completely relaxed. Alone at his table, facing the spectators directly, with the defence to his left and the tribunal to his right, he appears to hold centre stage, and his presence, when he speaks or rises from his chair, will dominate the room. The courtroom is austere, there are no decorations anywhere to suggest the majesty of justice—no flags, crests, no mullioned panelling, no dark weighty oak. Only a large, light room and the silent, serious tribunal.

There are rustles of paper, murmurs of spectators as the court awaits the entrance of Belshaw. Then at 9:15 a door opens behind the defendant's table and Professor Belshaw, accompanied by a gendarme, walks in. He bows his head to the tribunal and counsel, then stands waiting to Paschoud's left, scarcely a metre from the spectators.

The spectators are astonished at the sight of him. This is the man whose name has been trumpeted in headlines for over a year. He has been accused of so much, directly and by innuendo, he has begun to loom very large in the imagination. And now—he is so small! That is the first thing one notices, the glaring, unmistakable first impression. He has lost weight, his brown suit hangs loosely on him, the sleeves come almost to the middle of his small white hands. Thick, very brown hair, neatly cut around the nape of the neck. White sideburns and a short salt-and-pepper moustache above a prim mouth and little round chin. He seems almost like a boy wearing his father's suit, with gold-rimmed glasses and a dyed wig, ready to play a part in a drama meant for grown-ups. His neck in particular shows the signs of his lost weight. It has been creased and lined with strain, sudden aging and sagging flesh.

The plump, satisfied, jowly look of a year earlier is gone, and before the tribunal stands a very small man, utterly calm and composed, with his sharp and exacting intellect his only remaining weapon in the battle to come.

The gendarme, in a well-pressed grey uniform with enormous gold buttons, seats himself in a chair behind Belshaw, at the door. It seems a pointless precaution.

22

A Vaudois trial is opened by the president who must first swear in the jurors and then read out the charges. Next the president reads out relevant material from the dossier, interrogates the accused, and then calls the experts and witnesses who testify in the order he has prescribed. The president has a great deal of latitude in how he handles this part of the trial, and in what questions he asks. Witnesses and experts must answer any questions the president chooses to put, unless they are protected by a code of professional secrecy or are close relatives of the defendant. The accused, on the other hand, is not required to answer questions put to him, nor is he subject to contempt charges for lying as are the witnesses. However, when it comes time to set the sentence, the president can take into account any of the accused's refusals to answer, and any lies he has told.

President Guignard, in particular, believes in giving witnesses and defence a great deal of latitude in expressing themselves. While he will interrogate each witness and the defendant and put great pressure on them if he wishes, as is his right under the law, he also believes in letting witnesses express themselves freely. "We believe," Guignard said later, "that the witnesses render a service to justice. They must be allowed to express themselves freely, in all liberty. This is very important. Then we evaluate what they have said, and decide what weight and credence to give to it.''

If a witness appears to be lying, the president then—and only then—cautions the witness to reflect, and warns him or her of possible charges of contempt. Basically, however, all the witnesses are assumed to be doing their duty as citizens. They testify without oath, and say whatever they have a mind to. They must, of course, reckon with the president, judges, jury, prosecution and defence, who all have the right to question them, and to try to break them down if it seems important to do so. Guignard feels that the defendant, too, must be pressed to reveal his character and motivations, because if he is found guilty, the law requires that these be taken into account when setting the sentence.

The first part of a Vaudois trial, the reading of the accusation and the president's interrogation of the witnesses and the defendant, corresponds to the prosecution making its case under the common law. When this is over, the prosecution asks questions, then the defence puts forward its witnesses. When all witnesses and experts have been heard and questioned by president, prosecution and defence, and the jury has had an opportunity to ask the defendant and witnesses any questions it chooses, the prosecution makes its summing up. Then the defence puts forward its final plea. The prosecution can respond, but the defence has the last word.

Once the trial is over the tribunal sits immediately and renders its verdict. A majority decision of the whole tribunal decides both verdict and sentence. The president speaks last before the vote is taken. He has the force of his personality and experience behind his views, and can instruct the judges and jury on the law, but in the end they must make up their own minds. Having heard all the evidence and arguments, they are equal in weight to the president. At no point during the trial have they been excused, even while points of law are debated. They have heard everything the president has heard.

Even spectators are rarely dismissed from a Vaudois trial, however prejudicial the matter under discussion, since the openness and public scrutiny which have been lacking during the *instruction* are considered crucial during the trial itself. So the jurors and also the spectators may hear evidence from both sides that would never be heard by jury or spectators under common law: they hear witnesses who are not sworn to tell the truth repeat hearsay and prejudicial opinion; they hear the opposing party answer the hearsay and opinion with other testimonials; they hear unsigned depositions read out from the dossier, and also hear the defence's evaluations of the evidence so deposed and of the witnesses who gave it.

In the case of the Belshaw trial, the shape of the trial, the peculiar ordering of the evidence, the tremendous pressure put upon Belshaw by the president's questions, although proper under Swiss law, were to take their character from President Guignard and from his view of his responsibilities. Veteran Swiss court reporters were later to call the atmosphere in the Aigle courtroom "astonishing" and attribute it in part to Guignard's intense and mercurial nature.

But whichever president directed this trial, it could not help but be sensational, as Vaud attempted to try Professor Belshaw on psychological grounds for a crime which, the defence would argue, might never have been committed at all.

23

Looking down upon the six men before him, sombre in the grey morning light, the president opens the trial by swearing in the jurors: "Do you promise to give the most serious attention to the proceedings which are here beginning, to not falter in the exercise of your function as *jurés*, neither through interest, nor through weakness, nor through fear, nor through favour, nor out of hatred; to make your decision entirely upon these proceedings, according to your own conviction and your own conscience; to communicate with no one about this trial, even with other members of the tribunal, until after the judgement; finally to guard the secrecy of the deliberation and of the vote of the tribunal?" He then calls the name of each juror and states his profession: a teacher, a clerk, a restaurateur; men involved with the wine industry as growers or merchants. Each in turn, looking solemn, raises his hand and recites, "I so promise."

Now President Guignard, fixing his glasses firmly on the bridge of his nose and staring fixedly at a sheaf of papers, begins to read the charges rapidly in a sing-song Swiss accent.

"Between the 6th and the 13th of January, 1979, perhaps following a dispute due to the discovery by Betty Joy Belshaw, née Sweetman, of the liaison of her husband with Margery Wilson, Cyril Belshaw, by a means which has not been determined, in the couple's apartment in Montana, the Jolilac, or en route between Montana and Paris, probably in the district of Aigle, intentionally killed his wife, after which, having wrapped the corpse in three plastic garbage bags, he transported it in the trunk of his car and threw it down the slope from a lay-by on the Aigle-Le Sépey road, at the Larrevoin bridge.

"The corpse, in an advanced state of putrefaction, and partially eaten away by wild animals, was recovered on March 28th, 1979, 7.3 metres from the lay-by."

The court slowly stills as the president continues, reading out the charge that the accused then reported his wife missing in Paris. Later, reads Guignard, Belshaw wrote her dentist for her dental records and falsified them, whiting out with liquid paper six indications of work done and substituting his own markings in black ink. The charge makes clear that as very little material evidence remained, the State will base its case mainly on psychological evidence.

While the president is reading, Belshaw stands very straight, looking directly, unswervingly, into the eyes of the president, who never looks up from his sheaf of papers. The spectators, for the first time, get a glimpse of the remarkable *sang-froid* of Cyril Belshaw, which has so daunted the investigators. Only when the president reads out that Belshaw has now been in detention for 380 days—the time between the arrest at Roissy and the first day of the trial—does any change of expression appear on his face.

Finally the reading of the charges is complete. Belshaw sits down. The president looks down upon Belshaw, pushes his glasses up on his nose, and asks him if his birthdate and name are correct as read. Belshaw assents, and the president, with a smile, wishes him a happy birthday. Belshaw acknowledges this with a small formal nod. Guignard is about to begin reading from the dossier which he, alone among the members of the tribunal, has read, when Stoudmann rises to make a procedural argument.

The Canadian journalists sit up and take notes as Stoudmann launches a restrained but nonetheless bitter attack against the RCMP. He states that, contrary to both Swiss and Canadian law, the first interview with Belshaw was taped without his knowledge. Furthermore, Stoudmann goes on, the transcriptions of the tape reproduced in the dossier are inexact, in part actually incorrect, and important parts—particularly threats made by the Vaudois police—have been left out.

Guignard looks down at Belshaw, and asks him if it is true that the edited transcription of the tape contains omissions and errors. Belshaw smiles like a professor when a student has asked him an easy question and explains as if to a student: "For example, Fischlin said, 'If you were in Switzerland, you wouldn't be able to get away with something like this, things wouldn't go like this,' and that remark wasn't in the transcription."

"Did you see that as a threat?" asks Guignard.

Belshaw nods. "Yes, yes I did."

Back and forth, the president, Stoudmann and Heim discuss the taped interview, growing heated as more and more allusions are made to improper behaviour by Fischlin and Wyss. Paschoud, in particular, shows by his interjections how strongly he feels about the way this matter has been handled. Belshaw, he says, was completely devastated by the attitude of the police in this interview, and by the fact that Wyss and Fischlin did not respect the rules. Belshaw reiterates his agreement with these points when the president asks his opinion. He speaks in short, precise, grammatically correct French sentences, with a strong English accent.

Stoudmann tells the president that Belshaw was never warned of his rights and that the transcription of the interview was never signed by him—that the RCMP officer had a tape recorder microphone secreted in his clothes. It was a "savage interview", Stoudmann concludes, contrary to law and contrary to justice. Later the police covered it with a formal interview, but the damage was done.

Heim protests. "We do not deny that the taping of that interview

by the Canadian police was illegal according to our penal procedures, and may very well have been illegal, as well, in Canada.
But this does not make the transcript inadmissible in court. The
Swiss federal precedents are quite clear on this point. Illegally obtained evidence is acceptable, the court has ruled, if the same information could have been obtained legally.'' Quoting precedents,
the prosecutor demonstrates to the court that the law on such matters
is clear. He tells the tribunal that the only real sanction the law
provides against illegally obtained evidence in such cases is disci-
plinary measures against the judge or policeman involved in ob-
taining it.

"Furthermore,'' the prosecutor continues, ''it would be against
logic and common sense to remove the edited transcript of the tape
from the dossier after the prosecution and the president have both
seen it. The proper time to do this is during the *instruction*. The
defence did try to have it removed at that time; I ruled against it,
and the *tribunal d' accusation* upheld my ruling. If, now, the defence
wants this tape transcription removed it would make much more
sense for them to ask, as well, that the president be replaced, because
of the influence reading this transcript may have had upon him. And
this they have not done.

"And, finally, it makes no sense, and it would be poor procedure
indeed, that a significant element of the dossier telling against the
accused should escape both this tribunal and any higher court which
may later be involved, when both the accused and the defence are
familiar with it—whatever its actual importance.''

The argument grows heated. Heim's legalistic approach seems
to anger the defence, who obviously feel strongly about the tapes,
and the faces of president and counsel redden as they argue about
the legality and implications of the tapes. While Heim is making
his defence of the tapes, and explaining that they fall between the
two systems, Stoudmann murmurs ''Yes, neither one nor the other,''
and rustles a sheaf of paper revealing his agitation. His voice is
bitter.

It is a dilemma which appears difficult to solve, and seems to
embody within it the problems which have faced the Swiss in their
attempt to carry out the *instruction* and trial with the intrusions,
from time to time, of common-law procedures. Finally the president

calls a fifteen-minute recess. Everyone floods out into the corridor, and the president, defence and prosecutor take the time to cool their heated tempers.

The attack on police methods is not an ordinary approach in Vaud, and it has angered the president and annoyed Heim. But when the court is called back into session the president, ruling contrary to the precedents quoted by the prosecutor, announces that the tapes of the interview will be set aside "because they were obtained by procedures contrary to our conception of justice". This is the last that is heard, officially, of the disputed interview, although later it appears that both prosecutor and president are trying to get Belshaw to admit to statements he made during this interview and which are now admissible no other way. They will not be successful. Neither man will ever refer to what he has read, but can no longer properly use. The ruling will also be recalled later as proof that the president was directing the trial fairly, no matter what his personal opinions— which were soon to become clear—may have been.

Now Guignard begins to read from the giant dossier, over a foot thick, which stands before him in two large bound volumes. He reads in the same droning voice and the spectators frequently cannot make out precisely what is being said. Many of them are unfamiliar with the local intonation and the poor acoustics make it difficult to hear well towards the back of the room. Yet, despite this, the suspense in the courtroom grows, as the nature of the allegations begins to make itself clear.

Guignard is reading from the *pièces*, numbered sections of the dossier, which provide the background information upon which the prosecution is basing its case. Much of what he reads is unsubstantiated opinion, and he appears to be reading out bits and pieces in no particular order. Some of the information presents a serious problem of journalistic ethics to the English-language press. Such unsubstantiated allegations would probably not be allowed in North American or British courts. Here the Swiss press will report them, frequently referring, for example, to Margery Wilson as Mme. W. The English-language press would normally feel free to report whatever happens in court. But this? There is a frisson in the courtroom when Guignard reads out the account of Belshaw and Wilson in the red sportscar on the University Endowment lands. He reads in a statement from Wilson to the RCMP about her unhappy marriage, about how her husband called her a whore and threatened to strangle her, how she feared for her life and arranged to go to her parents' house in time of trouble.

Guignard reads out that no evidence of Betty ever having made the trip to Paris has been discovered. He recounts apparently contradictory actions of Belshaw after Betty's disappearance. He reads out evidence that Belshaw and Wilson lived together in Montana-Vermala the summer before Betty's arrival and travelled together to Ferney and Paris.

At one point during the reading of the *pièces* there is a brief interchange between Guignard and Belshaw. Belshaw, in his pedestrian French, admits calmly to having falsified the dental records, as stated in the charge, and says he will explain later.

The spectators are now silent, as the president finishes his chanting of the *pièces* and calls the first witness. In this first half hour the president has destroyed the previous image of the world-renowned anthropologist and model husband, and replaced it with a story of a philandering and deceitful man whose actions after the disappearance of his wife were equivocal and dishonourable.

The first witness to be called is a Lausanne medical dentist and police technical advisor, Claude Imobersteg. He walks to the witness chair, which sits with its back to the defence table, directly facing the tribunal, and takes his place, looking calm, but very much aware of the packed courtroom. Imobersteg looks straight at the tribunal and identifies his own record of the teeth. The jurors take notes as he testifies that the Le Sépey Corpse had three gold crowns on one side, and one on the other.

However, they put down their pens and look up as Imobersteg describes how the dental records were falsified with liquid paper and then photocopied. The records first deposed were, in fact, the photocopies of these altered charts. He testifies that when Belshaw was first asked if his wife had gold fillings he had answered, "I don't remember."

Guignard turns to Belshaw, and says to him, "It's impossible that you wouldn't have noticed. You were married so many years, you made love every night, how could you not have noticed?"

This is the first example of the president's approach to Belshaw:

his personal tone, his sarcasm, and the way he throws in his own opinions on matters which seem at least to non-Swiss observers out of his scope.

Imobersteg goes on to testify that at first, based on the records provided by Belshaw, he had excluded the possibility that the Le Sépey Corpse could have been Betty Belshaw. Then he began to think about it, and asked for another record.

Willy Heim, the prosecutor, asks him, "The more you mulled it over, the more uneasy you became?"

Imobersteg replies, "Yes, I thought x-rays would help, so we asked for them, even though Belshaw had denied that they existed. And *voilà*, the complete record arrived."

Then it is Paschoud's turn to question this witness and his first question immediately antagonizes President Guignard, harking back as it does to the sore points of the earlier discussion about the behaviour of the police. "Are you," Paschoud wants to know, "the habitual consultant for the police on such matters?"

"I see where you're going," Guignard tells him. "Don't suggest we're all in collusion."

Paschoud defends himself, and the president returns to his questioning of Imobersteg. The dentist makes it clear that he compared a great many records to the Le Sépey Corpse and that none matched, except Betty's.

Then Guignard asks, "You are absolutely certain, there is no doubt whatsoever in your mind, of your identification of this body as Betty Belshaw?"

Imobersteg sits very straight and says in a clear voice, "There is no possible doubt. I confirm it absolutely."

The next witness to be called is Inspector Wyss. He testifies, in response to the president's question, that the police asked Belshaw for the dental record and pictures of Betty. He describes the succession of events which led up to their receipt of Belshaw's falsification of the dental records. He explains to the president that the falsification was done in two stages. First Belshaw, using liquid paper, effaced the notations of work done. Then he marked indications of other work, on other teeth, work which in fact did not exist. He photocopied this altered chart and then destroyed the original. Then he made six photocopies of the falsified charts. One he sent to

England, two to Switzerland, one to France, and the remaining copies he kept in his own files.

Under repeated questioning from the prosecutor, however, Wyss admits that this is only *his* version of what happened. All he knows for certain is that the charts were altered with liquid paper and ink, and that the altered charts were photocopied and distributed.

Unsigned depositions taken in Canada by the Swiss police are now read aloud. From now on and throughout the first day, it will be difficult to follow the significance of the ordering of the evidence. It seems as if the president is just putting out all the evidence and testimony which the prosecutor will later use to build up a coherent case.

The depositions contain summaries of the characters of Cyril and Betty Belshaw, as the officers had defined them during their seven-month *instruction*. Mrs. Belshaw is described as emotional, a perfectionist and hypochondriac. She is alleged to have taken sleeping medication. Belshaw is described as cold, proud, intelligent, self-satisfied, ambitious, solemn, calm and sly. Wyss testifies that these are correct accounts of the information he gathered in Canada. The defence asks Wyss whether or not he and Fischlin told everyone in Canada that Belshaw's guilt was certain, thus eliciting this negative picture. Wyss denies it.

He testifies, in response to a question from the president, that the police asked Belshaw for the dental records and pictures of Betty. Heim asks, ''He spontaneously confessed to this falsification?'' Wyss agrees that this is correct.

Next Fischlin is called. He looks very nervous, and as he recites his name one can see his Adam's apple bobbing up and down.

The light reflecting off the snowy roof grows stronger and it becomes difficult to see in the courtroom, as Fischlin describes how, sometime in July, following a conversation with the *juge informateur*, he arranged to go to Canada. He then tells how great were the difficulties there. The Canadian police could have refused, Fischlin says, but they authorized the interview; then Belshaw refused to co-operate further.

Belshaw takes issue with this and corrects Fischlin. ''I stated, through my lawyer, that I was prepared to co-operate completely.''

In his cross-examination, Paschoud reads aloud a letter from

Canada, protesting about the way the police handled themselves in Canada. "He was under no suspicion in Canada," Paschoud reminds the tribunal. It appears, from the faces of the tribunal, that these attacks on the police are doing the defence no good.

Police evidence is now deposed stating that no one remembers seeing Betty Belshaw in Beaune where the couple were supposed to have stopped for the night on their way to Paris. And that Belshaw, who normally paid by credit card when travelling, had paid cash for his meal there and not kept the receipts—receipts which might have shown whether or not two people had eaten.

Parts of the French police report are read aloud. It states that Belshaw was calm and cool when he reported his wife missing. His demeanour struck the police as unusual. It goes on to say that despite Belshaw's testimony that both had stayed at the Hotel Novotel no one could confirm that Betty was there, and there was no record of her ever having been in Paris.

Testimony is read aloud from the waiter who brought up two breakfasts for the Belshaws at the Hotel Novotel the morning after their arrival. The waiter said there was no sign of Mrs. Belshaw and that Professor Belshaw told him she was in the bathroom.

A report from Betty's doctor is read out. In it he states that Betty never had a lapse of memory.

Then follows a series of bits of evidence which will be explained more fully later. A photo of Mrs. Wilson which has been identified by various witnesses is passed around. The spectators and jury are growing weary. There is a steady mumbling from the spectators, and the jurors rustle their papers, as an account from a meteorologist is read stating that there was seventy centimetres of snow when Belshaw left for Paris. The court is told that Belshaw's car was snowed in between January 4th and January 11th, when it was taken to a garage. It was returned to Belshaw on the 12th. Therefore he could not have travelled in it between those dates. Then depositions state that Belshaw told Major Smith in London that Betty had her passport and little money when she disappeared in Paris; that Belshaw had written a letter to an English friend, Lady Firth, saying that he had informed the British and Swiss police.

It is hard for the jurors and spectators to see the significance of all these facts piecemeal, and an air of boredom is settling over the courtroom. Then the president, with a twinkle, reads out evidence that Belshaw had ordered a catalogue of pretty girls modelling sexy underwear. It is passed around to the two judges, but not the jurors; the men snicker over it, as they quickly riffle the pages. Belshaw received this catalogue after Betty's disappearance, the prosecution contends, and this has been discovered by an exhaustive analysis of every cheque and credit card voucher signed by Belshaw—many of which are read aloud.

The catalogue has put the court into a good humour, and even the exhaustive reading of Belshaw's expenditures fails to dispel it. Paschoud complains about the quality of some of the translations of documents, and offers his own which are obviously better. After this, when each translated document is read aloud Guignard asks Paschoud if there is a more elegant translation.

The tribunal hears more details about Wilson and Belshaw's travel together the summer before Betty's arrival. They hear that on April 2nd in a conversation with Major Smith in London, Belshaw told Major Smith his wife had suicidal tendencies. It is very hard to make any sense of this jumble of evidence.

Only later will it become clear that these *pièces* form the bones of the State's case. Eventually they will be formed into a skeleton, revealing the shape of that case. For the basic facts crucial to the prosecution have now been laid before the tribunal: that the Le Sépey Corpse was Betty, that Belshaw carefully and meticulously falsified her dental records; that no one saw Betty on the trip between Montana and Paris and there was no evidence to prove that she had made the journey; that Belshaw's demeanour after his wife's disappearance was suspicious; and that Belshaw had had Wilson with him in Europe before his wife's arrival and had continued seeing her, in a clandestine way, in Vancouver. The various depositions laying out Belshaw's character also make up part of the prosecution's case, for without them the tribunal will not be able to evaluate the significance of his actions after Betty's disappearance.

Yet at this stage, most of the *pièces* read aloud serve only to confuse, or at best to whet the appetite for more, and there is evident relief among jury and spectators when, shortly before one o'clock, the president calls the lunch recess.

24

It is snowing heavily as the journalists and lawyers leave the court-house. Belshaw is nowhere to be seen, and President Guignard, the judges and jurors are eating somewhere in a reserved dining-room. Outside various groups of two or three spread out to the various small restaurants in the vicinity of the *Place du Marché*, to eat the *plats du jour* or *biftek* and *pommes frites*, and drink the local Dorin wines.

Heim, Stoudmann and Paschoud and the Swiss journalists go in one direction. Various North American journalists go the opposite way, and gather in a little restaurant to exclaim over the trial. They are nonplussed by the reading in of so much hearsay evidence, and uncertain how to handle it. They can hardly believe the testimony about Wilson and her husband, and worry over what to do about it. Some are worrying over their French, stretched to its limit by the poor acoustics and the Swiss accents. They check with each other to be sure that they have all heard the same thing. Then they argue over the Swiss mentality, and what the evidence of infidelity will mean to the jurors. One young woman states with authority that Swiss men are never unfaithful to their wives, and that the evidence of Belshaw's infidelity will go over badly with the jurors.

On returning to the courthouse, Paschoud and Heim, who are standing in the ante-room, are approached and asked questions. Is it true, asks one woman journalist of Paschoud, that Swiss men are never unfaithful? Paschoud enjoys the question. "We have it all worked out here," he explains with good humour. "You know, all Swiss men must do three weeks of military service ? Well, during the year they behave beautifully, but on their three weeks they can all have a *petite amie* ... , it is the perfect system. No, no," he continues, growing serious, "it is not like it used to be, here in Switzerland. With television, movies, people are sophisticated now-adays and morals are no different here than anywhere else. The jury will understand the affair. It will make no difference to them."

"Is Mrs. Wilson coming to testify?" asks another. Paschoud looks sad. "She is a married woman, with small children. How could she come? But she has done everything she can to help ...

she has sent her statement." Then, smiling, to the journalist who has asked him about Swiss infidelity, "If you were having an affair with me, would *you* leave your family to come all the way to Switzerland to testify? No, no, one couldn't expect it." Paschoud seems concerned to make his point. But surely it is obvious that a married woman, whose husband has not known any details of her affair and who has attempted to keep that affair a secret, dare not go to Switzerland to testify for her lover. Her detailed deposition is the best possible compromise the defence could have expected.

Harry McLaughlin is seen striding anxiously around the waiting area where the crowd of journalists is attempting to corner Paschoud, Stoudmann and Heim. "I can't believe this trial," he says. "Why bother to try him at all? It's a kangaroo court." He shakes his head in astonishment, and bites his upper lip nervously. One wonders how much he has understood, as his French is virtually non-existent.

Then it is 2:00 p.m., the court is about to resume. The English-speaking journalists rush for the front seats, the doors close, Belshaw comes in, looking calm and sedate, with his gendarme. He smiles at the tribunal, and his smile has a certain dignified sweetness. The women journalists stare at him, trying to see what the attraction is that has drawn a young woman to risk her family and security. They can't see it. His reticence, his total lack of *joie de vivre* are his predominant characteristics. He sits waiting, contained, reserved, so proper. The afternoon session begins.

Now the technical experts are to testify. A plastic bag is opened, and the spectators crane their necks to see it as it is unwrapped at the end of the bench and the famous garbage bags are brought out. The gruesome evidence of the state of the body is read aloud. The court is told how the body had been wrapped in three garbage bags, which had been torn away by wild animals. A piece of a fourth, of a different kind, was found lying some distance from the body. It is assumed that this had nothing to do with the other three and was just part of the refuse found at the site. Earlier reports filed in the dossier stated that the garbage bags had red ties. The defence tries to make something of this error, but it appears insignificant and the court is told that the ties were in fact white. As the medical witness discusses the state of the body, badly decomposed and partly eaten, Belshaw remains perfectly calm.

However, when the president, reading from the dossier, reads out that Belshaw did not respond to the request from the police to provide the dental records, but instead insisted upon writing for them himself, he shakes his head in negation and his neck grows red.

Then Guignard turns to Belshaw, looks down on him and, taking up his inquisitorial role, begins to question him directly about the falsification of the dental records.

"Let us admit, Professor Belshaw, anyone, in a moment of passion, could kill his wife, but this—I can't understand. I have for you all the sympathy a magistrate can have for an accused ... but this! It's beyond understanding!"

Belshaw replies, carefully, finding and using the exact word in French in each sentence. "I couldn't support the psychological trauma of such an identification, without my family. I needed to be in the presence of family and friends. I could bear it only after being home with my family ... I waited to be back home. I was finding it unbearable, the prolongation of uncertainty, months of hope, hoping she would return alive.... I wanted to think of her alive."

"If you were so upset," Guignard persists, "why did you write to your daughter in May,"—he reads from the dossier—" 'The police are on their third round'? That sounds pretty flippant to me."

"I was alone in the apartment, without enough work to do; *bouleversé*. I wanted to think of my wife as living." Belshaw's voice trembles slightly, and he seems to be struggling to control himself as he continues, "She hated publicity, she wouldn't have liked all that—to be all mixed up in that mud.

"And then," he goes on, growing calmer, "you must realize that during the weeks when I had nothing serious to do, nothing to occupy my mind, I had had three emotional crises which had made me *fou*, irrational. I didn't think of the consequences, I didn't stop to reflect. That is why, with the dental record before me, so technical ... something involuntary came over me. The dental chart ... it had nothing to do with a living being!"

Guignard leans forward, growing heated; he raises his voice and his gestures become animated as he berates Belshaw: "Did you intend to remain forever uncertain about the fate of your wife? You say you didn't want to think of your wife like that...."

"I didn't want to imagine something like that!"

Guignard continues to press Belshaw; he reviews the gory description of Betty's remains, trying to shake Belshaw, but Belshaw remains adamant. The court is electric as the president reveals his conviction that Belshaw is guilty, and he continues to attempt to break him.

"If you had killed your wife ..." the president begins.

"I didn't kill my wife! I thought only of the dental record, and the possibility that my wife might be dead, and at that minute I couldn't bear ... I was cowardly, I know. I was a coward. I'm not proud of my state then. The moral and legal consequences of what I did have seared my conscience."

Then Heim interjects, "It was fifteen days between the time you wrote for those records and the day you falsified them, fifteen days. How can you say you did it involuntarily, in an emotional state ? You could have given the name of the dentist to the police, but no, you wrote for the dental records yourself. You must have had the intention, from the beginning, of falsifying them."

A letter is read aloud, in which Belshaw wrote that he was anxious to have an identification.

Guignard continues to push. "You say you wanted to have an identification, couldn't go on; but it is you, you yourself who have prevented that. It is that which is so horrible. There's a contradiction on the face of it. You wrote to your daughter, 'I can't face it,' when you had written for the dental records but not yet falsified them. You had already—admit it—made up your mind to what you were going to do."

The president now has the bit firmly in his teeth, yet Belshaw answers each question and never loses his aplomb. "My conscience weighs on me," he tells Guignard. "It's serious what I did, it was done in a moment of weakness ... morally, it weighs upon my conscience." This is said as a statement of fact, and seems only to further anger Guignard.

"Let us admit, Professor Belshaw—how many people when told about the finding of a body say they can't face it and falsify the record? Wives, husbands, sons, daughters, how many of *them* falsify the record? How many do you think? How many? How many?"

Belshaw, ashamed, looks down at his hands, folded over one

another on the table before him. "Very few. Very few."

"Less than zero per cent! In fact, it has never happened!" Guignard sits back, triumphant.

But Belshaw has regained his momentary loss of composure. "How many people have had their wives disappear as mine had done? And then twice have had their hopes raised and then dashed?

"You must remember, there were several events which upset me profoundly. First there was Major Smith, who talked about many cases where a totally unexpected suicide took place. He questioned me deeply when I was in London and had gone to visit the Salvation Army because I heard they had a lot of experience in such affairs.

"Then, while I was at York, at the conference, I had a message from the Canadian High Commission that the Paris police had some news for me. This raised my hopes, so on the Monday I went to Paris but—they had no news for me. I was like this," he raises his hand high, holding it flat in the air, "and like this," he lowers it sadly.

"Oh yes," Guignard says, "but when you sat there working carefully with your liquid paper and your ink and your glue it doesn't sound like you were up and down and so emotional."

"At that time," Belshaw explains, "I had finished my work at Montana. I had sent the manuscript of my book to be typed in Canada. There was nothing to do. All the beauty of the scenery ... without Betty. Then I began to realize, for the first time, that she was gone forever, and would never come back. Yet I couldn't accept it, I kept hoping for a miracle.... To accept that that corpse was her! ..."

The prosecution returns to reading in evidence of Belshaw's behaviour in an apparent attempt to confront him with contradictions. A statement from a fellow anthropologist and friend of Belshaw, a Mr. Friedmann of UNESCO, is read in. In it Friedmann states that he saw Belshaw soon after Betty's disappearance and that he was remarkably calm. His indifference to Betty's disappearance was notable, Friedmann says.

Another statement from a friend of Belshaw is read aloud. This is from Lady Firth, wife of Sir Raymond Firth. The Firths were friends of the Belshaws. They had known them since Belshaw's graduate days, more than thirty years before. In November, the Belshaws stayed with the Firths in London and in Dorset, before continuing to Switzerland. In the statement read aloud, Lady Firth says that Betty had appeared perturbed, that once she had slept an entire weekend. Another time, when the Belshaws stayed at the Firths' apartment in the Firths' absence, the bed was broken. The journalists look at one another at this testimony, totally unable to see the significance of it.

Next, evidence is given about the situation of the Jolilac, and the position of the Belshaws' apartment, on the ground floor. Then there is evidence from the dossier about Wilson and Belshaw living together for a week in an apartment very near the Jolilac. Later these pieces of evidence will be used to build up the prosecution's version of what really happened. Now it appears out of context, and confusing.

Then medical evidence begins in earnest. Dr. Genillard of Aigle testifies that the body was found stretched out, on its side, naked and wrapped in plastic sacks.

The forensic doctor, Professor Marc-Henri Thélin, testifies that it was impossible to tell much from the state of the body. They could not determine how Mrs. Belshaw died.

The defence presses Thélin. ''Then how can you be sure she met with foul play?''

''But she was naked ... wrapped in garbage bags!''

''Yes, but what medical proof do you have?''

Thélin seems to miss the point. ''I have told you, the corpse was completely naked, and had been wrapped up by a second party.''

Finally Heim lends the defence a helping hand. ''Isn't it possible that she died a natural death, and then someone else came along and denuded the body and disposed of it?''

''Oh. Yes, yes, that's possible.''

The toxicologist Alex-Rudolphe Gujer, who examined the body for evidence of poison, testifies next. He states that he looked for evidence of poison, but the advanced state of putrefaction made it impossible to determine anything with certainty.

President Guignard presses Gujer, and Heim too asks him questions. They try to determine whether there was any trace of sleeping medication in the body and if not whether this was, in itself, proof that Betty had *not* been drugged by a soporific at the time of her death. The toxicologist explains that there are various types of sleeping pills. Some are stable, and could have been found if they existed.

Others would have passed away since the time of death.

"What about the kind of sleeping pills you buy without a prescription?" Guignard asks.

"We don't know. We just don't have enough experience in these matters. There are some sleeping pills which would have vanished from the body in the time which had elapsed. Ordinary pills would have lasted. We have consulted widely on this. The best specialists in Switzerland don't know. We studied all the available literature, we called in Carl Nillson from Copenhagen, the European expert on such matters. We just can not state conclusively how she died or whether she had taken soporifics before death."

After the technical witnesses have finished, Inspector Guignard, one of the two officers who called upon Belshaw to ask for his wife's dental records, takes the stand. He explains that he and Inspector Reichen told Belshaw that they were trying to identify a body which had been discovered. "We had been notified that his wife had disappeared. We asked him first to give us the name of the dentist who looked after his wife's teeth. But he preferred to write for the records himself. We had no idea he was a suspect; it was simply a matter of trying to identify a body. But Belshaw refused categorically." Inspector Guignard goes on, "He said he wanted the matter handled with discretion, because he knew the dentist personally."

Now it is Belshaw's chance to give his side of his story, about which so much has been said by the prosecution. Speaking with his usual calm, but with a trace of annoyance in his voice he tells the president, "I didn't refuse to give them the name of the dentist. The two officers discussed among themselves whether it would be faster to get the records from Interpol or by my writing directly to Dr. Nishiguchi."

The defence begins to press Inspector Guignard. For a while he sticks with his story that Belshaw refused to give them the name of the dentist. But as Paschoud pursues the matter, repeating Belshaw's statement of how the two officers had discussed the matter between themselves, and considered the time it would take to get information from Interpol, he seems suddenly to give way. "Well, I guess I don't remember if he actually *refused* to give us the dentist's name."

More questions from Heim and Paschoud elicit nothing. It becomes obvious, as it will again and again, that Belshaw's memory of the past is so much more clear and exact than the memories of those opposing him that he is able to carry his point. It is apparent from Inspector Guignard's face that, until Belshaw made his statement, the police officer had forgotten the discussion between himself and Reichen. Being reminded of it, he lost heart, and was no longer certain of his contention that Belshaw had refused to give them the name of the dentist.

Next, Inspector Reichen testifies. He too states that he had not the least suspicion that Belshaw might be involved in any foul play. And he too admits that he cannot remember if Belshaw *refused* to give the name of the dentist.

The next witness is of a totally different stamp. She is identified as Mrs. Babcock, an old friend of the Belshaws since 1945 who lived not far from them in Montana. An attractive woman who appears to be in her late fifties, she is wearing an expensive dark brown winter coat which she does not remove while testifying. Mrs. Babcock, speaking in a quiet refined voice, and with an air of intelligence, tells the court that she received a letter from Betty before Christmas, and a telephone call from Cyril, about plans for getting together socially. She also testifies that on the 19th of January she talked to Belshaw on the phone, and he commented that he was annoyed with the Swiss police and the way they were handling Betty's disappearance. It is, obviously, to stress this point that Mrs. Babcock has been asked to testify for the prosecution. Belshaw had told her, as he had told others, that the Swiss police did not appear to be doing anything. He had complained about them to his friends, yet never called them directly himself. This is a point the prosecution will stress repeatedly.

President Guignard picks up on it. "Don't you think it odd, his irritation with the Swiss police, if he hadn't seen them at all?"

Mrs. Babcock answers with composure, "Why no. It was natural for him to be worried. His wife was missing."

The president asks Mrs. Babcock if she found Belshaw "proud, sly, self-satisfied, ambitious".

"He was proud of his work, his family, but not himself. He was always kind to me, and my husband knew him well during the war in the Pacific. They got along well together, the Belshaws. They worked well together, and were great lovers."

The spectators are growing restless as the president calls the next witness, the real-estate agent who handled the rentals at the Jolilac, Mme. Wuest. She is an arrogant-looking woman, in her forties, with artificial-looking streaked hair, and she too has not removed her coat. It is a heavy beige suede with fur trim; with it she wears matching boots.

Mme. Wuest tells the president how she made an inventory of the apartment a few days after renting it, and says that the Belshaws gave her the impression of being agreeable tenants. She recalls how in November 1978 she came to the Jolilac apartment to replace a refrigerator and had a brief talk with Mrs. Belshaw. She remembered Mrs. Belshaw saying her husband was away.

Then she tells the story of Belshaw coming the summer before the sabbatical to rent the apartment. He had an *amie* with him, and after looking over the apartment, he said, in the presence of his *amie*, that it looked fine to him, but that he would have to telephone his wife. The remark and its context made a strong impression on Mme. Wuest.

The president hands down to her an 8×10 glossy photograph of a woman and asks her if that is the person who accompanied Mr. Belshaw when he looked over the apartment. No, Mme. Wuest says, his *amie* was older.

But Belshaw interjects, and says in a tired voice that yes indeed, it was Mrs. Wilson with whom he had been looking at the apartment that day.

Mme. Wuest goes on to confirm that after the 1st or 2nd of January the Jolilac was three-quarters empty.

Mme. Wuest has a way of holding herself and a coldness of tone which produces an unpleasant effect on the spectators. Perhaps it is partly the elaborate make-up, the carefully dyed and coiffed hair, the expensive coat and boots, the arrogant tone of her replies to the president. But later, when the prosecutor casts her into an important, if minor role in the murder plea, the spectators will remember, and believe that she could indeed have been malicious, or at least a catalyst, in a possible series of events which is beginning, dimly at this stage, to take shape.

The next witness to testify identifies himself to the court as Zdravko Vrgovic, Jugoslav, concierge. This then is the man who told the press that he had seen Betty alive a week after Cyril reported her missing in Paris. Yet his story has so far formed no part of the prosecution's case and now it is hard to understand how it can help either defence or prosecution.

Vrgovic is nervous. He crosses his legs, revealing flashy shoes with built-up heels and an expanse of beige sock. He tells stories of how he saw Mrs. Belshaw during the time when his mother was visiting from Jugoslavia. It is obvious that President Guignard does not believe him, and he presses Vrgovic, trying to show that the concièrge has confused the dates. The questioning, however, is inconclusive.

Vrgovic tells Guignard that one night he heard loud noises in the Jolilac which lasted for about an hour.

The president is sceptical. "Could it have been little children running in the halls, or in the next apartment?"

The concièrge is sure that that is not possible.

The defence presses him on the point, until weakly, and obviously not believing it, he admits that it *might*, just *might*, though he didn't think so, have been children in the halls.

Then Heim asks whether or not Vrgovic could have confused another woman with Betty. As Heim presses Vrgovic, the last bit of certainty seems to ooze from him; he appears to have been affected by the scepticism of president, prosecutor and defence, and his assurances that he really did see Betty in January trail off.

He is questioned briefly about the garbage bags at the Jolilac, and it appears that the ones commonly used were either used for the kitchen, and a smaller size than the ones Betty was found in, or used in the laundry room and a larger size.

Paschoud asks Vrgovic what was the height of the drift of snow between the Jolilac and the Bellevue next door in January 1979.

"Approximately a metre," the concièrge answers.

"Could someone have dragged a body from the apartment and put it into a trunk of a car pulled out into the parking area of the Bellevue ?"

"I don't think that would be possible."

"Could someone have taken a body out the front door and put it into a car waiting in the parking area of the Jolilac itself?"

"Yes, that's possible."

The next witness to testify is a hostile-looking young woman who identifies herself as Miss Janine Hurliman, a former student of

Belshaw. Speaking in short sentences, and volunteering nothing until asked, Miss Hurliman testifies that she was a former student of Belshaw and that some time after his wife's disappearance she telephoned him to get some advice about her academic career. They agreed to meet. Belshaw picked her up at the railway station at Sierre and drove her to his apartment, where they had their conversation. They spent the night together although, she tells the court, they slept in separate beds and, she states, absolutely nothing improper passed between them. In response to the president's questions she says that she and Belshaw had talked about his wife's disappearance, that he wasn't indifferent. He was simply a reserved man who hid his feelings. Hurliman is sullen and does not look at Belshaw, who stares indifferently at the bit of her profile which is visible from the angle at which the witness chair is placed.

Hurliman is followed on the stand by Jean-Claude Antille, a doctor who practises in Montana. He says that in the third week in December Betty consulted him about a sore throat. Aside from this she was in fine health, he saw no signs of any other physical or mental ailment.

On February 8 Cyril Belshaw had an appointment. He came to see Dr. Antille about a cardiac weakness, and only mentioned in passing that he had been waking early and wanted something to control his tension because of the effect it might have upon his heart. He explained that he was suffering from anxiety, but when Antille asked if there were any personal problems, Belshaw replied that there were not. He did not mention to the doctor that his wife had disappeared, and the doctor had not asked.

The next witness is M. Bernard Eggs, an optician from Montana. He tells the court how Betty bought glasses from him, and how his records show that she had received them on January 6th. From this he concluded that although he could not remember specifically, he must have seen Betty on that date, as he always adjusted the glasses personally.

Eggs, who is dressed in a lush suede coat with a short plush collar, and has a very adenoidal voice, seems to antagonize President Guignard, who presses him repeatedly on how he could be sure that it was Betty herself who picked up the glasses.

Eggs is unshakeable. That is how it must have been. His calm certainty annoys the president, who at one point prefaces one of his

questions to Eggs with, "Well, I'm just a petit-bourgeois, but ..."
In the end, Guignard unwillingly accepts Eggs' assurances that Betty
must have been alive on the 6th, and from then on this date is
accepted as being the last one on which anyone saw her alive.

It is now close to 7:00 p.m. and everyone is very tired, except
Guignard, whose vitality, humour, temperament and charm seem
impervious to the hour as he calls the last witness, M. Tschopp
from the office of tourism in Montana. Tschopp reads aloud, from
his own records, the temperature and snowfall for each day from
the 6th of January to the 13th, when Belshaw drove to Paris. The
temperature during this time never rose above zero Celsius and snow
fell every day. By the time of Belshaw's departure for Paris seventy
centimetres of snow had fallen.

Then the first day is over. The spectators stream out, relieved and
exhausted from the roller-coaster of emotion, and the confusing
testimony.

In the corridor Heim is telling one of the journalists, "Yes, it's
true, we have no material evidence. We don't know where the
murder was committed, we don't know how, and we don't know
why. We are basing our case on psychological evidence."

Everyone goes out into the cold snowy night. Most of the journalists head back to hotels in Montreux, Lausanne and Geneva since
the one major hotel in Aigle is closed for repairs. Belshaw is taken
back to his cell in Bois-Mermet in a police car, a drive of almost
an hour over the snowy roads.

That night, reflecting over their Beaujolais Nouveau, or rushing
to meet their deadlines, journalists puzzle over the implications of
the first day: the confusing nature of the *pièces*, the astonishing
sang-froid of Belshaw on the stand, and his ability to stand up to
the tremendous pressure of Guignard's interrogation. Now the
State's witnesses have been heard, tomorrow it will be the turn of
the defence.

Paschoud and Stoudmann will have to defuse the picture of Belshaw as a cold, sly, proud philanderer. They will have to explain
away the falsification of the dental records and try to show that Mrs.
Belshaw really went to Paris. No wonder Paschoud is unable to
sleep. He is convinced he will succeed; after all he believes completely in Belshaw's innocence. But the prosecutor's case is such
a spider's-web of little details and hypotheses. The case which has

absorbed Paschoud for over a year is now reaching its climax, the man he regards as a friend is back in his cell in Bois-Mermet. Paschoud lies awake trying to see where the prosecution is going and making his plans on how to forestall them.

For the observers who have not yet made up their mind, the first day has been bewildering. Confusing as the evidence has been, there is a great deal of it which tells strongly against Belshaw. Yet his demeanour is the most puzzling of all. What does it mean? Is he an innocent man showing grace under pressure, or a guilty man brazening it out, arrogant in his belief that he can outwit the Swiss through his superior intellect? This seems to be the greatest puzzle of all.

25

Thursday, December 5th. It is snowing more heavily, the skies are grey, but the air is a bit warmer, as journalists and spectators hurry into the well-heated modern *Hôtel de Ville*. They walk along the long corridor and cluster in the waiting area, forsaking the comfortable sofa and chairs to stand bunched in front of the door. The first day's testimony has made clear how important those front seats are, and the journalists rush in, as soon as the *greffier* opens the door. Two well-known Swiss crime reporters, Myriam Meuwly of *24 heures* and Pierrette Blanc of the *Tribune de Lausanne-le matin* graciously give up their front seats to anxious Canadians. The six-foot tall AP stringer who has not arrived early enough to get a front seat accuses the Canadian women journalists of selfishness and retires, miffed, to the third row. From his height on the bench, President Guignard looks down upon all this bustle, and then calls the court to order. Belshaw enters, nods and smiles politely to the tribunal. They look at him but do not smile back.

The president begins by telling the court that he will be reading out more of the *pièces* and questioning the accused. Then the defence will bring forth their witnesses. He also explains that he has been presented with a new piece of evidence, a deposition from Harry McLaughlin, "a magnificent statement". He then reads out a French translation in a clear sonorous voice:

"The law of Canada is quite clear that citizens are entitled to know if criminal charges have been laid against them. If a person has been charged, or if charges are being contemplated against him, he is not required to make any statement and indeed, his refusal to make a statement cannot be the subject of any comment in court and it is most improper for the prosecutor or anyone else to bring it to the court's attention that the accused remained silent or refused to answer.

"One of the most cherished rights of the Canadian judicial system is the right of citizens to refuse to make statements that would tend to incriminate themselves.

"An accused and anyone suspected of any crime has the inviolate right to remain silent.

"Accordingly, it was with these principles of law and practice in mind and also because the Swiss officers would not advise me if charges had been or were going to be laid against my client and also because the Swiss officers would not advise what additional questions they wanted to ask my client (he already had been subjected to a lengthy interrogation in the absence of counsel previously) that I quite properly, under the Canadian system, advised my client not to answer any further questions.

"The course followed by me and upon my advice by my client was correct and proper under the Canadian law and practice. Indeed, the RCMP officers attempted to explain to the Swiss officers that there was nothing improper in the position we took in refusing to answer further questions."

The phrase "one of our most cherished rights" sounds particularly good in French, and it appears that the tribunal is very favourably impressed with McLaughlin's statement. The president, by introducing it himself, and praising it, has shown his capacity for objectivity just at the time that many of the journalists, unfamiliar with the inquisitorial role of the president under the civil law, were becoming convinced that Guignard was incapable of impartiality.

Prosecutor Willy Heim comments, "Of course, it is not for us to criticize the Canadian system."

"But that was just what was done in the dossier, on this subject," Paschoud reminds him.

"I see your point," Heim nods.

Guignard then reads out a long letter from Betty Belshaw to her daughter Diana. The letter, dated January 2nd, recounts the doings of Adrian over the holiday, and tells how Cyril and Betty celebrated New Year before a real Christmas tree, drinking champagne and clicking their glasses to the New Year. It shows that Betty Belshaw was in good spirits during the holidays.

There follow more bits and pieces of evidence. It is as if the president wishes to accentuate and fill out in detail all the points on which the prosecution will base its case. Yet he himself does nothing to connect them up. This will be done by the prosecutor, later.

Guignard reads aloud the letter of Cyril to Diana in which he asks her to phone Dr. Nishiguchi and have the dental records sent right away. " 'Perhaps I am cowardly,' " reads out Guignard, " 'but I can't face it. I think I have an idea of what may have happened. She was on her way to the library ... and she decided to go for a walk by the Seine. She slipped on the banks. Perhaps that is too simple, but we must find a simple explanation we can live with.' "

The president then reads out Belshaw's *curriculum vitae* and an exact accounting of his income and financial worth. The figures show that the Belshaws' affairs were in order and that they had no financial difficulties.

The jurors look serious and bored as Guignard drones on, reading about Fischlin and Wyss's trip to Canada, about evidence that Belshaw and Wilson stayed together in a hotel in Paris for several days in June 1978. They listen without a great deal of interest as he reads out a statement from Professor Friedmann who says that when he talked to Belshaw and Diana Belshaw a week after the disappearance, they told him the Paris police had said there were 3,000 disappearances a year. They discussed the matter and Friedmann was astounded by the calm and apparent indifference of both Cyril and Diana at the disappearance of Mrs. Belshaw. As this letter is read Belshaw sits disapproving, his head resting on one hand.

The garbage bags, of grey plastic, are brought forward again and opened for the inspection of the court. A smell of disinfectant permeates the courtroom as they discuss the fact that such bags were manufactured in October 1978 and were available at Montana at the time of the disappearance. Again the good faith of the police is brought into question, as it is recalled that Fischlin and Wyss told Belshaw that the bags were available *only* in Montana, which it appears was not the case.

President Guignard shows his displeasure. "I will uphold the law of the defence of which I am the symbol," he reminds the parties.

He then reads aloud the entire report about Belshaw and Wilson on the UBC Endowment lands. Then Wilson's explanation of the incident, as she deposed it to McLaughlin, is read in. She was a student, she stated they were discussing a paper.

Belshaw puts in, "We were in the car with the light on, looking at a paper. Not a button was undone."

A statement of Dr. Melville Shaw, Betty's Vancouver doctor, is read in—a police report which says, "Shaw asked us our opinion about the behaviour of Cyril Belshaw. We told him that we were personally astonished at how unconcerned he was about the death of his wife; he acted as if the whole thing concerned someone else.

"Dr. Shaw said that he had exactly the same impression after he had a discussion for over three hours with Belshaw after he returned from Switzerland. He felt Belshaw must be a very sick man, and even expressed fears that he might do something horrible to his children."

However, following this statement, the president again reverts to his impartial role and brings out another statement by Shaw, denying the implications of the first statement and saying that he was certain Belshaw could not have done such a thing. "The officers came to talk to me," Shaw explained in this second statement, "and asked me if I wanted to see the pictures of the body. They opened their briefcase, took out some pictures and showed them to me and I was shocked and horrified. They then told me they had evidence that proved that Belshaw had done this thing. After that I said, well, if he did that and talked the way he did then he must be very sick and I am afraid he will do something horrible to his children. I wouldn't have said that if I hadn't been so upset by the pictures, and been given that assurance by the police. I have no criticism of Belshaw's manner concerning his wife and her disappearance.''

As the matter of Dr. Shaw is discussed, Belshaw looks disgusted, and shakes his head.

Next a long statement from Mrs. Wilson is read aloud. It tells how she met Belshaw for the first time when she was a student and speaks of the love affair which developed during 1978. The statement continues: ''At the end of 1977 and the beginning of 1978 I had on rare occasions intimate relations with Professor Belshaw and in June 1978 I stayed with him in Switzerland and France for about ten days.'' She says that the affair provided relief for her from a difficult marriage. Belshaw and Wilson corresponded through intermediaries and spoke on the telephone. She states categorically, ''I never at any time envisioned the possibility of marrying Professor Belshaw, and he felt the same. The possibility of his divorcing his wife to marry me was out of the question.'' As for the car incident in July 1979, it was a question of an exam. She wanted his advice, so she called from her office to his, he was in, they met, she picked him up in her car and she drove. He was the passenger. It was a two-seater car with a gear shift in between. As she tried to talk about the exam and drive, Belshaw suggested that her driving was erratic and that they should pull over. They parked in a well-lit area, with the car light on. ''I deny absolutely,'' says Wilson's statement, ''that there was any physical contact between us—that Professor Belshaw 'climbed off me' and had been stretched out on the front seat.'' When the RCMP officer approached the car, she could not find her driver's licence, so Belshaw showed his. She identified herself with her social insurance card.

Paschoud takes issue with the words ''have sex'' as a translation of ''intimate relations''. He tells the court that the phrase ''intimate relations'' in English doesn't just mean having sex. It means, to caress, to hug, to touch. The distinction seems important to him, but the rest of the court are enjoying the whole incident. The men smile at one another and there is a clubby atmosphere in the courtroom. The president, after a discussion about the English phrase ''climbed off me'', asks if Belshaw will confirm Wilson's deposition.

He nods. "It's exact," he says, raising a finger, "except for one thing I must say. What Constable Fleet did is disgusting to me. We were next to the Physics Lab, it was well lit, the car light was on." Belshaw looks angry. "I have admitted we were having sexual relations, yes, but something like that? Sex in an automobile. That's absolutely disgusting!"

Belshaw has been so calm while gruesome details were read out about his wife's body, he has listened with great dignity to police reports which were insulting to him, heard statements of friends read out which he might well have considered as betrayals. But now, with the courtroom tittering over one alleged sexual peccadillo, he is outraged, insulted.

And the observers might well wonder what is the point of dragging in an incident which could only prove embarrassing to Mrs. Wilson and a threat to what remained of her marriage. After all it had taken place well after the death of Betty Belshaw. The affair itself was not denied by Belshaw. In fact, not until the prosecution's final summing up will the rationale behind stressing this incident become clear.

After this interval of relatively light relief, the president continues his reading from the dossier. A letter dated January 16th, 1980 from Lady Firth is read out. "He notified me of the death of his wife...he seemed very calm."

The president reads that in January Belshaw made numerous calls to the Paris police asking if there was any news. In February he told them that he was losing hope.

Backtracking in a confusing way, Guignard now reads out a statement from a Dr. Hertzman that on April 17th, 1979 Betty visited him. She was upset, afraid she had cancer and no one would tell her.

The lunch break comes as a relief. In the corridor Paschoud tells curious journalists that the sojourn of Wilson and Belshaw in Europe had not been planned in advance, and that allegations that Belshaw had paid for Wilson's ticket to Europe were untrue. She had been at a conference in Europe, and had taken the opportunity to join him. A Canadian journalist asks if it is true that Belshaw will be found guilty if the defence can not *prove* him innocent—the reverse of the common law. No, the tribunal needs only a reasonable doubt to acquit, Paschoud explains. But if they are convinced by psychological evidence they can convict.

At the *Hôtel du Marché,* the French and Swiss journalists have pushed two tables together and are chatting with Heim and Paschoud. At another table, the correspondents from *Le Figaro* and from a Paris tabloid discuss the psychology of Belshaw's attitude with a Canadian journalist. As have the other European journalists, they try to get information about Belshaw's love life in Vancouver, chew over the gossip they have picked up in the corridors. The petit-bourgeois character of the jury is significant to them, and they speculate aloud about how the glamorous life-style and international renown of Belshaw will appear to the jury.

At two o'clock President Guignard opens the afternoon session by returning to his attack on Belshaw. He begins to question Belshaw about the incident, alleged earlier, when Betty slept for a whole weekend at the Firths'. It is obvious that Guignard has some idea about this incident, and its importance, but it is hard to see from his questions just what this idea might be.

"Now tell us," he begins, leaning down towards Belshaw from the height of the bench as if to press upon him the full weight of justice, "why did your wife sleep all weekend?"

"*Then* we thought she was exhausted physically. But let us get things straight," Belshaw corrects the president. "In fact, she slept until noon, she ate her lunch in bed, then got dressed, and we walked in the garden. And don't forget, this was just after we had had a car accident."

The president is nonplussed. "Where is that in the dossier, that she got up and walked in the garden? I didn't see it anywhere." He riffles through the pages and looks at Heim, who has no help to offer.

"In retrospect," continues Belshaw while Guignard, who is still leafing through the papers, is hardly listening, "it was an error, that I didn't suggest she see a doctor." The car accident, he explains, was obviously a greater shock to her than he realized at the time.

Guignard changes the subject. "How do you explain your indifference, as described by so many witnesses, and as shown in your letter to Diana and in many other incidents?"

"I suppose," says Belshaw, considering,"that in certain social conditions I am under control, as I am at this moment. If I am with people who are close to me I let go, but for others, I keep my feelings to myself.

"When I visited the Paris police and the Canadian consul I was numb. Often, in such a state I act mechanically. I passed that night trying to remember everything I could so I could make my statement without forgetting anything important."

"How is it," Guignard asks, "that you planned your trip to Paris so long in advance, then two days after the disappearance you abandon Paris?"

"I thought my wife might be in England or Canada. And everybody knew our address and phone number in Montana. The police told me there was nothing I could do in Paris. When the children came, we discussed if there was anything practical we could do. I even telephoned Paris ... they said there was no point in coming."

"But," Guignard argues, gesturing at Belshaw, "people in Canada had your address in Paris. You had written them giving them that address."

"I have to say I just wasn't acting rationally."

The president throws up his hands in disgust. Then accusing Belshaw, "Why didn't you suggest to the police that they look for her on the road between Paris and Montana?"

"I never thought of that."

"But it makes sense to look there!" says the president scowling.

"That was not how I looked at it at all. That was not my idea of my wife at all, that she would have run away. She had never run away, never left the house or me for even a night.

"I had several conversations with Mr. Nasrallah at the Paris Embassy, about whether it would be useful to inform the Swiss or English police, and I thought he had done so. It was only when I got a call, later, from Mr. Mooney at the Canadian consulate in Berne, asking if I would agree to their informing the Swiss and English police that I realized it had not been done. I was very surprised. I thought he was doing it."

The president wants to make his point absolutely clear. "But *you*, you yourself, *you* didn't call the Swiss police?"

"Yes, that's correct." Belshaw nods to accentuate the fairness and accuracy of the president's point, as if to suggest that from accuracy he has nothing to fear—that nothing could please him more. He continues in his measured French, "Mr. Mooney, the Canadian consul, indicated that he was in frequent contact with the Swiss police, and I thought that was the way to do it."

"But," says Guignard, "in England you didn't see the police, you saw Major Smith of the Salvation Army."

"Yes, that's right. There I had a different motive. I thought a search was already underway. So I went to the Salvation Army because they had great experience with missing persons. Perhaps they would find something which had escaped me."

"When a person is in such a position they try every avenue," persists Guignard. "Yet you, in France you informed the police and not the Salvation Army; in England you told the Salvation Army and not the police."

"In Paris the police discouraged me from going to the Salvation Army. They didn't think it would do any good. That interview with Smith, I was absolutely devastated by it. He had brought out so many emotional things. I cried and walked the streets."

The president continues his attack, angry and accusing. "How do you explain the fact that your wife was found nude, wrapped in plastic bags—that she had disappeared in France and turned up wrapped in garbage bags and thrown away like a piece of garbage?"

Belshaw replies, "I don't know at all, it's a horrible thing." Looking miserable he tells the president, "I have no explanation. I have theories, hypotheses...but no explanations."

"And why have you refused to collaborate with the Swiss police?"

Now Belshaw is angry. He thought he had made it crystal clear that it was not his fault that the Swiss police had not been informed. "Never! Never!" he cries, looking directly at President Guignard.

But Guignard has not at all been convinced on this point. "You called your lawyer..."

"At the end of a hard working day they announce the disappearance of my wife, and right away they begin to attack me. They didn't even have the courtesy to give me a moment to recover. Four hours without stop, and I was at the end of my resources. I called my daughter Diana, then I called my lawyer. And he told me it was not necessary to continue."

"And now," accuses the president, heavy irony in his tone, "you think you were hunted by the police."

"No. Attacked. I was in agreement with my lawyers. If the police had given us a list of written questions we would have responded. It was only at the end of October that the police finally gave me their questions in writing. They were exactly the same questions I had answered before. So Mr. McLaughlin decided that as there was nothing new I need not bother to answer.

"McLaughlin and I talked it over, we decided we needed a Swiss lawyer to help us deal with the Swiss judicial system. So I retained Maître Paschoud.

"I intended to talk deeply with Paschoud about how I could help the inquiry. I needed a lawyer's help."

Then looking directly at the jury, Belshaw says with the air of a man half-pleading, half-scoring a winning point, "You have inscribed on your crest the motto of Vaud, *liberté* and *patrie*. In order to respond, to collaborate, one must have liberty. Liberty to become informed."

Now President Guignard looks down upon Belshaw without smiling, without any traces of the strong feeling he has shown a minute before, totally seriously.

"You can be convicted, acquitted totally, or acquitted because there is a reasonable doubt and you must be freed," he says. "If after all that has happened there is the choice of condemnation or acquittal, could you accept acquittal by the benefit of doubt?"

"It's not what I want," Belshaw replies with conviction. "I had nothing to do with the death of my wife, and only an acquittal would be just." Suddenly, Belshaw's feelings break through. Passionately he strikes the table with the sides of his hand. "It's insupportable that people could suspect me of such things!"

"All right," says President Guignard, turning to another subject. "When you were arrested at Paris, and were under this accusation which weighed so heavily upon you, yet you refused extradition." Guignard berates Belshaw. "How could you allow these heavy accusations to rest against you, unanswered?"

"That's not my view of the matter," Belshaw replies. "I considered the request illogical. It had no basis in fact, it was ridiculous. As a matter of fact, it made me angry."

But Guignard is not satisfied with this answer, and he presses Belshaw, leaning forward and frowning at him.

"There are two points to consider," Belshaw explains with an air of condescension. "I understood, from Maître Badinter, that I could be kept in preventive detention for a long time. And that is in fact what happened."

Guignard explains to Belshaw the Swiss preventive detention regulations.

"First," says Belshaw, developing his argument unperturbed, "I knew that when one is in detention it is very rare indeed that one is let out on provisional release; and second, I thought that most of the information needed for the inquiry would be in Canada. That I could best help by consulting with my friends, my records there, and so on.

"You mustn't say," Belshaw continues pedantically, "that I escaped justice by going to Canada. There is, after all, an extradition treaty."

Guignard disputes this point heatedly, leaning forward and gesturing at Belshaw, who listens politely and then explains as if the president were a student of his. "In the beginning I wrote to my friends, to Mr. Nasrallah, to Mr. Nemetz [the chief justice of British Columbia], to the police, to everyone who could help. Yet in the end the police state that I systematically flouted the inquiry. That is simply not true.

"My files were all mixed up, years of files, and to answer your questions I was beginning to set aside all the papers which concerned my wife." Belshaw goes on to explain patiently to Guignard that all this gathering of information needed to be done in Canada. And how could he do it if he were in preventive detention in Switzerland?

Prosecutor Heim has some questions. "When, in early 1979, Inspectors Guignard and Reichen asked you for identification you gave them a falsified dental chart because you feared that your wife would be identified, yet you deposed a coloured photograph of your wife."

Belshaw disagrees. "That is not exact. The photograph was for identification if my wife were alive, the dental charts if she were dead."

"Did you know," Heim asks him, "that the corpse which had been discovered couldn't be identified?"

Belshaw replies quickly. "At the time those officers came to see me I had no knowledge of the Le Sépey Corpse."

Heim presses him. "But the *Nouvelliste du Rhône* of March 29th told of the discovery. It was in that newspaper, you were a reader of that newspaper, you must have known of the state of the body."

"But I must tell you that my interest in that newspaper was only for my studies. I don't remember reading the article. Judge Chatelain told me about it; *then* I noted that in the article the woman was described as being between thirty and forty years old. If I had read it I would not have thought it concerned Betty."

"Now, now, Professor Belshaw," Heim insists, "that would make sense if you were just Professor Belshaw, scholar. But you were also Mr. Belshaw whose wife had disappeared. It seems only natural, normal that you would have noticed such an article."

"Perhaps. But I didn't notice it."

Heim continues to press. "But the article was so specific! It stated that the woman had four gold crowns." Heim goes on to read aloud from the article, pointing to his own teeth, and giving the exact description of where each gold crown was located.

Belshaw is not in the least cowed. "When my wife smiled you couldn't see the gold crowns." And he continues, with an air of triumph, "I don't even remember which of my own teeth are crowned."

But the prosecutor has resumed his questioning and misses this last little sally.

"Professor Belshaw, the article is a fact."

"Yes," responds Belshaw, "but your interpretations are not facts."

"As for the Wilson story, about you and her in the car, do you confirm that none of that is true?"

"Absolutely."

Heim is trying to sneak up on Belshaw. "You saw Mrs. Wilson once a month at your house, about once a month you had sex with her?"

"Yes"

"Then why," Heim asks suddenly, "did you have your discussion in a car and not in your house?"

Belshaw explains calmly, patiently, as to a child who has heard something many times before and stubbornly refused to grasp it.

"I was in my office, and spoke to her by telephone: she was in her office. Then I joined her near her office, where her car was parked. We thought the matter could be discussed in just a few minutes ... it was ten o'clock. We drove around, but she was driving very badly, so I asked her to pull up. We stopped by the Physics building, which was very well lighted."

Heim changes the subject. "I know everyone said you were happy with your wife, but you showed off your affair, you displayed your mistress. You spent twelve days with her, you stayed with her at Montana when you knew your wife was coming there later, you slept with her there at your apartment. You were indifferent to your wife!"

"No," says Belshaw, endeavouring to clear up this new misunderstanding. "It was not like that. It was low season, there was almost no one there. In any case we spent most of our time elsewhere."

Heim pursues the matter. "Come now, you slept with her there. Couldn't someone say, Oh, your wife has changed? Let's admit it, you were indifferent to whether or not your wife found out."

"No. I considered it, and I decided the risk was slight."

"What would have happened if your wife had found out?"

"If my wife had found out, her reaction would have been ... to criticize me very harshly, to complain strongly, there would have been a scene, there would have been words ...."

Heim is very quick. "There was such a scene!"

"No."

"Have you ever struck your wife?"

The questions are coming very fast now, Heim is on his feet, facing Belshaw, looking at him, daring him to try to evade the questions.

"Never in our life."

Heim reads from the dossier, "'I may have struck her, she may have struck me'—so you said about a fight in the early sixties."

"Once, my wife slapped me."

"Your son said there were scenes during his childhood."

President Guignard turns a page in the dossier and interjects, "Your wife may have struck you once or twice?"

"No."

The president reads from the dossier. "It says in many places, the testimony of many witnesses, that she was formal, conventional, proper and didn't believe in extra-marital relations.''

Belshaw frowns, and rebukes Guignard. ''That's a complete caricature.''

Guignard and Belshaw begin to discuss Betty's character. Beyond them the sky grows steadily darker, it snows harder and flocks of small black birds wheel over the roofs and chimney pots, now blurred under a blanket of snow. The Alps are no longer visible.

Guignard has not succeeded in wringing any admissions from Belshaw about his wife's character. ''Keep in mind one thing,'' Belshaw is concluding: ''for my wife, people were more important than rules.''

The prosecutor returns to his probing. There is something he is trying to get at, but Belshaw is thwarting him. ''I can't help but think of Mrs. Belshaw, and her feelings for you. How *could* she have borne such things?''

''The most important thing to keep in mind is that my wife wasn't intolerant concerning things like that. She didn't attach too much importance to the physical act.''

Heim seems satisfied at the answer. The women spectators look at one another and raise their eyebrows.

Heim now turns the pages of the dossier and begins to read out the list of what Betty was wearing when she disappeared. Carefully, slowly, and with heavy irony he reads: ''a suit of green wool, a beige Burberry raincoat, a beige blouse, chestnut-coloured shoes, gold Longines watch with worked band, platinum wedding ring, emerald engagement ring, green travelling bag, green wallet, bifocal glasses with brown frames .... How could you know all this, so precisely, and then not notice she had gold crowns?'' He turns to the jury. ''I defy you, *messieurs,* to tell us this afternoon what blouse, what skirt, what shoes your wife is wearing today. It's stupefying Mr. Belshaw! Yes, laugh, you're having fun....''

Belshaw, who has been laughing along with the jurors' nervous titters, wipes the smile from his face, and resumes his more serious demeanour. ''I noticed these things because they were the same things she wore for dinner at Beaune, because I am very sensitive to things like that, because I was with her when she bought that suit and she usually wore that blouse with it. And as for knowing the brand name of her bra [this fact had been mentioned earlier] it is perhaps interesting for you that when I was in Europe by myself she got me to buy her bras. She had found that the brand she liked best was only sold here, and she wore it always.''

"But to remember everything!" Heim cries. "And then to tell them all that, and not to mention her teeth, her gold crowns to anybody.''

"But they weren't visible.''

The two argue about the gold crowns. Guignard and Heim find it a very telling point, that as observant and clear-headed a man as Belshaw should have been completely unaware of those four gold crowns.

The prosecutor finally moves on. "On the 29th of March the article about the discovery of the Le Sépey Corpse appears in the *Nouvelliste*. The next day you leave for London where you go and see Major Smith and talk about suicide. A curious coincidence.''

The jurors turn their attention from the prosecutor and stare at Belshaw. It is as if they have just seen the significance of Belshaw's behaviour in the matter of the falsified dental records, and his trip to England.

But Belshaw is totally unshaken, totally calm. "It was no coincidence. You base your opinion on the article, but I didn't notice or read that article.''

Heim will not accept Belshaw's assurance. "You *must* have read that article! The natural thing would be to call one of the journalists, or the police, for more information.''

Belshaw appears not to like being told by someone else what the natural thing is. "The trip was planned well in advance,'' he reminds the prosecutor with irritation.

There is some discussion about why Belshaw went to the Salvation Army while he was in England. Belshaw explains that the Army is known, in London, for its work in finding missing persons. He explains to Heim that many of Betty's friends and attachments were in England, and he thought perhaps she might have gone there.

"Why did you tell Major Smith that your wife had suicidal tendencies and deep depressions, when you knew it wasn't true,'' Heim asks him.

"No. It wasn't like that at all. Major Smith told me that people are often suicidal without their families having any idea, without their giving any indications beforehand. Up until then I thought I would have seen some sign of such a thing. When Major Smith told me this wasn't true, I was stunned.''

Heim reads aloud from a sworn statement by Smith which says that Belshaw had said Betty was depressed and suicidal.

Again Belshaw shows his remarkable recall, and his ability to turn what appear to be suspicious statements into innocuous ones.

"Yes," he tells the prosecutor. "That's true. What I said was that in the sixties my wife had had a serious depression. At that time it was a question of medical tension, but afterwards things were better, and it wasn't like that any more. It was a thing of the past. My wife had had problems for which she was treated medically in 1964 or 1965.

"You see, Major Smith asked the most profound questions, like a doctor. He was trying to put together a medical history." Belshaw goes on to explain that Smith searched into the past, dredging up everything which might explain, or give clues, to Betty's disappearance.

Heim moves on. "Why in your letter to your daughter of May 3rd did you describe yourself as a 'coward' afraid to face things, why did you so describe yourself—*before* you had falsified the record?''

"It was the first time I analysed things from my own point of view....*M. le procureur,* you confuse the thought and the act. I described my state of mind, but I hadn't thought of committing the act.''

Heim continues to press, trying to get Belshaw to falter, to admit the contradictory and ambiguous nature of his actions after Betty's disappearance. "Why, when your wife hadn't returned to the hotel on January 15th, why didn't you phone to see if she had gone back to Montana? Why didn't you phone the concièrge at the Jolilac? It seems the first thing you would do.''

This is one of the questions observers most want answered. It has come up again and again in their discussions. To many it is the major stumbling block to a belief in Belshaw's innocence. For when someone's spouse has disappeared, the most natural thing in the world is surely to telephone home. The jurors look at Belshaw with attention, and the courtroom is hushed.

"I was completely at sea...the idea never entered my head. I just never imagined that my wife would have run away. She had *never* run away."

The prosecutor chuckles, and comments to the tribunal, "A very intelligent response." He presses on. "Your wife must have disappeared in 150 or 200 metres, between the Métro exit and the door to the library?"

Belshaw smiles his sweet small smile. "No, not at all. I don't agree that that is what happened."

"But on the Rue Richelieu, between the Bourse and the library is only 150 or so metres. In any case, not a very great distance. You left her at the Bourse station, at 10:00 a.m., you were to make some purchases, meet at 1:00 ... and you are trying to tell us that she disappeared without trace in that small area?" Heim smiles and looks at the tribunal. "Tell us, did you have an argument at the hotel that morning?"

"No."

"Everything was completely normal, tranquil, you left her in the best of humour?"

"Well, there were a few things...in the week before she seemed to have a couple of things on her mind. Perhaps she was a little depressed after Christmas, a bit worried about her work—whether it was going well, plus worries about her life at the university ... she had perhaps just a little more on her mind than usual."

The afternoon is beginning to wane. It is only 3:00 but the light coming in through the great windows at the far end of the room is growing dim.

Belshaw is beginning to tire. At times his fatigue shows as he falters, searching for the exact word in French; but he never seems to hesitate, even for a moment, in answering the hostile questions of the president and the prosecutor. Now, however, as he explains once again to Heim about the falsification of the dental records emotion breaks through into his voice. With an air of complete sincerity, a sob in his voice, he tells Heim, "I can't imagine that I could ever hurt my wife. I couldn't do such a thing to her body." Speaking with passion and conviction, looking directly into the eyes of the prosecutor, he continues, "It's because I couldn't imagine such a thing that I could falsify the dental records."

Belshaw is now given an opportunity to explain why he ordered the underwear magazine, and had it sent, care of Betty, to the Firths' home in London. Although it was ordered, according to Belshaw, before his wife's disappearance, it arrived afterwards. "It was advertized in the London *Observer*," he explains, obviously convinced that this alone had given it respectablility. My wife and I wondered what it was, after seeing the ad from time to time, so we ordered it. We laughed about it together. I have a curious nature."

Guignard looks amused while Belshaw describes the catalogue *Babette*. The president has an extraordinarily charming smile, and from time to time he gives Belshaw the benefit of his warmth and sympathy.

Then, however, the president's sympathy vanishes as he questions Belshaw about hiring a clairvoyant. Guignard appears to find this contemptible and each time he uses the word Professor to address Belshaw his tone is mocking, almost insulting.

"I don't understand how you can call yourself a professor. Could a professor do such a thing? And if you *had* managed to get in touch with this psychic, what would you have done? Gone to the police with the information?"

"Yes. I didn't have much faith in it, but some of my friends suggested it. At first I was sceptical, because it isn't my way of thinking. I asked a colleague of mine in Holland, Is this man Croisé reputable? He told me he was, so when I was in Switzerland, I wrote to him, but there was no response. Eventually we found out that Croisé had had a nervous breakdown."

Guignard seems really angry. Perhaps it is the final insult to him that Belshaw would write to a psychic and yet not bother to contact the Swiss police directly. "What astonishes me, *Professor* Belshaw, is that you would have recourse to a clairvoyant and then, at the same time, falsify the dental charts, when they were the only *real* evidence for solving the mystery, and making a positive identification of the body. And you call yourself a professor. Your actions are totally beyond me."

Belshaw doesn't reply. He now seems very weary. He has endured so much: the hostile questioning, the ribald laughter over his sex life, the sneers of the president regarding his behaviour.

He has sustained with dignity each of the attacks launched by the prosecution. Each question, each accusation has been met by a logical explanation. Not once has Belshaw been at a loss to explain his behaviour, not once has he been caught out in a lie or a direct contradiction which is not susceptible to a reasonable explanation.

Yet the total effect of all this is different from the sum of its parts. When the observers consider all the things that Belshaw has explained away they are still puzzled. Most worrying of all is his behaviour immediately after Betty's disappearance. It is logical, it is rational but still... It is hard to imagine that if anyone's spouse has disappeared in a foreign country they would just inform the authorities and then leave in three days. Wouldn't one call the hospitals, perhaps even go around with a picture? Why hadn't Cyril immediately called home to Montana-Vermala? Why hadn't he phoned friends or acquaintances in Switzerland and Paris to see if Betty, perhaps miffed over a trifle which he had not even noticed, had suddenly gone to see one of them?

Every married person can recall times when he is startled to learn that his partner has taken deep offence at a remark which to him seemed perfectly innocuous. On such occasions the angry partner might go to a friend, fail to show up at a rendezvous, even return home. Yet Belshaw had not checked these obvious avenues. True, he had given reasonable explanations of why he had not done so. And each made sense in themselves.

And then there was his remark, "She wouldn't have liked to be all mixed up in that mud." Was it possible that Cyril Belshaw would have found it too embarrassing, too humiliating, to call up Mrs. Babcock, for example, to see if Betty had gone to her, thus admitting to Mrs. Babcock that he did not know where his own wife was? Extraordinary possibility, that pride should override concern—but possible for a man with Belshaw's temperament.

But even this explanation fails when it comes to Belshaw's not calling the concièrge at the Jolilac right after Betty disappeared. Here was a woman who, according to Belshaw and acquaintances in Vancouver, had had periods of confusion, or lapses of memory, in the past. He must, as time passed and his anxiety increased, have thought of the possibility that, if she had suddenly become confused, disoriented, had checked her papers and seen written there in the space for "temporary address" the Jolilac in Montana, she might have set out to return there. So why did he not call the concièrge and ask him to check the apartment? Worrying, worrying fact, which his explanation did not really explain.

The spectators and journalists whisper among themselves. There is no doubt that Belshaw's demeanour on the stand is impressive, but the cumulative effect of all these incongruities, even though each one has been explained away, has left a peculiar taste in the mouth.

26

Now at last it is the turn of the defence, and the spectators wait anxiously for the appearance of Diana Belshaw, whom they expect to be the first of the defence witnesses. But Paschoud has other ideas.

Paschoud intends to defuse the significance of some of the testimony which gave the impression that Betty could not have accepted Cyril's infidelity. He is anxious to show the universal esteem in which Belshaw is held, and to erase the effect of those police reports.

His opening surprises the court. He begins by questioning Belshaw about a love affair that he had in the early sixties. Belshaw has obviously been prepared for this, and at first he answers Paschoud's questions in a cold matter-of-fact tone.

"Yes," he says, trying to undo the effect of some of the earlier questioning. "I had an affair in the sixties. My wife found out about it. The person was a friend of my wife, and that was unpardonable." Now he is losing his aplomb, as he reveals these private matters to the silent courtroom. His voice trembles, "I recognized that. My wife and I discussed it. In the end, she forgave me, and she told me, 'If you do something like that, don't do it with a friend of mine.' " He bows his head. "I was absolutely in agreement with that, and I promised."

Everyone in the courtroom laughs, and the women journalists look at one another and shake their heads. They can understand what the defence is trying to show here—that Betty was tolerant of Belshaw's affairs so long as they were not with her friends—but that is not the implication that they as women draw from the story.

Some of them wonder if the "medical depression" Betty Belshaw experienced in the mid-sixties was caused by her discovery of her husband's infidelity. Could this have been the cause of the fights the president and the prosecutor had referred to when they read out "I may have struck her, she may have struck me, in the early sixties"?

But Paschoud continues obviously oblivious to such an interpretation of this evidence. "Did your wife know Mrs. Wilson"?

"She wouldn't have recognized her if she saw her in the street." His air as he says this shows that to him this is the definite proof that Betty could have accepted the affair with Mrs. Wilson. The matter is closed, his tone seems to say, and no more needs to be said about it.

The defence now brings forth its first witness. He is Professor Grotanelli, anthropologist from Rome, a stoutish man in a grey suit and unshined boots. He is the first of many character witnesses the defence has assembled in their attempt to undo the effect of the police reports. However, Professor Grotanelli produces an extremely unfavourable reaction upon the tribunal and the spectators, as had Mme. Wuest, the real-estate agent for the Jolilac, before him. Perhaps it is some cultural antipathy between the Italian and the Vaudois, perhaps it is Grotanelli's manner which seems to suggest the arrogant man of the world telling the petit-bourgeois the truth of the matter and warning them not to be so ignorant as to disbelieve him.

Grotanelli testifies that he has been a friend of Cyril Belshaw for many years. That he saw him at a conference in New Delhi in December of 1979, and has visited him in prison in Lausanne. Grotanelli explains to the tribunal that anthropology is the study of different societies of the world, of different ways of thinking, acting and living. He tells them that Belshaw is not a physical ethnologist, but rather a cultural ethnologist, though in response to a question he concedes that every anthropologist must be knowledgeable to a certain extent about physical anthropology. He goes on to state that Belshaw was elected as president of the International Union of

Anthropologists and Ethnologists, the biggest in the science of anthropology, a society which covers all the countries of the world. Also, Belshaw is editor of the journal of this association. This is not merely an honorary position, Grotanelli explains; there is a great deal of work involved. Leaning back in his chair, looking relaxed, Grotanelli tells the tribunal that Belshaw is an eminent colleague, and a friend. "I haven't many I call friends," he says, "I think before I use this word.

"I am older than most of the people in this room," Grotanelli goes on. "I have lived as a scholar, soldier, traveller, intellectual. I have seen much. I know that Professor Belshaw is capable of mastering his feelings—he is not unlike my other colleagues—we can all master our feelings—I say he is capable of mastering his feelings even in such circumstances. I would never for a moment accept the idea that Cyril Belshaw could have murdered his wife. In so far as one person can know another, it is my absolute conviction that Cyril Belshaw is totally incapable of committing such a crime."

There are no questions for Grotanelli, and the next witness to be called by the defence is Ken Burridge, a long-time friend and colleague of Belshaw and an ally in the ups and downs of academic politics. Burridge took over the chairmanship of the Anthropology and Sociology department at UBC when Belshaw resigned. He has come all the way to Aigle at his own expense to testify on behalf of Belshaw, and his demeanour appears to make a very favourable impression upon the tribunal. He is totally unemotional and reticent, not unlike Belshaw himself, and so, perhaps, is a corroboration of all that has been said by the defence, and by Belshaw himself, about the significance of such demeanour. Burridge, however, is at a disadvantage, for he must speak through the court translator.

This last is a rather stout, homey middle-aged woman, who is seated on a chair directly in front of Belshaw and about a metre from the witness chair. Within a few minutes it becomes obvious that her English is not as good as that of the defence lawyers and of Heim; they constantly have to correct her, lending an air of farce to all the English testimony. The jury listen to the questions, the answers, the translations, the corrections of the translation; they observe the polite annoyance, and the frustration of the counsel on both sides. Their own inability to understand, the lengthening after-

noon, the heavy layer of suspense which hangs over the courtroom
as everyone wonders when Diana Belshaw will finally be called to
testify, create a sense of slowly building anticipation.

Burridge identifies himself and a brief series of questions and
answers emerges from the welter of translation:

Q Are you the superior of Cyril Belshaw?
A Yes, as the head of the department.
Q So you know him well?
A Yes, for twelve or thirteen years.
Q And you knew Mrs. Belshaw?
A Yes.
Q And saw them frequently?
A Yes.
Q Do you think it credible that he, as you know him, could kill
   his wife?
A No.
Q Have you been astonished by his attitude, his indifference
   when his wife disappeared?
A I didn't see any indifference.
Q What did you see?
A Much distress.
Q Did he tell you about it?
A Yes, in a letter from Paris.
Q Did he take up a normal life on his return from Switzerland?
A He tried to.
Q Is he still a professor at UBC today?
A Yes.

Burridge speaks in a subdued voice. He answers only the question,
volunteers nothing, and looks calm but uncomfortable. When the
defence has finished its questioning Guignard asks what would happen if Belshaw were to be found guilty. "He won't be," Burridge
says shortly.

"But if he is?" the president insists.

"We'll deal with that when and if it comes up," Burridge replies
coldly.

The next witness is Mrs. Scott, a small, meek-looking woman
dressed in a plain skirt and shirt and a white blazer. She is identified

as a social worker, and a long-time friend of Betty Belshaw. She has come to Switzerland with her husband, Professor Scott, who is to testify next. Mrs. Scott is soft-spoken, well-bred, and appears shy. The translator has more difficulty with her slightly vague answers, and there is much laughter and sarcasm about the translation, much of which goes by Mrs. Scott, who looks bewildered and uncomfortable at the frequent outbursts of giggles from the spectators but bravely tries to keep her self-possession.

Mrs. Scott tells how she was a friend of Betty for twenty-five or twenty-six years, and how the two wrote to one another three or four times a year when Betty was away. Paschoud asks if Betty had written that she was tired or overworked. Mrs. Scott answers that Betty said she was very busy.

"Did the police call upon you in Canada. Do you remember the interview?" Paschoud asks.

"Yes," Mrs. Scott replies. "They interviewed me for forty minutes. Two Swiss police and one Canadian. When they came I told them that if there was going to be a written version of the interview I wanted a copy. But they told me no, it was to be only an informal chat, and that no record would be made."

Fischlin and Wyss, listening, look very serious.

"Did you tell the police that you were surprised that Belshaw did not talk about the disappearance of his wife?"

"No."

"Are you surprised about that today?"

"No, he talked about it with me and my husband."

"And did you find his attitude normal?"

"He was deeply distressed. When he came back to Canada we saw him on several occasions, and we talked about it."

Paschoud asks her, "And could you imagine the possibility that Cyril Belshaw might kill his wife?"

"Absolutely not."

"Because they were a devoted couple?"

"Yes."

Now Paschoud is treading carefully. "And how do you feel now that you know he had a 'friend'?"

"I only heard about that recently," Mrs. Scott answers, her voice almost inaudible. "He didn't have one when she was alive....I didn't know whether or not he had one when she was alive."

"If he did?"

"He didn't."

"But if he did," Paschoud presses her, "would it change your opinion?" The spectators wait breathlessly for the answer, conscious of the irony of Mrs. Scott's testimony, and of the fact that she cannot have heard what happened yesterday, and has not been able to read any of the Swiss newspapers which have so blatantly given headlines to the love affair. The translator stumbles; finally Mrs. Scott gets the question in English, "Would it change your opinion if he did?"

"I suppose it would." There is an audible gasp from the spectators. Mrs. Scott now seems to have said that if Belshaw had been unfaithful to his wife it would change her opinion about whether he was capable of killing her. Yet the question was so far from the previous answers, the translation so confusing, that it is very possible that Mrs. Scott did not understand its implication.

Paschoud asks Mrs. Scott if it is true that Betty was rather conventional. "Yes, in many ways. Not formal," Mrs. Scott explains, "not strict, but a person who liked to see that things were done correctly. A perfectionist."

The prosecutor tries to follow up Mrs. Scott's earlier *faux pax*. "If you now heard he had had an affair when she was alive ..." But the translator becomes so confused and overwhelmed at the attempt to render this sentence in English that the courtroom dissolves into laughter and Heim, smiling, abandons the question. Instead he asks, "If Mrs. Belshaw had heard that her husband had had a mistress in your neighbourhood, what would have been her reaction?"

"Distress."

"Yes, but would she have accepted it?"

"I can't answer that."

As Mrs. Scott joins the previous witnesses in the spectators' area of the court, there is a murmur of voices. The stream of translation seems to have left the jurors restless and confused, but people wonder among themselves why the implication of Mrs. Scott's remarks has not been more stressed by the prosecution.

Professor Scott, Mrs. Scott's husband, is next to testify. Scott is a highly respected scholar with a national reputation in the field of economics. His specialty is the economics of natural resources and he has been a good friend of the Belshaws for many years. He tells the court, with many interruptions from the translator, now hopelessly demoralized, that he found Belshaw's reaction after Betty's disappearance totally natural, that Belshaw undoubtedly loved his wife, that it would be impossible for Belshaw to have killed her. Scott explains that Belshaw had never reacted to anything with violence, and that he had never seen an argument between the two, not even a serious dispute.

"Would she have reacted violently if she heard he was having an affair?" asks Paschoud, apparently oblivious to the effect of relying on a witness who has already shown himself rather imperceptive about the Belshaws by suggesting, contrary to Belshaw's own testimony, that the two never argued.

"It's hard to say, but I would predict a calm discussion." The women journalists snicker. "This trial would be different if there were women on the jury," murmurs one to another.

"Have you ever seen Mrs. Belshaw not able to control herself?" Paschoud asks Scott.

"No," Scott replies. In answer to further questions he tells Paschoud that Mrs. Belshaw was warm, affectionate, and friendly. He explains that though she had formal values, they did not affect her conversation nor her dealings with other people.

"Was she understanding with her family?"

"She discussed that kind of thing with my wife, not with me, but I would say she was close to, and tolerant with her family."

Next, briefly, Paschoud introduces a Swiss anthropologist as another character witness for Belshaw. His chief value seems to be that he is one of their own, a Swiss from the Suisse Romande. This professor, Olivier Centlivres, from the University of Neuchâtel, testifies, as have previous witnesses, that Belshaw is a renowned scholar, an upright man, a friend, and that it is "unlikely" that he could have killed his wife.

There has been a sense that some of the character witnesses knew only the very proper public face of the Belshaws and comparatively little of their private life. This is not the case, however, with the next witness. For now, finally, comes the moment that all the spectators have been waiting for. Diana Belshaw enters the courtroom. Diana Belshaw, who is so close to her father, who was at Montana immediately after her mother's disappearance and saw her father at this crucial time. Diana, who has been reported in the Canadian press to be totally committed to her father and absolutely convinced of his innocence. *She* will not treat the court to pedantic logical explanations, nor hide her true nature behind the manner of a very intelligent teacher impatient with a slow pupil. In Diana the court will have a young woman, in the most dramatic circumstances, testifying to save her father from conviction for murder.

She moves with the grace and presence of an actress, and takes her seat in the witness chair, after bestowing a look of tender concern upon her father, who seems to grow in strength at her entrance and to regain some of the energy which has been draining from him during the day.

Diana is of medium height, about five-foot five, and slender. She is dressed in a loose brown jumper, and creamy silk shirt with big flowing sleeves. She has long wavy chestnut hair and white creamy skin, and wears dark-framed glasses. Her face is very attractive, and she has an air of intelligence and sensitivity.

The president identifies her to the court as Diana Belshaw, born 1949, actress. He then leans forward over his bench, and speaking very gently, tells her that she doesn't need to answer any question which she finds upsetting or too difficult.

Diana nods. She answers the questions put to her in a soft, gentle, low voice. Her French is very good, her accent and intonation excellent, the turn of phrase almost poetic. She describes how she was closer to her father than her mother, although on good terms with both her parents. She agrees with the Swiss police report of her interview with them that she had described her mother as emotional, energetic, serious about her professional obligations, working too much, hypochondriac and moody. Her father she had characterized as more calm, rational, and as living a life conforming to his thoughts.

She testifies that her parents had never struck one another. The jurors stare at her intently as she sits, her hands twisting over one another slightly in her lap, her legs in their long cream-coloured boots crossed decorously, if tensely, under her chair.

"How would your mother have felt," the president asks her in a considerate, solicitous tone, "if she heard of your father's liaison?"

Diana, emotion trembling in her voice, replies in short, flowing

French sentences, "She would have felt disappointed, she would have cried," and, pressing her hands to her breast, "she would have been wounded to the heart. Oh, she would have been angry!"

"Could she have accepted it?"

The court is hushed. On her answer to this question, Diana's credibility lies. The other witnesses, in their answers, have been so superficial, so glib, about a question which must, after all, go to the heart of the relationship between two people. Diana hesitates, the pause heightens the drama. Softly, very softly, her hands clutching one another, she says, "I don't know."

The courtroom relaxes. It is the right, the only answer. Now she has the jurors, the judges, the president, the women journalists, in her hands.

"Would she have stayed with him," the president says, looking even more paternal, concerned, than before, "if she knew he had a mistress whom he saw once a month?"

Again Diana hesitates, thinking, then "...My mother loved my father very much, and he loved her. I can't answer."

Now Diana, accompanying her flowing French with graceful gestures, answers the defence's questions. She explains that it was she who unpacked her mother's suitcases from the Paris trip, which her father had set aside, unopened.

Close to tears, her voice breaking, she tells the court, "I had to unpack her things, I had to sort them."

Stoudmann asks her, "Was there soiled lingerie in those suitcases?"

"Yes," says Diana, "I had to wash it...."

Seizing on this point, suddenly thrown into the trial at the end of the second day, as the first concrete evidence that Betty had, in fact, been to Paris as Belshaw has contended all along, Stoudmann wants to make absolutely certain that no one has missed it. "Are you *absolutely certain* that there was soiled lingerie?"

Diana seems oblivious to the implications of her testimony. Close to tears, she seems to be reliving the terrible moments alone with that suitcase, going through her mother's things. "Yes," she tells Stoudmann. "I had to sort through her things, I had to unpack them, I had to wash her lingerie ...."

The defence moves on. "How were you informed of your mother's disappearance?"

"My father left an urgent message for me at the theatre in Calgary. I telephoned him—this was the 16th of January. He told me that my mother had disappeared the day before, he gave me the details, he cried on the phone. We both cried a lot. I telephoned him several times after that first conversation."

"How was he?"

"He was lost, devastated, upset, tormented. He didn't know what to do, where to turn. He needed someone."

"When you arrived in Geneva your father met you. Had he recovered?"

"We embraced, we cried, we tried to talk, it was difficult." Looking at the jurors, almost pleading with them, "he was *never* cold, just reserved, shy ...."

"You went to Montana, you went through your mother's things, perhaps to find a clue to what had happened."

"I looked through her things. We talked of it all the time, we tried to support one another, tried to think of happier times ... but always, the nightmares. We had to be strong with one another."

Diana cries out, "Our family is very private, we keep to ourselves, we find it difficult to show our emotions to the world. And also, we hoped, each minute, each day, if she came back, everyone wouldn't have to know ...."

Belshaw wipes away tears which stream from his eyes, a white handkerchief balled in his hands, his face expressionless. The tribunal and spectators are moved, the mood in the court is sombre, and there is dead silence and a growing intensity as Diana's emotional testimony continues.

"In our family we are private. One of the first things my mother told me, that I remember my mother telling me was, never cry in public. That's private, not for everyone. But there was so much warmth," her voice is full of emotion, "so much affection in our family."

The jury looks impressed, chivalrous, as they lean forward spellbound.

"People who knew your mother have said she was conformist and rigid, conventional."

"Not at all, that's not right! She wasn't rigid. For the last eight to ten years, though, she was very nervous."

"Did your mother know about, and accept, liaisons of yours?"

"Not the first, but after that she did."

"You know about this catalogue *Babette*. Could your parents have ordered a magazine like that together?"

Diana smiles. "Of course; we're not living in another age." The jury laughs; if Diana has made a little joke, they are going to appreciate it. "Of course, it's amusing."

The defence repeats Belshaw's explanation of why he falsified the dental records and asks Diana if this motive, this explanation— protection from scandal and publicity—makes sense to her.

"Yes, my father was alone in Montana for four months, because of that...he was completely alone, always the nightmares, his greatest desire was to protect my mother from scandal .... If one never knew what happened, one could always hope, *n'est-ce pas?* But if one knew something terrible ... it's so difficult!"

"Could your father have killed her?"

Firmly, with absolute conviction, Diana replies, "It's not possible."

Paschoud reads aloud a letter from Belshaw to Lady Firth. " 'Almost before she got off the plane Diana said to me, "No guilt, none of that, we'll remember the happy things." It's not so easy, alas.' Why did you say that?"

"We all felt a sense of responsibility. I blamed myself because I wasn't there at Christmas, my father because he travelled so much. We thought of things—if we had done this or that it wouldn't have happened."

"Do you think if there were an argument between your parents, do you think your mother would have run away?"

"Oh, maybe she would have gone out for a quarter of an hour, slammed the door...."

"But suicide?"

"It's possible."

"But could one kill the other?"

"No. She was always worried about cancer, that's why she didn't like x-rays."

There are a few more questions. Then Diana takes up her seat among the spectators, next to the Scotts and Professor Burridge. The jurors follow her with their eyes, concerned, admiring. Two have shed a few tears and use the moment to dry their eyes.

The journalists are attempting to recover their objectivity and to break the spell which Diana has cast over the courtroom. *"Un peu trop actrice,"* murmurs one of the French journalists to the other. One of the Canadian women journalists, an old hand, confides to a less experienced colleague, "You know what Dorothy Parker said about Shirley Temple? 'It makes me want to fwow up.' " But others including the two Swiss journalists disagree. "Moving." "Sincere." "I believe every word," they tell one another. Tomorrow the Swiss women will write that Diana has produce a *"declic,"* turned the trial around, perhaps saved her father. At this moment it is hard to imagine the tribunal feeling anything but filial protectiveness towards Diana. No wonder Willy Heim has not dared to ask her any questions at all, not even dared to question her about the soiled lingerie.

There is no doubt Diana believes in her father and his innocence. And she has convinced the tribunal of her sincerity. It has been a bravura performance.

27

The last witness is Diana's brother, Adrian, and he is definitely an anti-climax. He seems a miniature Cyril Belshaw in his demeanour which is so reticent and restrained that it is impossible to deduce anything from his testimony.

Adrian is introduced, and the courtroom is told that he was born in 1953 and is a school teacher in Sechelt, the lower mainland of British Columbia. Adrian is in fact working on his doctoral thesis while he teaches, but his academic achievements are not mentioned when he is identified to the court. He has the same very brown hair as his father, and the same creamy youthful skin as his sister. He has an air of youth, innocence, and naiveté and seems, as does his father, very out of place in this Vaudois courtroom, facing the thirteen men sitting at the bench who are all so serious, so stolid, so large-boned, in their dark suits. Adrian is dressed in a cream jacket, light pants, a dark tie and wears a moustache in the same style as his father's. The jurors look at him with interest, but they seem drained after Diana's testimony, and very tired.

In response to Paschoud's questions, Adrian, sounding shy but speaking easily in French, testifies that his family are emotional at home, but more reserved for the outside world.

"Did your mother accept your girlfriend?" asks Paschoud.

"Yes," Adrian answers. "She liked her very much. When we came to Montana together at Christmas, my mother told us to take her and my father's bedroom, as it had a double bed." Adrian recalls other kindnesses his mother had shown to his girlfriend when the two had come to Switzerland for the holiday, the holiday which Betty remembered so fondly in her letter to Diana and after which she disappeared.

Paschoud asks if there were any untoward events during their stay in Montana at Christmas, and Adrian tells him there were none.

"Did your parents every fight?"

Adrian responds that yes, once, when he was young, he remembers a fight which "traumatized" him. His mother had shouted and shouted, and his father had calmed her.

When he was young—that would have been in the sixties; one cannot help wondering again if this was the period when Betty, at home with two small children, learned of her husband's infidelity. But it is an inference Paschoud does not make—and certainly one which Adrian appears to be unaware of. For Paschoud goes on. "How would your mother have felt if she had heard your father had liaisons?"

"She wouldn't have been happy, but she would have accepted it."

"Did you all have a good, happy Christmas?"

"Yes. My parents were getting along very well."

Adrian goes on to say that the Belshaws showed their feelings only to one another.

"Do you do that?"

"I try. I don't always succeed." Adrian describes his father's state of mind after the disappearance. "I have never seen my father in such a state before. I said, 'It must be the most difficult thing

that you have ever had to bear.' He said 'Yes', and he cried.''
Adrian goes on to tell the tribunal how throughout the marriage
Cyril wrote poems for Betty, and brought her breakfast in bed, and
gifts from his travels. He describes a relationship full of small
kindnesses and courtesies, of mutual consideration between the parties.

"Was your father normal when he returned to Canada?'' the
defence asks.

"Not at all. He was a broken man after my mother's disappearance. I think he just wanted to withdraw into himself and his work,
and forget what happened. He *tried* to lead a normal life.''

Paschoud asks, "Was your father a good driver?'' Belshaw smiles
at the question, and Adrian does too, relaxing a bit.

"He loved his car, felt good in it. Perhaps one could say he was
un peu maniaque.''

There are a few more questions for Adrian, and then the president
announces that the witnesses' testimony is finished. Court is ad-
journed until tomorrow at 9:00, for the final pleas of counsel.

So the second day of testimony is over. Belshaw rises, and the
gendarmes help him into his beige Burberry. One solicitously
smoothes down a flap. They go out, and then the court is dismissed.
In the corridor Heim is talking to the journalists. "A very tough
little man,'' he says. "A very difficult case. Anything could happen.'' He seems to be enjoying himself, enjoying the suspense and
the mystery of the case. It is easy to understand why Badinter said,
"I would give anything to be there, to defend it. It is the most
mysterious case I have ever seen.''

It is late, well after six, and very dark in the *Place du Marché.*
The snow which has been falling all day has coated the cars and
the streets are icy and slippery. All the journalists are exhausted,
drained, as they brush the snow from their cars and set off back to
Montreux, Lausanne, or Geneva. Those with urgent deadlines try
desperately to find phones in a city which is now dark and shuttered.
The Swiss journalists agree that Diana has shifted the balance in
the court, and will write what they think with a frankness impossible
for their North American counterparts.

And so, on Friday morning, over marvellously good hot *café au
lait,* fresh croissants and Swiss apricot jam, other observers, and
the members of the tribunal itself, will read their frank opinions.

"BELSHAW DEFENDS HIMSELF EVERY STEP OF THE WAY," trumpets the headline of *24 heures.* "BUT WHO KILLED BETTY?" it asks in 48-point type. "Who killed Betty Belshaw?" writes Myriam Meuwly. "The enigma remains unresolved at the end of the second day of testimony....Because someone certainly threw this body to the bottom of a ravine on the road of Les Mosses, after having deprived it of life. But one other question remains to be answered: who is Cyril Belshaw? Submitting to the intense interrogation of President Guignard, Chief Prosecutor Heim, and lawyers Paschoud and Stoudmann, the professor showed himself firm without every faltering—but not exempt from emotion—as he explained and defended the apparent irrationality of his deportment since the official disappearance of his wife...and during the enquiry which followed. Anguish, solitude, and the refusal to believe his wife dead alone made this scientist act contrary to good sense. Is this enough to change the minds of the jury, and the conviction of the president, which for the moment, seems already made? If something was still needed to trigger a reversal of the current, which until now has been adverse, Diana, 31, daughter of the accused, certainly provided it at the end of the day by her testimony."

As for the *Tribune de Lausanne-le matin,* it trumpeted in headlines almost as large: "BELSHAW: 'I HAVE NO EXPLANATION.' 'I had nothing to do with the loss of my wife.' "

"Before the criminal tribunal of Aigle," wrote Pierrette Blanc, the best known crime reporter in Lausanne, "Cyril Belshaw hammered the table with both hands. For the first time the Canadian professor came to life, his face flushed purple. Finally he could say his piece. And not a moment too soon. During the entire day he answered the questions of the president and the prosecutor without ever making a false step. He explained himself on every obscure point without hesitation, with a remarkable *sang-froid,* which was interrupted only by a few outbursts which broke through the self-control that characterizes him, and which has often passed for indifference."

The Swiss press, it seemed, had decided against the version of a man who was "cold, self-satisfied, and smug". Instead they presented their readers with a picture of a man bravely enduring the heaviest questioning, never making an error or a false step, a man of true emotion who controlled himself heroically. As for Diana, *she* had saved her father, their articles told the readers—if he were to be saved. The second day of testimony had not lessened the mystery, the reporters explained, nor laid bare the truth of what had happened to Betty Belshaw, nor revealed who, really, *was* Cyril Belshaw. But whereas after the first day there had been a general view that it would be impossible for Belshaw or his defenders to answer all the accusations weighing against him, the second day seemed to have left the impression that Belshaw's courageous demeanour on the stand, and his daughter's loyalty, affection and sincerity might have turned the case around.

Now it would be up to the lawyers on both sides to put the pieces of the case together and so produce a mosaic, a picture telling a coherent story and one that the tribunal would believe to be the truth.

28

It is still snowing on Friday, as the journalists arrive at the *Hôtel de Ville*. The ante-room is more crowded than before. Townspeople, attracted by the press coverage, are crowded in seats before the door. One in particular, a plump woman with heavy layers of overcoats, a dyed black bun, a busybody mouth, and heavy snow boots, has a ghoulish look that causes the reporters, perhaps a little guiltily, to draw back in distaste.

When the doors are opened at 9:00 a.m., extra folding chairs can be seen in the aisles and at the back of the room. Diana, Adrian, the Burridges and the Scotts are clustered together, looking drawn in the early white light of the overcast morning. The journalists do not approach them.

At 9:05 Belshaw comes in, looking wary and tired. The president calls the court to order, and then, to the surprise of the spectators, announces that the judges and jurors will now be permitted to ask questions of the previous witnesses. The meteorologist again gives the exact amount of snow that fell each day in Montana in mid-January.

Inspector Margot is now called to the stand and one of the jurors asks him whether or not the police tried to find out in Canada if anyone else might have been responsible for Betty's death.

Margot, in his clear, quiet voice, explains. "During the inquiry our convictions weren't formed all in one instant. They developed gradually over the course of the inquiry. We looked into everything. We envisaged every possibility. We weren't picking on Mr. Belshaw."

"Did you try to find out if anyone had seen Mrs. Belshaw at the hotels in France?"

"Yes, but the system is different in France. The *hôteliers* don't keep the same kind of records as we do."

"Did you interrogate the inhabitants of Le Sépey?" asks another juror.

"Yes, in the whole area. We talked to the people in the farms, the cafés, all along the route. The whole region was interrogated, to no effect."

The juror with the grey suit and the Argyle socks addresses Belshaw. "Who in the family was in charge of the finances?" Belshaw explains that the household finances were his area, but his wife made some of the major purchases, such as clothing.

"Who looked after the taxes?" asks the juror.

"We both did our own."

The juror is interested. He pursues the point, trying to find out how the Canadian system works, and to understand why Belshaw did not save the cash receipts from his trip to Paris. Belshaw explains. As he makes each point he gives a little nod to accentuate it, but the juror does not nod back. He just listens, and occasionally makes a note.

Finally these matters are cleared up to the juror's satisfaction and Willy Heim rises to begin his address. Slowly Heim walks to the front of his table. The pale light streams in, putting his long intelligent face in shadow. He speaks intently, without notes, gesturing, bending forward, raising and lowering his voice dramatically. From his first word the courtroom is hushed, and he holds their attention for ninety minutes as he unrolls his dramatic narrative.

"On the 15th day of January 1979 Mr. and Mrs. Belshaw have breakfast and then leave the Novotel Bagnolet by Métro, she to go to the Bibliothèque Nationale, and he to do some shopping at the Galeries Lafayette," Heim begins. "At about ten o'clock, they part, and she gets off the train at the Bourse exit of the Métro, about 200 metres from the entrance to the Bibliothèque Nationale. She never arrived at the Bibliothèque—because her reader's card wasn't presented."

Heim turns suddenly to the jury and raises his voice, "Abruptly she decides to return to Montana. Without returning to her hotel for her suitcase she takes the next train for home."

Heim outlines the train schedule and shows that Betty would have arrived at Sierre at 7:20 in the evening. "She did not go to her apartment to freshen up, or to sleep, for there are no traces of her anywhere. Perhaps she went to a restaurant to eat, and there or at the station she met a stranger who offered her a ride. Perhaps he made advances which she repulsed, there was a struggle, and this unknown person killed her. He then put her body in his car, drove her to Le Sépey, removed her green suit, her beige blouse, her lingerie, her green vinyl travelling bag, her wallet, took off her gold Longines watch, and, with some difficulty, her emerald engagement ring and her platinum wedding ring. He wrapped her body in three garbage bags which he happened to have in his car, and then threw it down a slope."

Heim lowers his voice. "He could not have known the area well, as the place chosen had a small tree which, by pure chance, stopped the descent of the body. Then this unknown person disposed of the suit, blouse, underwear, shoes, handbag and jewelry.

"If only there had been an investigation then," cries the prosecutor, "perhaps some evidence of this story might have been found. But on his return to Montana on the 19th of January, Professor Belshaw strenuously avoided telling the Swiss police of his wife's disappearance, although he insistently pursued every avenue of search in Paris and London. And why?

"Because Mr. Belshaw never believed in his wife's disappearance from Paris! There he had made enquiries of the concièrge at Bagnolet, he had alerted the Paris police and the Canadian Ambassador. He had telephoned his children in Canada."

Heim pauses. "But he had never telephoned his apartment or the concièrge at the Jolilac to see if his wife had returned!

"And when a body was found in Le Sépey, he made no connection with the disappearance of his wife. Although he had a subscription to the *Nouvelliste du Rhône* and must have seen the incredibly detailed description in it—a description which mentioned all the points of identification, describing in great detail the teeth and their gold crowns, an extraordinarily precise description of the teeth—it must have struck such an accurate observer as Professor Belshaw—a man who knows the brand name of his wife's brassière—[turning to the jury] how many of *you, messieurs les jurés,* know the brand of your wife's bra—he is such an observer, knows so many details about her....a man such as this *must* have read the article as yesterday he stated it was irrelevant because it concerned a woman of between thirty and forty!"

Heim pauses. Perhaps these points are not as telling as he believes. For how many of us know what crowns or fillings our lovers or spouses have? Especially if such dental work is not easily visible, as Betty's was not. No. Belshaw's contention that he did not remember his wife's gold crowns is reasonable. Nor is it so remarkable that he noticed and remembered his wife's clothes. Many men take an interest in such things. They make up the surface appearance which to such men is of great importance. The contradiction between Belshaw's accuracy of recollection on the one point and his ignorance on the other is more apparent than real. In any case, the prosecutor has failed to prove that Belshaw saw the article in the *Nouvelliste*. Even if he had seen similar articles which appeared in all the local papers at the same time, they too stated that the woman was between thirty and forty. If Belshaw truly believed his wife had disappeared in Paris, his behaviour in regard to these newspaper accounts was not as strange as the prosecutor would like to have the tribunal believe. Further, it is disingenuous for the prosecutor to tell the tribunal that Belshaw *must* have seen the article because he remembered the estimated age of the body. For Belshaw clearly stated, when the prosecutor put exactly this point to him, that he noted the age discrepancy only when the *juge d'instruction* showed him the article—long after the events in question.

But Heim continues. *"M. le président, Mm. les juges, Mm. les jurés*—on April 2nd Professor Belshaw left for London, and there he went to see Major Smith of the Salvation Army, told him of the disappearance of his wife, and stated that she had suicidal tendencies and was subject to periods of profound depression.

"Curious! Curious!, *Mm. le président, les juges, les jurés*, because nothing in the investigation has confirmed this; the accused himself said such was the case in the early sixties, but there is no evidence whatsoever to support his contention."

Heim stops pacing and lowers his voice to a conversational tone. "Apparently, on the 2nd of April, according to Belshaw, it had still not occurred to him that the Le Sépey Corpse could be his wife.

"Now. If Mrs. Belshaw disappeared in Paris between the Bourse exit and the Bibliothèque Nationale, the discovery of her body, not in the Seine but near Le Sépey, precludes all explanations but the one I have given. Because is it likely that she was killed by someone on the Rue Richelieu who was sufficiently detached to take her body to Le Sépey? Totally unlikely!"

Here one must agree with the prosecutor. It is estimated that customs officers open the trunk of one out of every three cars which cross the border between France and Switzerland. Why would a malefactor take the risk of carrying the body of a woman killed in Paris over an international border?

The prosecutor goes on. "If Mrs. Belshaw had suddenly decided two hundred metres from the Bibliothèque to return to Montana, she would have gone by her hotel to pick up her bag. If she had returned alone to Montana, she would have stopped by her apartment to refresh herself.

"Would such a respectable person have followed from the railway station or restaurant a stranger who later raped and then killed her?"

At this, a look of sorrow replaces the look of annoyance which has marked Belshaw's face. His arms crossed over his chest are tense, but his legs, crossed neatly and composedly, are still. He doesn't move in his chair.

"Why would a stranger make such an effort to render her body unrecognizable?" continues Heim, "and take such a risk in transporting it from Montana to Le Sépey? And is it likely that such a person would have had garbage bags in his car?

"So, you see, we come, almost irresistibly, to the extraordinary conclusion ... *M. le président, Mm. les juges, Mm. les jurés* ... Mrs. Belshaw was never in Paris!

"The accused signed the forms at the hotels for both of them, and paid for two. And, although he ordinarily pays by credit card—as is the habit of Anglo-Saxons—as he paid for the gas on this trip—he contends he paid for meals for two at Geneva, Beaune, and Bagnolet by cash. But the three receipts have vanished. The defence has tried its best to find a trace of Mrs. Belshaw on this journey. *No one* saw her at Geneva, *no one* saw her at Beaune, *no one* saw her at Bagnolet. NO ONE saw her at all!"

Here one must remember the very important, uncontested statement of the defence. No one remembered seeing Cyril Belshaw either.

But the prosecutor has another telling point. "And the receipts which might have proved she was there? Professor Belshaw told the *juge d'instruction* he threw them away!

"Even in the case of Beaune, where the hotel does not serve breakfast and they went down the street to a restaurant to eat, there are no signs of them. Professor Belshaw paid by cash, and the receipts are gone. These things are extraordinarily troubling."

Heim now reminds the court that, although it was totally unnecessary, Professor Belshaw signed in at the hotels as 'Cyril Belshaw and Betty'. Why did he do this when his previous custom was to sign only 'M. Belshaw'? In France the registration form at hotels requires only one signature, and this person is not required to give the name of his companion.

Heim turns to the jury, looks at them, drops his voice. "Now we come to the testimony given yesterday by the very charming Diana. It was put forward by the defence, perhaps to show that Mrs. Belshaw indeed went to Paris, and to show that Diana found the used lingerie of her mother at the end of January when she unpacked her mother's baggage.

"*M. le président, Mm. les juges, Mm. les jurés* ... the fact that this story of the used lingerie came out for the first time yesterday afternoon renders it suspect. For two years the contention has been that Mrs. Belshaw was never in Paris—this is the cause of all the suspicion, of all that has happened, of all Mr. Belshaw has suffered—and now,'' he cries out, his voice filling the courtroom, ''we learn that her daughter has known of this evidence since January 1979! Why wasn't it brought forward during the so-detailed *instruction*?

''This statement is totally unverifiable. The lingerie could have been left in the apartment. The statement is totally without substance!''

Heim repeats that the whole of Mrs. Belshaw's trip to Paris is a fiction of Mr. Belshaw, used to announce her disappearance. He suggests that if Belshaw went to the trouble of creating this fiction, it is because he killed her. No stranger would go to so many pains to hide her identity. Although the autopsy doesn't tell how she died, the forensic experts observed a pinkish cast to the roofs of the teeth, and some authorities believe this suggests strangulation. However, not all the experts agree and Heim doesn't insist upon it.

''What we *can* affirm, however,'' Heim continues, ''is that no one is as likely as Cyril Belshaw to have killed her, to have taken off her clothes, removed her rings, wrapped her in three plastic bags which we know had been available in Montana since October. And Professor Belshaw admits to having purchased similar bags.''

''Who else but he could have transported her to where she was found? After the 12th of January, there were very few people in the apartment block; a dispute, even a violent one, could have passed unnoticed. What place would have been better suited to the deed than an apartment? He could easily have put the body on the terrace and lowered it to the little square which led to the underground parking of the neighbouring apartment building, the Bellevue.

''Nothing would be easier than to take a body out of the apartment this way, and then load it into the car, unless a wall of snow running the entire length of the hedge of trees had built up at that time, and prevented him from carrying the body from outside his apartment to the Bellevue driveway.

''If that were the case there would be no other solution for Belshaw than to transport the body in the elevator up one floor to the lobby, to the main entrance, and then to carry it to the car. This certainly would not have been easy, but it would have been possible for a man animated by the energy of despair.

"Unless we were to contend that the accused, the night before his departure for Paris obtained his wife's agreement that the couple go for a drive in the car, and then administered a sleeping medicine to her in order, later, to strangle her in her sleep when she was already in the car. This is a possible version of the events, but it does not fit in with the image I have formed of Professor Belshaw.

"In any case, the trunk of the car could easily hold a body the size and weight of the victim; transport of the body would be no trouble for the Citroën of Mr. Belshaw.

"No one could have more easily committed the crime than the accused. Only one person had reason to conceal the identity of the body, to take off the clothes and the rings. There was no reason for a stranger to do this."

Heim pauses, then fills the room with the resonance of his voice as he cries out: "No one else would have reason to render the body unrecognizable!

"It was necessary that the body never be discovered—but if discovered, not identified. That is why, when the police asked him to supply them with means of identification, Belshaw, a man who has surely seen dead bodies during his time as a soldier [Belshaw shakes his head back and forth in negation] a man with such authority, such *sang-froid*, this impassive and highly-controlled man, this man who controls his feelings at all times, and controls himself with reason...we are supposed to believe this man loses control."

Turning to Belshaw and addressing him directly Heim demands, "When the Vaudois police ask you for the dental chart—you who knew the body had been found [Belshaw shakes his head slowly in disagreement]—and you show you must have known that by your actions, you must have known that the body might be your wife— yet you arrange that you will be left in this hideous suspense...." The prosecutor repeats this last phrase, *"incertitude affreuse"*, with enormous intensity, staring at Professor Belshaw.

"You are not a religious man, you have said"—Heim fixes his eyes on Belshaw and, speaking very slowly, walks towards him— "but how could you bear the idea of your wife's remains in such a place, forever without burial, like a piece of putrefying meat?" Belshaw winces and pales at this phrase. "In every civilization, they respect the dead!"

The prosecutor returns to his place, and takes up the thread again, in a lower tone laced with irony. "Instead you play this lamentable comedy, you tell us these absolutely incomprehensible stories...these stories we have heard about Belshaw's emotional reaction. They lack substance, they lack reality.

"This man deliberately, rationally and consciously falsified the dental records. He began this charade by writing on April 13th to the dentist himself and asking that the records be sent to him personally and that the matter be handled confidentially by the dentist. When the charts arrive he proceeds to all sorts of operations with glue, liquid paper; making twelve corrections, he photocopies the originals, then photocopies the doctored charts, destroys the originals. All this shows cold premeditation, cold execution. He has had plenty of time for reflection, he is fifty-eight years old, an eminent professor," Heim cries; "he is the president of an important international society!

"And he purposely falsified a scientific document."

The prosecutor suddenly addresses Belshaw directly, "I say to you, man to man, eye to eye, that a husband capable of this is capable of anything!"

Belshaw makes a gesture of despairing denial.

"Then the body is found. It is identified. He has not envisaged this possibility; he has not expected he would have to entertain this risk—that is the obvious reason for what he has done."

Calmly the prosecutor continues, "The nature which falsified those records is a fact. We can draw conclusions from this fact." Again he drops his voice, almost whispering. "If Professor Belshaw killed his wife, why?

"The enquiry has furnished us with information. We know that the Belshaws were a *couple unique,* and that they and their children constituted a "perfect family". All the evidence shows these sentiments, shows how strong was Mrs. Belshaw's family feeling.

"Belshaw, it is true, deceived his wife, but his married lover was not free and even though she complained about her husband, she hadn't the least intention of remaking her life with the accused.

"In any case I don't see Professor Belshaw deciding one fine day, in order to live a better life, to get rid of his wife, painstakingly preparing his *coup,* and coldly carrying it out, believing he had all the trumps in his hand.

"That the adultery of the husband should have played a role in this affair, appears certain. But it is not crucial to see in it the *motive* of the crime.

"Belshaw—one must come back to this—deceived his wife. At first he did not want to admit his infidelity, making the pretence that he had had no affairs since the sixties, and it was very difficult indeed to induce him to name his partner.

"Ill luck willed it that, on the evening of the 19th July 1979, in Vancouver, he was surprised in an equivocal position in a car with a neighbour, Mrs. Wilson.

"Questioned later Mrs. Wilson admitted that she was Belshaw's mistress and that she had passed about ten days in his company at Montana in the month of June 1978.

"And the inquiry on this subject makes clear the following:

"In 1972 to 1973 Belshaw and his wife stayed for the first time in Montana for a year, in the Mischabel apartment building.

"Belshaw again rented an apartment in this building between the 1st of June and the 4th of July 1978. It was there that Mrs. Wilson, his mistress of two years, came to join him. It was in her company that, on the 21st of June 1978, he came to find Mme. Wuest to sign the lease of the Jolilac apartment. After this he took Mrs. Wilson to Paris making three stops along the way.

"Now," says the prosecutor turning to face the tribunal, fixing his eyes upon the jury, and spelling out his points in a ringing voice, "why, given the relations which had been already going on for such a long time with Mrs. Wilson, why when he was living alone, and could now receive her in his house or go with her to a hotel, did he choose the discomfort of a two-door sportscar?

"Did he fear that this liaison would be discovered and a connection would be made with his crime?

"Living ten days with Mrs. Wilson at Montana, where his wife was to rejoin him several months later, Belshaw, however, gave a clear proof that he did not fear people talking and that he cared very little if his liaison were discovered by his wife."

Speaking very slowly, the prosecutor hammers home his point. "Why is it that what is permissible at Montana during the life of

Mrs. Belshaw, is no longer permissible in Vancouver six months after her death? When during the same period, by his own admission, he was not afraid of taking women out to restaurants and concerts...and even bringing them home?''

Heim's point is made. It was *this* liaison that Belshaw was concerned to hide; it was Wilson, who had been at Montana before Betty, whose connection with him was dangerous. This contention shows for the first time why the prosecution has made so much of the discovery of the couple in the sportscar.

Heim, quieter now, but continuing, inexorably, to join the links of this chain of logic, reminds the tribunal of the deposition of Mrs. Grey, the sister of Betty Belshaw, one of the many read out in the jumble of depositions on the first day. Mrs. Grey characterized Betty as a woman who disapproved of all extra-marital affairs. Heim laughs at the possibility that Betty would have accepted the affair. The fact that she tolerated the extra-marital love affairs of her children was not at all relevant to her attitude towards her own husband. After all, Heim reminds the tribunal, smiling, ''we must all make allowances for youth.'' He recalls the deposition, read in by the president, of Dr. Greenburg, the former head of the UBC English Department and an old friend, who had said that Betty strongly disapproved of extra-marital affairs, that she was very strict where morals were concerned. And Adrian remembered being ''traumatized'' by the conjugal scene which took place once before....

''Imagine that in January 1979 she discovered the liaison,'' Heim continues. ''Perhaps someone said, 'My, you've changed in six months'; perhaps a chance word of Mme. Wuest seeped into her consciousness.'' Heim gestures, tapping his own head, while spectators recall the sour character of Mme. Wuest. ''Hasn't Belshaw admitted that once during a scene between the two there was an exchange of blows on this subject? Could not such a thing take place again? Imagine the scene, between a woman, terribly moral, rigid, emotional, jealous—one can imagine this after thirty-seven years of marriage; the jealousy, gentlemen, the jealousy!

''Imagine a calm man who suddenly explodes.

''Mrs. Wilson says her husband was violent....If an established professional man can threaten his wife, if the philosopher Althusser could strangle his wife, why couldn't Professor Belshaw, in a moment of passion, kill his wife?

"Such things *have* happened. Perhaps he pressed a place on her neck, and without meaning to, asphyxiated her. It's not impossible to imagine the scene:

"She cries, shouts, blows are struck. The man continues to explain, apologize, until finally exasperated, he loses control—and kills her.

"It is after this that he sets out to dissimulate. He can no longer understand how he could have done it. He can't bear it, he doesn't know why it has happened, the thing which has happened is insupportable to him.

"So he undertakes the required task." As the prosecutor speaks these lines, the sky, which has been grey, suddenly clears, and the jagged peaks are visible, veiled in snow. "And this good wife and mother is abandoned thousands of miles from her family, her friends, her country, to the mercies of the wild beasts.

"Who else but the accused committed the falsification?

"Who else but the accused had the reason to kill Mrs. Belshaw, and who else but the accused went to so much trouble to prevent her identification?

"It is you and you alone, Cyril Belshaw, who had this interest. I don't believe you committed a premeditated murder. I think that if you killed your wife, it was without having wanted to or meant to. It was an accident, in the course of a dispute where you lost your habitual *sang-froid,* you who are so proud of being master of yourself.

"Yes, this frightful thing happened, you killed your life-time companion, and you did not have the courage to face it. The gentleman that everyone acknowledged you to be, the brilliant scholar, the character you have so patiently built up for yourself—you could not accept appearing in the eyes of others, in your own eyes, as a murderer. It was necessary to erase at any cost this stain, to make it disappear.

"*M. le Président, Mm. les juges, Mm. les jurés*—at the beginning I gave you another version. Now it is clear that that was an absurdity. The unlikelihood of it! The illogicality of it!"

The prosecutor exhorts them, his voice rising on a dramatic crescendo, "You must have the courage of your experience of life, of your psychological experience; you must have the courage of your convictions. Don't be mislead by vague doubts. Let it not be said that with intelligence, *sang-froid* and good lawyers one can escape justice, the law and the prison.

"I don't ask for first-degree murder because there is no certainty of how she was killed. It is not impossible—but it is more probable that he killed without premeditation. Premeditated murder doesn't correspond to his personality, it is out of his nature.

"That is the reason I demand, for Cyril Belshaw, twelve years with *réclusion!*"

29

As Heim finishes and sits down, there is absolute silence in the courtroom. Everyone slowly awakes, as if from a spell. Even Paschoud and Stoudmann are looking stunned. The prosecutor's dramatic style, his thrilling crescendos and spellbinding diminuendos, his gestures, even his sarcastic asides, have created an extraordinary sense of drama.

It is close to the lunch break, and the president asks Paschoud if he would like to speak after lunch, or if he thinks he can finish his *plaidoirie* before. Paschoud seems to be still recovering from the effect of the prosecutor's speech. He stumbles slightly over his words as he tells the president that he would like to begin right away.

He riffles his notes and licks his dry lips. Fatigue, from the sleepless nights he has had worrying over this case which has come to mean so much to him, shows in his face, in the tremor of his hands. He begins to speak, in a conversational tone, looking directly, on their own level, at the jurors. Whereas Heim seemed to address them from the height of his position, his forensic power, his majesty as the State representative, Paschoud is talking to them man to man. Gathering his courage, he begins.

First he tells the court that he is not a great trial lawyer like his colleague the *procureur-générale*. "I am just an ordinary lawyer, but it is with my heart that I will try to convince you.

"Some months ago," Paschoud continues, "certain people, among them magistrates of this canton, having learned that I was going to defend Cyril Belshaw remarked, 'Ah, what a *belle affaire!*'

"Not at all! For me, it is no *belle affaire,* it is nothing like that. It is not a matter of an interesting trial story for a reader to relish, or a game, or a duel—single combat between the prosecution and the defence, an oratorical battle with the prize going to the most eloquent.

"No, the *'affaire Belshaw'* is a difficult, a tragic case, which concerns the death of a woman, and now the life of a man, her husband. It has deeply upset me and totally preoccupied me since the 15th of November, 1979, when I found myself for the first time before Cyril Belshaw for a half hour at the prison of Fleury-Mérogis in Paris. At the end of the meeting we looked one another in the eyes and I explained to him that if he were really guilty it would be better to tell me right away. He would be protected by the code of secrecy between lawyer and client, and no one would know of this avowal, or even that I had been to see him. He could then choose another defence lawyer and say to him whatever seemed best."

Paschoud looks directly at the jurors now, speaking in a conversational tone, as if he is telling each of them, privately, what is in his heart.

"But as for me, I told him, I could not plead for him in all conscience and with a whole heart if I ever came to believe he were guilty. If that were to happen I would renounce my responsibility and his position would be extremely difficult.

"Cyril Belshaw swore to me with tears in his eyes that it was not he who had killed his wife. And since then, until this very moment, step by step, day after day, my conviction of his innocence has been reinforced. Nothing has happened to shake it."

This remarkable opening statement astounds the observers from common law countries. Such remarks, coming from a defence lawyer in another country, might very well be cause for a mistrial. But here they are apparently considered proper. And most likely, considering the high esteem in which Paschoud is held, such a deep conviction in the innocence of his client will carry great weight. Instead of thinking "Of course his own lawyer believes in him," or "How dare he testify as a character witness for his own client," perhaps the Swiss will think "That is Paschoud speaking, and if *he* believes in Belshaw ..."

Paschoud continues, telling the jury why he has called in Stoudmann to assist him, explaining that he himself was away during part of the *instruction,* and also that Stoudmann is an expert on criminal law, about which Paschoud feels himself particularly inexperienced. He explains that he will deal with the personalities of the Belshaws and with their relationships and with certain specific areas of the dossier. Stoudmann will deal with the facts, and with the law which the defence will cite in order to support their pleas of not guilty. Paschoud then pauses, straightens his glasses, shuffles his notes, and begins, addressing the entire tribunal.

"One. Who was Mrs. Betty Belshaw?

"After having read and studied the quantities of material about her, about her personality, after having perused her letters, her diaries, and the statements collected about her and for her from those close to her, from friends and acquaintances, I feel as if I see her before me, as if I had known her and spoken to her, as if she were a friend of mine. Let us see if we can illumine her personality.

"She was an instructor at the University of British Columbia in Vancouver, British Columbia, where she taught English.

"She had two sisters. One was Mrs. Joan Swaill; she was the closest to Betty, and they saw each other often and corresponded frequently. This sister described her as a very gay person, very energetic, enterprising, but, like people of that temperament, often subject to bouts of depression.

"Other people interviewed described her as follows: 'very organized, friendly and likeable', 'a private person, loyal, energetic, intelligent, extraordinarily loving to her family.' A Professor Greenburg describes her as 'formal, conventional, not in agreement with the concept that a couple live together if they are not married, believing in marriage and in the particular quality of the individual'. But this gentleman indicates that he had not seen Betty since 1973, perhaps she changed subsequently? In any case he also called her 'dynamic, a hard worker, and someone who had to take Valium to sleep'. Others described her by saying, 'well-disciplined, severe, a very British education, she wears the pants in the family'; 'effervescent, dynamic, alert, lively, always under pressure'; 'a marvellous person, great sense of humour, a good friend, loved her children, adored her husband, believed in marriage'; 'reticent about her private life, proud of her husband, made scenes with her secretaries, hard to get along with'; 'brilliant, intelligent, determined, meticulous, always under pressure, emotional'; 'cordial, warm and spontaneous'; 'always worried that she might have cancer' ....

"One must make clear that all these somewhat contradictory testimonials were gathered unilaterally without written, dated depositions and without being signed, by the investigators sent to Canada. And they were taken under the influence of those investigators' preconceived ideas and their propensity not to transcribe anything unless it agreed with their preconceived theses.

"And finally, let me read to you what her doctor, Dr. Shaw, who looked after her from 1955 to 1972 and saw her four or five times a year, said. He spoke of her as a very pleasant person who was very intelligent, but anxious, slightly hypochondriacal, and plagued with headaches and palpitations.

"And so, putting these statements together with the testimony of the witnesses heard during this trial we can now see the principal facets of the personality of Betty Belshaw. She was intelligent, sensible, gay, and very active. She loved her family and her work deeply. In more European terms we could say that she was incontrovertibly an admirable and adorable woman!''

Paschoud pauses, looks around, shuffles his notes again, laying aside some of the 6 x 9 sheets he holds, and continues.

"Two. Who is Cyril Belshaw? I am not going to repeat here his *curriculum vitae* which the investigators have transcribed in detail and which you have heard read aloud in the *pièces*.

"The witnesses whom you have heard, those who voluntarily gave their statements in the course of police interviews in Canada, or by letters voluntarily deposed either with Maître Badinter in Paris or later with me here, *all* have unanimously declared that Cyril Belshaw is a man of quality, on the professional level as well as on the human level. There are only two discordant voices, which I will explain later.''

Paschoud briefly runs through some of Belshaw's most important achievements, and then reads from statements in the dossier, "Friends, acquaintances, colleagues and relatives say of his character: 'a calm non-aggressive, tranquil personality; the couple understood one another well'; 'a person of the highest integrity, a gentleman on all points, a loving husband, a good man, highly regarded.' His sister-in-law Joan Swaill writes: 'a devoted husband and provider, an honourable man deserving of every confidence.' Colleagues say, 'distinguished professor, I have the highest regard for him'; 'eminent scholar, a man of principles and integrity, honourable on all points'; 'a man in whom one could have every confidence, of great sensitivity, calm and controlled'; 'a well-deserved reputation for honesty and conscientiousness, good and kind, a man for whom I have affection and respect.' And from Professor George Woodcock, who has known him for twenty-five years: 'He and his wife and children formed an exceptionally united and harmonious family, and they were a united couple.' Others say 'a person with high principles, a spotless reputation'; 'impressed by his integrity; he has been an exemplary father to his children and a devoted husband'—and the man who said that knew him for more than twenty years! 'We have been next-door neighbours for fifteen years and our families are very close. We hold this man in high esteem as a father, husband, neighbour ... we have the highest regard for him.' 'Honourable, open, loyal and honest, great integrity of character.' 'Violence would be inconceivable from him, he is a man of integrity, sincere, straight, and they are a couple in complete harmony.'...

"I stop here and ask this question of each of you, before so many depositions filled with such high praise—would any of us receive such testimonials? Reading these, one after the other, I ask you this ... and remind you that these are sincere and cannot be the expressions of a simple complaisance, but only of very exact and specific opinions.

"There were only two voices which disagreed. These two were among those whose interviews were transcribed without a written, signed statement, and we made protests about them, among others, due to the manner in which they were reported by the Vaudois investigators. These were the only ones among all of the Belshaw's friends who insidiously suggested doubts about Cyril.

"First there was the statement of the Morandas. This couple characterized Betty as 'orderly, friendly and well-loved'; however, 'Cyril was'—already they use the past tense!—'ambitious, and was the object of a very active resentment in the department of anthropology.' Now we have heard the chairman speak, Dr. Burridge, and he said quite the contrary. Then the Morandas reveal the possible origin of their misrepresentations when they state, 'Cyril was responsible for, or present during, the capital execution of two young people in a Pacific island a long time ago.' This has been formally contested. It is pure imagination, a page of a novel, and the investigation pursued in London revealed that there is absolutely nothing to it.''

Thus does Paschoud dismiss one of the negative reports which has most troubled him, personally, on reading the dossier. He is, it seems, unaware that Professor Moranda, formerly a colleague of Belshaw in the Anthropology Department, and his wife, also a professor at UBC, were opponents of Belshaw in some of the political infighting which characterized the department in earlier years, and perhaps for that reason felt fewer compunctions about injecting a less than positive note into their interview with the Vaudois investigators. The Morandas, too, were unlike the Scotts and Burridges who fit into a more discreet and genteel academic mould. The Morandas had shown themselves to be less rigid, more lively, more prepared to take unorthodox views, more prepared to walk openly into controversy. Temperamentally the Morandas were very different from the Belshaws, and the two couples had frequently found themselves on opposite sides of disputes.

"As for the other note of disagreement," continues Paschoud, "it is that of Dr. Melville Shaw, and it is worth the trouble to stop a minute here, too, and examine it." Paschoud repeats the two statements read in yesterday. He reminds the tribunal that the first, unsworn, statement was taken when Shaw had been suddenly shown the gruesome photographs of Betty's decomposing body and told that the police had information which showed that Belshaw had committed the crime. The second statement was the sworn one, and in it Shaw testified to his faith in Belshaw's innocence.

"As for me," Paschoud concludes, "I would rather agree with Dr. Shaw's testimony as given under oath, than with the interpretation of Inspector Margot, even if his mother *was* English.

"To complete my discussion of the personality of the accused, here is how it is summed up by Inspectors Wyss and Margot, in the last page of their final report to the *police de sûreté*—which, curiously enough, no longer figures in the long dossier made available to me at the end of the month of August.

" 'Cyril Belshaw had a personality completely opposite to that of his wife. People around him described him to us as being calm, not expansive, solemn, intelligent, master of himself at all times, sly, ambitious, vain, and full of himself.

" 'Since the beginning of February 1980, we have had regular contact with Cyril Belshaw but have never been able to see his real self. He adopted a professorial attitude towards us, wanting always to be right. It has become clear that being contradicted exasperates him. Because of his pride, he cannot admit to having committed the least fault or error.' "

Paschoud sets aside the police report and continues, "For my part, having seen Professor Cyril Belshaw once a week for at least an hour, often two or three hours, over a nine-month period, having grilled him, argued with, questioned him—as did the police—but also having opened the door to confidences and comprehension, as for me, I acquired for this man respect and admiration."

By pursuing this point Paschoud shows that his own conviction remains, to him, one of the most compelling arguments in Belshaw's favour. He is telling the tribunal that he, Paschoud, believes in Belshaw, that he is putting his own honour and integrity on the scales of justice, to be weighed in Belshaw's favour.

Paschoud continues, "He is fundamentally honest and good; he is human with the greatness and the frailties that this includes. And he is sensitive, with the strengths and weaknesses which flow from this.

"He committed an inexplicable fault, he went astray, and then was weak and cowardly not to admit it until he was discovered.

"But he has paid. Very heavily....

"But as for having been able to kill his wife, I say and I affirm—as have all who know him and who know him better than I—it is absolutely impossible! It is excluded by reason of his entire past, by his mentality, and by his personality. But it is excluded also, and before everything, because he has never ceased to love his wife."

As he speaks, Paschoud has been gaining confidence. His words flow more surely, his personal conviction is apparent in every gesture and in the tone of his voice. Although he speaks conversationally, directly to the jury, without dramatics, his deep emotion is becoming apparent.

He continues, now treading carefully. "That there were here and there some differences, some disputes, some angry moments on the part of Mrs. Belshaw does not mean that this couple were not united as a family. In what household has there never been the least little cloud in thirty-seven years of marriage? If you are such a one, raise your hand and I will see that you get a gold medal!

"Among all the witnesses we have heard—and here there is not a single exception—everyone who knew and was close to the Belshaw family declared that they formed a united couple, perhaps even a model couple. They had two children whom they raised, cherished, and loved together. They shared everything in life, even their activities as teachers brought them together. They both liked reading, nature, good food, travel, vacations, the sea, mountains, skiing, poetry.

"That Mr. Belshaw was weak and had a liaison with another woman after many years does not exclude, certainly, nor in the least diminish, the love, affection and respect that he felt for his wife."

Paschoud has dealt with the personalities of the two, and he now addresses the jury with a slight note of irony in his voice. "Would it not be more likely, knowing that Mrs. Belshaw was the more lively, the more spontaneous, the more emotional of the two, that *she* killed her husband? It is a general, perhaps even an absolute, rule that the deceived spouse reacts with violence, and not the deceiver. To reverse the roles flies in the face of logic!

"And then, if one went along with the accusation just to the point of admitting the violent scene that has had to be invented to suit the case, a scene such as that must have left some traces. There would have been an assault, a struggle, a defence, things broken, noise, cries, scratches, marks, traces of strangulation, because that is the thesis of the accusation! Victims of strangulation have swollen faces, *their tongues protrude from their mouths.* Around the neck are lesions corresponding to the shape and size of whatever was used to strangle the victim. Yet there was nothing at all like that in the report of Dr. Genillard or the forensic doctor. Here also, one drowns in supposition.''

This is unfair of Paschoud. Has he forgotten that the throat was eaten away, as was part of the face? If such signs had existed, they would have been obliterated.

"There is one last element of fact to which I must draw your attention. Professor Thélin answered a question put to him by my colleague Maître Stoudmann and stated that rigor mortis intervened four to five hours after death. If so, how could the body have been put in the trunk of the car?

"But let us return to the psychological factors which are my area of concern, as I explained at the beginning of my plea. As I have just shown, there is no motive for the crime—as every mystery story shows is necessary. For what advantages could Mr. Belshaw have gained by the death of his wife?

"Financial? Certainly not.

"Personal satisfaction? That would be completely out of character. He is not a sadist!

"Fear? Of what?

"To remarry for love? We have shown that is not the case.

"Jealousy? There wasn't any.

"Why then?

"Is it possible that he killed his wife because she discovered, for the second time in her life, at fifty-nine years of age, that he was involved in an affair with someone who, even though she lived in the same neighbourhood, Mrs. Belshaw didn't know at all? And this person, a married woman, mother of two children, who didn't dream of divorce?

"It's unthinkable, irrational, unsustainable!

"A man of such *sang-froid,* an ex-serviceman, a man who rarely or never loses his temper, a man of this calibre, of this quality, of this intelligence? It's impossible!''

Paschoud rustles his notes, and the spectators look at the clock. It is well past noon. "Let us move on to point three,'' he says. The spectators sigh. After all, Paschoud has not gotten into anything meaty yet, and contrary to his assurances to the president, he seems to be only just getting into his stride.

"Three," announces Paschoud. "The particulars of the investigation.

"On the 28th of March 1978, a body completely denuded, and in a state of advanced putrefaction was discovered, wrapped in three sacks of plastic, down a slope by the Aigle-Le Sépey road, *about eighteen kilometres from the French frontier if one travels by St. Grygolph, and about twenty-five kilometres if one goes via the col de Morgins!*

"Without wishing to suggest anything, I point out again simply that the road between Col des Mosses and Aigle is the closest one that leads into the mountains from the other side of the plain of the Rhône, when one comes from France by the South bank of Lac Léman...." Here Paschoud is trying to suggest that Le Sépey is not *that* far from the French border and that Betty could have met with foul play in France and been brought to Le Sépey by her killer. But the circumstances are such as to make this a very unlikely supposition, so he doesn't press the point.

"At first the inquiry developed normally, aside from the slightly surprising report of the forensic doctor, Professor Thélin."

Paschoud goes on to summarize the inquiry of the police, stressing the rarity and brevity of the interviews between the *juge d'instruction* and Belshaw. He also again reminds the court of his conviction that Fischlin and Wyss acted in haste, and with preconceived ideas of Belshaw's guilt.

"Every measure they took was aimed only at finding proofs of Belshaw's guilt," Paschoud insists. "Everything that did not accord with their theses they deliberately ignored.

"When they questioned Cyril Belshaw they already suspected him, already saw him as an *inculpé,* or as a person on whom were directed not only suspicions but the certainty of the *juge* for whom they acted by delegation ....

"It goes without saying that I have, in other circumstances, acquired a great deal of respect for the *police de sûreté,* and particularly for the conscientiousness and tenacity displayed by certain inspectors.

"But in this affair, those who participated in the inquiry directed against Cyril Belshaw—and acted under the delegation of the *juge d'instruction*—went beyond their duties and their competence.''

Paschoud does not refrain from reminding the tribunal of Fischlin and Wyss' actions in Vancouver. ''On their first full day in Vancouver,'' he says, ''they participated in an interview with Cyril Belshaw called suddenly and without prior notification which took place in an office of the Canadian police, an interview taped without his knowledge, which lasted more than two hours.

''This manner of proceeding was contrary to Canadian proper legal proceeding as well as, in every particular, being contrary to our code of penal procedure and the inspectors knew it.''

In regard to Canada, Paschoud was mistaken: this procedure is legal under Canadian law.

''If I keep coming back to this interrogation of September 24th, as well as the transcriptions and translations, it is because these were included in condensed form in the articles of the dossier, and determined forever the attitude adopted afterwards, towards Mr. Belshaw, until his extradition to Switzerland.

''Let us suppose for an instant, *messieurs,* that Belshaw is not guilty of the murder of his wife, and let us admit, as he has revealed to me, that he was called at the end of the day to the police office at the University of Vancouver [UBC] there to find himself confronted by three inspectors who revealed to him that a body had been identified as his wife. He was completely shocked, horrified. These officers refused to tell him where, when and how the body had been discovered. Instead, right away they assail him with questions the contents of which were accusations. They say to him, over and over, that he is a murderer, and they call upon him to confess...because if he were in Switzerland he would be treated differently...then they go and search his house!

''If it is in this manner that one formulates an invitation to return to our country in order that an investigation may continue with his participation, it is necessary first to understand the significance of the word 'invitation'.'' This remark receives general laughter, except from the president, who sits stony-faced.

''What could be more normal, after this, that Mr. Belshaw put an end to this conversation and unexpected visit of more than three and a half hours which had fallen upon him like a bolt from the blue, and that he took the advice of a lawyer on the conduct to follow.

"Mr. McLaughlin, a lawyer in Vancouver, who is here today, advised him to put an end to the interview and to the visit that night. Then he demanded that the questions which the inspectors wanted to pose to his client be communicated to him; this request was refused.

"We arrive thus at the end of September 1979, and Cyril Belshaw has not decided if he is going to Switzerland or not, whether to accede to this *invitation*.

"But Cyril Belshaw now knows that the body of Betty Belshaw has been discovered, he informs his children, he asks via his lawyer of the Ambassador of Canada the name of a lawyer in Switzerland, and it is thus that I entered into contact with my colleague in Vancouver....

"I informed Mr. McLaughlin of the principles by which an inquiry is carried out in Switzerland, as well as the conditions and treaties of extradition which we have with other countries...because after the undisguised threats formulated by the inspectors in their "invitation" of September 24th, there was no doubt that on this side of the Atlantic, Cyril Belshaw was already considered guilty of the murder of his wife....

"Let us imagine, for an instant, that Cyril Belshaw had been the author of the murder of his wife. He would have had but one sole attitude to uphold, under the counsel of his Canadian lawyer...not to leave Canada—natural advice!

"He did not need to fear being accused of this crime in his own country, because the Canadian police have jurisdiction only for crimes committed within the territory of Canada.

"Such an attitude, which would have implied his renunciation of all his professorial responsibilities, and such a new beginning, whatever it might have been, would certainly have been possible, in some way or other.

"Cyril Belshaw faced these alternatives and did not hesitate for an instant; he continued to meet his professorial obligations, which implied his trip to Paris, where he was arrested on his descent from the airplane on the 11th of November. I saw him in prison there and thus arrive, having made a complete circle, at the beginning of my exposé.'' The spectators move restlessly while the jurors sit impassively, their eyes fixed upon Paschoud.

''In the course of my interview with him on the 15th of November 1979, I said to Mr. Belshaw that I had no knowledge whatsoever of French extradition law and counselled him to consult my colleague and friend, Maître Robert Badinter, in Paris.

''Maître Badinter has become a champion in the struggle against the death penalty and interrogation procedures such as they have in France, and in the whole world.

''He knew the code of penal procedure in our canton, and it was he, and he alone, who advised Cyril Belshaw to oppose extradition, because there was no material proof at all of the accusation of murder laid against my client.

''You know what followed ... and if I have gone into all this, it is to show that Cyril Belshaw, personally, is not responsible for what has passed in this area; he has followed the advice of his lawyers, in an area about which he knew nothing!''

For his Swiss listeners these are important points Paschoud has been making. He must show why Belshaw did not voluntarily return to Switzerland and why he fought extradition. For the Swiss these two decisions of Belshaw seem to be, quite clearly, signs of guilt. Paschoud is obliged, therefore, to try to communicate the common-law attitude to such matters, however inappropriate his arguments may seem to some of the non-Swiss observers.

Paschoud pauses, and again shuffles his notes. Now the audience senses that he is approaching his conclusion, and their attention, which has been wandering, focuses upon him. The courtroom grows silent.

''As for the attitudes of Cyril Belshaw...Aren't we all, all of us here, different from one another? These differences appear not only in physical or material characteristics, which form our distinctive exteriors, but they are even more noticeable in traits of character, by our different reactions; the currents of sentiment, of temperament, or of reason that each of us feels in the deepest part of himself and shows outwardly towards those events which together form the traumas of life.

''There is no absolute rule which allows us to determine what ought to be the normal reactions that must be shown by any specific person in the different unexpected and unpredictable situations in which he may find himself. In this domain the law of the greatest number doesn't apply, because each individual is separate—is an exception.

"How now can we judge, we Europeans, Swiss, Vaudois, steeped in our mentality, our education, and our manner of thinking? We are inhabitants of this continent, this country, and this region. How can we judge the reactions of a man who has been born, raised and passed his youth in New Zealand, and who has spent the greater part of his life in Canada?

"It happens, even to us, that we astonish our own circle by the way we react in certain circumstances. Aren't we sometimes astonished, surprised, dumbfounded by the reaction of those nearest to us, of those we thought we knew?

"Can we be certain, we ourselves, of what we would do, or have done, if we had been placed in the situation of Cyril Belshaw? When parents lose a child, or when a husband loses a wife, or a wife her husband, he or she, alone, in his grief, even if he is consoled, supported, surrounded by his children, will behave irrationally."

Now finally, Paschoud is directing his full appeal to the tribunal.

"*Messieurs*. Let us imagine for an instant, I beg of you, that this man is really a man of good faith, and that he has committed an error in a moment of tension something like moral distress. Yet, I affirm to you it was not possible for him to kill his wife!

"What punishment for this mistake has he not already suffered, morally! Can we imagine his humiliation, in having been obliged to drag in his children, to put to the test his friends, who have come voluntarily and at their own expense all the way from Canada—to see his private life exposed, displayed in public, digested by people over their morning tea and biscuits like their food, to have ruined his career and his reputation, to have been obliged to submit to thirteen months of imprisonment which will remain forever in his memory and give him nightmares...?

"What dignity in his suffering, what mastery of self, what abnegation; he could not even find strength or courage in the memory of his wife, who disappeared in broad daylight, in circumstances and for reasons of which he is ignorant!

"Whoever has lost a being dearer to him than his own self can only feel compassion for the pain of Cyril Belshaw. His sole consolation, for himself, is in the memory of many little signs which remain of the one who is gone, such as the notes that she wrote in her personal notebook on November 29th, 1979. Mr. Belshaw read this only after the death of the one he mourns. Is it perhaps a premonition, a mysterious warning of the future which awaited her?''

Then Paschoud takes up a sheet of paper, and in a moving voice reads aloud the translation of a section of Betty's journal.

'' 'As I sit in the car which is moving at a great speed southward, I think of this fragile thread by which we are held to life, and I think of what I would like to leave behind for those I love. Not only material things, which will come to them in any case, but the knowledge of what is beautiful in life, the love of children, of husband, and the joy that they have given me.

'' 'The hope that they will remember me in the good years of laughter and adventure, and not in the years when I was half-ill with fatigue, and the ill-humour that goes with it. The places where we were happy, as they come to me, without any special order—just a string of memories which come to my mind as we drive along at 120 kilometres per hour....

'' 'The new snow, powdering the hillside covered with green foliage, which reminds me of Enna on the morning of Epiphany ... and all the mosaics and columns of the temples of the Acropolis, spring at Delphi, at Corinth or Mycenae, when Adrian read the street names in Greek. Diana with the goddess Athena. Rome so cold and damp and suddenly the sun on the Forum, the bohemian, the bohemians in Ireland, the crossing by boat, Edinburgh, the first train and the scramble for seats, and before that, the station in Montreal with our seventeen suitcases...Fiji, the huts, the beaches, the reef.

'' 'It is snowing again, fine flakes with a line of migratory birds.

'' 'The house, our dog Pushkin, Christmas, birthdays, days in the garden, days by the fire, dinners, friends, our twenty-fifth anniversary when Papa and Adrian did everything!

'' 'Long Beach, the Okanagan, camping with no hot water...school, prize-giving with tears in our eyes.

'' 'The sun shines, it's hard to write, another day I will write all these memories for you.' ''

Paschoud pauses. Then takes his seat. There is a moment's silence, then the courtroom shakes off the spell cast by Betty's voice, speaking from the past, and the implications of her words. There is a collective sigh, a murmur, and then the court is dismissed.

30

It is well past one o'clock when the spectators spill out into the streets in search of lunch. The journalists catch Heim to ask him the significance of the sentence he has asked for Belshaw. He explains that he must ask for *réclusion,* and that the twelve-year sentence, with the year Belshaw has already spent in detention, and one-third off for good behaviour, would come to five or six more years.

The journalists are trying to put the pieces together. "What time would the Belshaws have had to leave Montana to arrive at Beaune by 6:00 on the 13th?" one asks.

"No later than ten in the morning."

"What about this rigor mortis claim by Paschoud, he's got it wrong, hasn't he?"

Heim agrees. Rigor mortis comes and goes. It would be possible, if enough time had elapsed after death, for the body to be put in the trunk and then be stretched out where it was found.

Someone snags Margot. "I don't understand Paschoud's remarks about the tongue sticking out and lesions around the neck," the journalist says. "Wasn't all that destroyed by the animals who had been at the body?"

"Yes," says Margot. He looks angry and is distressed by the attacks on police behaviour. In particular by remarks of Paschoud repeating allegations, made by witnesses, which the police had removed from the dossier before the trial. "Why did he bring *that* in?" he asks. "We *had* to ask about such things, people make allegations which it is our duty to clear up. But if there is nothing to them we take them out of the dossier so they don't come up in the court and cause pain. And then *he*, the defence lawyer, repeats such things." Margot shakes his head angrily. "It's unconscionable! We kept them out. *He* brings them in, and he blames *us*!"

Margot doesn't want to talk any more. But Heim and Paschoud talk freely, and soon journalists, spectators and the lawyers are ensconced at tables in nearby restaurants, arguing heatedly over the morning's pleas.

The president has allowed only a short lunch break, and soon everyone reassembles to hear Stoudmann's address. He rises, elegant and contained, holding his notes at arm's length, and looking over them at the jury.

"The *affaire Belshaw* is an enigma," he begins. His voice is composed, his delivery polished. "And our epoch does not like enigmas. They remind man of his weakness and force him to admit failure. They go against our way of thinking, and against logic. Reason can not penetrate them, and that is why we find them intolerable. So the temptation is great to gloss over such mysteries; to give a rational explanation where none exists."

Stoudmann, in his black gown, his glasses sliding slightly down his nose, looks directly across the width of the room, from the defence table, towards the tribunal. He pauses, to let the force of what he has said penetrate, and the jurors look back at him, attentively. For in his opening remarks he has surely put his finger on a crucial point. The prosecutor's case depends on finding the most reasonable explanation for events which otherwise must remain inexplicable. But *must* there be a rational explanation?

Stoudmann continues. "This is what the prosecutor has done. The mystery is solved; and everything is logical, reasonable, conforming to the facts. And we can be comfortable.

"But it is not enough to be reasonable. We must have the truth, and the truth is not always reasonable.

"Now. Let us return to earth. Let us look at the testimony, the material evidence. The accusation is that he killed her. But we don't know *if* she was killed, nor *how* she was killed, nor *when* she was killed, nor *where* she was killed. The whole case is totally artificial, a total fabrication.

Stoudmann reads from the charges, mockingly, " 'apparently he killed her ... *probably* in the apartment ... possibly on the road ...' All we really have is a body and a suspect. And he—for a long time he was just an unhappy man who had lost his wife.

"It was only after the famous falsification that the investigation began to attempt to prove his guilt. I am going to discuss the circumstances from the disappearance to the 7th of May falsification of the dental records. I will show that Professor Belshaw behaved normally or understandably."

Stoudmann has laid the philosophical base for his plea. He has told the tribunal that is not enough to think that Belshaw is the most likely suspect, that his being guilty is the least improbable of all possibilities. Now he is setting out to show that Belshaw's behaviour after his wife's disappearance was not that of a guilty man.

"After Betty Belshaw disappeared, he reported her missing. He was told to wait. He went home and made an inventory of what his wife was wearing; her clothes, jewelry and so on. The next day he went to the Bagnolet police, and to the Canadian embassy, where he visited Mr. Nasrallah. Again he was told to wait. Perhaps, it was suggested, his wife had gone away, and would return. But Cyril Belshaw was not satisfied, because he knew his wife would never do such a thing. He called Diana, and he cried on the telephone. He stayed in Paris for several days. Then, there was nothing more he could do there. He returned to Montana.

"On the 22nd of January Diana arrived." Belshaw, listening, looks as if he can hardly bear to hear all this once again. The courtroom is very quiet, waiting to see if Stoudmann can explain away the equivocal nature of Belshaw's behaviour. "Later Adrian arrived. Together they discussed every possibility, including suicide, an idea which would surface later.

"Professor Belshaw telephoned the Canadian embassy. He believed he had told them to notify the Swiss police to look into the matter, and that, therefore, he had dealt with the matter in the proper, Anglo-Saxon way. The accusation that he did not inform the Swiss police is therefore not correct. In the context, his actions were appropriate. And we can see this from a letter he wrote on February 17th to Mr. Mooney, the Canadian consul in Berne, which said 'I thought you had already told the Swiss and English police'."

Stoudmann is referring to Belshaw's behaviour in regard to the

Swiss police, which has been a matter of dispute. He is reminding the tribunal of the fact that Mr. Mooney contacted Belshaw to ask if he wished the Swiss police informed. Belshaw wrote at once to say that of course he did, that in fact, he thought the Swiss police had already been informed. But it does still seem remarkable that Belshaw himself had never called the Swiss police to see how they were getting on.

Stoudmann now continues, putting Belshaw's earlier complaints about the Swiss police in context. "That is why he could write to Lady Firth on the 8th of February saying that he had informed the Swiss police. He thought it had already been done by the Canadian authorities. Yet it was only on the 19th of February that the embassy actually informed the Swiss police.

"So it is clear that his behaviour was perfectly normal. He was consistent as well in his attitude towards others. He showed himself cool to his more distant acquaintances, and emotional with those close to him."

Now Stoudmann goes on to discuss Belshaw's state of mind during this period. Again he repeats Belshaw's description of his feelings, of his mounting anxiety as he passed day after day alone in the empty resort village burdened by the stress of wondering what had become of Betty. Stoudmann recalls Belshaw's decision to go to London to break out of his solitude. There is nothing new here, but Stoudmann's account of Belshaw's state adds a certain authenticity to the story Belshaw has told previously, and the president, judges, and jurors look thoughtful.

Next Stoudmann turns to the problem about which the prosecutor was so forceful: the question of the article announcing the discovery of the body which appeared on the front page of the *Nouvelliste*. "As for the article in the *Nouvelliste*," Stoudmann goes on, "Cyril Belshaw has steadfastly maintained that he never read it. He left for London without knowing of the discovery of the body at Le Sépey. So he went to the Salvation Army and to the conference at York. While there he received a telephone call advising him to go at once to see Inspector Prost in Paris. But when he arrived in Paris he discovered there was no news for him. Then, on the 13th, two inspectors pay a call upon him—Inspectors Reichen and Guignard knock on his door. His hopes, which have been aroused and dashed, are aroused once more. But the two policemen say nothing about a body, they just request the dental records and a picture.''

Once again the tribunal hears, this time from Stoudmann, the defence's explanation of why Belshaw decided to write for the dental records himself, of his desire to avoid gossip and unpleasant speculation in Vancouver.

Stoudmann goes on to build up his own version of the falsification. Using evidence from the dossier, he attempts to show Belshaw's state of mind up to and including the period when the falsification occurred. ''A letter written by Belshaw on the 14th of April to Diana shows this uncertainty,'' Stoudmann tells the tribunal. ''In it he describes himself as upset, in a changeable state of mind. He wanted to know, yet he did not want to know. This has nothing to do with Cyril Belshaw the intellectual. It is a different matter altogether. On April 20th he wrote to a psychic. Surely this shows his state of mind—shows us how he was unravelling. For what else can it mean when a man of science consults a specialist in the occult?

''On the 3rd of May he wrote to Diana, telling her how the pressures were breaking him, how he feared there was no longer any reason to hope. He said he was a coward, afraid to face the identification procedure. He was beginning to crack.

''On the 7th of May he received the dental records. And he could not face them. He cracked. He could not bear the identification. That dental form, so technical, drove him to an irrational act. Too long he had been master of himself and held himself completely under control. Face to face with those dental records he cracked completely.''

Here Stoudmann breaks off to discuss the technical matter of whether or not you can forge something which is not an official document. It is his aim to prove that the dental records are not *titres,* not evidence according to the law. ''For a document to be a *titre,*'' Stoudmann contends, ''it must be a 'writing,' something which translates human thought by words or symbols which can be *read.* But the dental chart is a diagram or a drawing.... It carried no notation by the dentist.'' So, Stoudmann concludes, as it is not a *titre* in the legal sense, its falsification is not a forgery, not a crime.

"But the falsification of the dental records has given the police a suspect," Stoudmann continues. "All that is left is to turn him into the guilty party. The police thus sift through a veritable flood of evidence, hoping to find something on which to convict Cyril Belshaw.

"Yet all we have is a body and a suspect.

"As for the 'pink teeth'—cited as evidence of strangulation by the prosecution—this is a meaningless contention." Stoudmann quotes from the greatest European forensic specialists whom the defence has consulted on the matter. They all say that no significance should be attached to the evidence that the roots of the teeth had a pinkish cast. Stoudmann tells the court this contention must be considered totally without foundation.

"Natural death cannot be excluded. Or a sexual psychopath could have raped her and taken her clothes. And let us not forget that her rings were valuable.

"But now, with the body known to be Betty's, let us turn for a moment to the question of the motive." Stoudmann accepts the story of Belshaw's liaison with Wilson, but disputes the prosecution's logic in finding in it a motive for murder. "He always admitted that he had had an affair with Mrs. Wilson," Stoudmann reminds them. "But how could it matter enough to be a motive when it meant so little to the two involved in it? How could it precipitate such a violent action when it played such a small part in the lives of both of the lovers?" Stoudmann discusses again the picture of Betty's personality. He reminds the tribunal that Adrian had said he was "traumatized" by a violent fight in the sixties. The incident stood out in Adrian's mind, only because it was so *rare*, Stoudmann tells them. The woman portrayed by all the depositions before the court could not have played the part for which the prosecution has cast her.

Stoudmann continues. "To accept the prosecution's case we must accept so many unproven hypotheses. Look at Professor Belshaw. Can you see this frail little man overpowering his wife, strangling her, dragging her body through the snow? Have you seen the size of his little hands?

"No, there is just too much to accept. In order to go along with the prosecution we must believe so much that is not proven: one, that Mrs. Belshaw knew of the affair; two, that she would have reacted in a violent way; three, that he would have then responded violently himself. After all, is it not more natural that when spouses argue they forgive one another, or they divorce? Yet it is suggested that he preferred to kill his wife rather than to divorce her!''

"As for the other evidence, there are the incidents which took place at the Firths'. On the Belshaws' first visit, the bed broke. During that stay, the Firths were not present, they had lent their apartment to the Belshaws. And in any case, what does this prove? As for the second stay, it is perhaps being suggested that Betty's long sleep was caused by her husband's having drugged her. Yet let us not forget, she herself explained the matter by saying she had been tired out from a heavy work-load. 'I was very tired,' she wrote to a friend in a letter, 'but now I am well again.'

"As for the other evidence—on the 30th of December Adrian and his girlfriend left Montana. On the 2nd of January Betty wrote to Diana, and continued the letter on the 3rd of January, so we know she was alive then. On the 7th of January the optician cashed a cheque for 900 francs for two pairs of glasses. The optician has said she *must* have been there then, so we can be virtually certain she was.

"Remember that the trip to Paris had been planned in advance. On the 7th Belshaw telephoned the Motel PLM at Beaune and the Novotel in Bagnolet to make his reservations for a week later. If he had killed his wife, why would he not have gone to Paris right away?

"I can believe that this man could have deceived the *juges,* the lawyers, and so on, but his children? It's absolutely monstrous!''

Stoudmann then goes over the evidence concerning Belshaw's car. He reminds the tribunal that it was covered with snow, whose depth proved the car had not been moved, and the battery had gone dead. It had to be started by a mechanic on the 11th, and thus could not have moved between the 4th and the 11th. This evidence, accepted by both prosecution and defence, is one of the few absolutely concrete facts on which all suppositions about Belshaw's activities during this period must be based. Stoudmann makes the most of this, and the jurors look thoughtful. Stoudmann hammers home the point. "If he had killed her before the 11th of January, he could not have moved the body in the car. And after that it was at the garage, till the 12th.

"If he did it on the 12th, he must have moved the body during the day. Certainly most unlikely. If not, then on the evening of the 12th. But if he moved it in the evening, where did he get the garbage bags? He would have had to go and get the bags the next day, and again find himself in the situation of moving the body during daylight.

"So we come irrevocably to this. We are obliged to imagine this little man carrying this five-foot six, 145-pound burden to the elevator, across the hall, out onto the roadway—eighty metres—on a Friday or Saturday night. Or he would have had to carry her over the one-metre-high wall of snow between the Jolilac apartment and the Bellevue apartment building next door. He would have had to be an alpinist to get the body over this wall of snow. This is an absolute impossibility in the prosecution's case!" Belshaw smiles fleetingly as Stoudmann calls him an alpinist then, quickly, his habitual expression of reserve returns as Stoudmann continues to make his point. "And *Messieurs*, look at those little hands!"

Stoudmann refers only briefly to the prosecution's contention that Betty was never on the trip to Paris. He reminds the tribunal that he himself retraced that journey with a picture of Cyril, as well as one of Betty, which he showed to the hoteliers and restauranteurs of Beaune. *Neither* had been remembered. So what did it signify if no one had remembered seeing Betty?

"If Cyril Belshaw were the Machiavelli he has been painted he would have reported Betty missing at a more opportune time—not reported her as having disappeared from the subway. He could have just as easily claimed she disappeared in the morning."

Turning to the prosecutor's closing remarks about Diana's finding her mother's soiled lingerie in the suitcases, and his statements about the difficulties with Diana's evidence, Stoudmann is scathing. After all, it is the prosecutor's fault if he or the investigators did not ask this question before. Does the prosecutor think that Belshaw is so diabolical, so Machiavellian as to have put the soiled lingerie there himself, for his daughter to find?

Stoudmann pauses and surveys the tribunal. Then gathering himself together he launches into his final plea.

"Who killed Betty Belshaw? Let us remember, that is not the question we must resolve.

"Did Cyril Belshaw kill Betty? To answer this, we must discover if there is enough proof, or if there is not. And when we consider this, we are faced with an absurdity: we do not even know enough about how she was killed to know if it was manslaughter or murder!

M. le Président, Mm. les juges, Mm. les jurés, in the end, when the prosecutor demands that you have the courage to convict, he demands something monstrous; he demands that you have the courage to err, to convict an innocent man! The spectre of a miscarriage of justice has not been mentioned until now because it has haunted this trial all along.

"There is no question of doubt...it is a question of a lack of certitude."

After discussing at some length the question of doubt, Stoudmann concludes, "The *affaire Belshaw* gives you an exemplary role as jurors. This is not, as is so often the case, a question of law or a judicial question. No, today your role is paramount. You are equal in weight to the judges and the president. Reflection, honesty, conscientiousness—these are human qualities which have nothing to do with law or knowledge of the law, but with you as human beings. At the very least, you must give Cyril Belshaw the bitter victory of an aquittal by reason of doubt. No matter what happens, Professor Belshaw will never be able to live as before, a weight of doubt and suspicion will be with him always. For in that sense, it is true that justice never relinquishes its victims intact.

"If you are honest, it is impossible to reach the conclusion that Cyril Belshaw killed his wife. And your conclusion must be one of superior quality: reasoned, complete, and one that precludes all risk of error.

"Remember, it is not enough that it is possible, even very probable—that is not enough to convict. There must be complete certitude; all doubts of his innocence must be completely banished from your mind. And so you cannot, you ought not to convict. Because no one knows how, when or why."

Stoudmann goes on to remind them of cases with much more evidence where mistakes were made. Again he reminds them of the manner of the disposal of the body, a thing which was completely alien to Cyril Belshaw's character. "You have seen, that is not Cyril Belshaw!

"*M. le Président, Mm. les juges, Mm. les jurés,* true courage is to admit the inexplicable. How was she killed? One day the murderer may be known and you will be relieved—and proud—to have acquitted Cyril Belshaw.''

There is a sigh as Stoudmann finishes. Admiration for his eloquence, particularly as he turned the tables on the *procureur-générale* with his final words about courage. There is a sense of a great five-act drama being played out. Not a cue has been missed, and it is as if the curtain has just come down on a magnificent fourth act. Each of the three men has risen to their roles. There was the *procureur-générale*, in an address which the press will call ''one of the finest in his career'', drawing together all the varied and confusing points brought out by the president on the first day, and creating vivid and living images of a story which his forensic skill made seem as real as fact. There was Paschoud, calling himself ''just a little lawyer who speaks from the heart'', giving the human dimension and breaking the oratorical spell of the prosecutor. And finally there was the eloquence and logic of Stoudmann, showing up the holes, the ambiguities and the weaknesses of the case for the prosecution.

The president calls a recess for the lawyers to prepare their rebuttals. As Heim comes out of the courtroom and crosses the foyer he waves at the journalists whom he has come to know in the last three days. ''A difficult case.'' He raises an admonitory finger. ''The most difficult case I have seen in my thirty years as a prosecutor. He's so very strong, this little man. Never have I seen such self-control!''

Then the recess is over. The spectators return, the tension is still high, the packed courtroom silent, as the president calls the courtroom to order.

First it is the prosecutor's turn. He has assembled a stack of books, judicial authorities, to dispute the learned claim of Stoudmann in regard to the charge of *faux dans les titres*. He disputes the idea that the falsification is not illegal. It relates to the ''establishment of a fact'', he tells the tribunal, and the dental chart is the thing which proves the fact.

He then turns to the point which has been made by both Paschoud and Stoudmann about rigor mortis. He explains that rigor mortis is cyclic, and says the protestations of the defence that it would have prevented Belshaw from putting the body in the trunk of the car are meaningless.

Then he has a word to say in defence of the police. Speaking with passion he tells the tribunal, "We cannot hold it against the police that they acted differently in an Anglo-Saxon country, in a different language, thousands of miles away from home. They are good, honest policemen, and I want to state this publicly."

Finally Heim returns to his contention that Belshaw knew that the Le Sépey Corpse was his wife's when he falsified the dental records. If he were really afraid to face the possibility of his wife's body being identified, he would not have provided the police with an excellent colour photograph. Yet he did this. He knew it was safe to do so, Heim insists, because he knew about the Le Sépey Corpse and so knew that a photograph would be of no use in identifying it.

The defence now has its turn in rebuttal. They have only a few minor points to make. Paschoud tells the jurors that when he went home to lunch, he asked his wife how many gold crowns he had, and she didn't know. Jokingly, he tells the jurors that when one kisses, one closes one's eyes. Then, with a smile, he turns the case back to the president.

And so, finally, according to the law of Vaud, the president gives Belshaw the last word.

He stands, controlling his voice with an effort, his back straight as a soldier's, as he says to the tribunal: "I loved my wife and I still love my wife. I have not committed murder. I have not hurt my wife. I could not do such a thing, I am not capable of such a thing." Then stumbling slightly over his words, his voice breaking, he says, "I am in your hands."

The trial is over.

In the foyer as the reporters mill around the exhausted lawyers, Margot goes up to Stoudmann.

"I really admire what you have done," he tells him.

"Really?" responds Stoudmann. "I find that very surprising."

"Yes, really, you did an excellent job."

They shake hands, Stoudmann looking surprised, and Margot adds, "As I told the prosecutor last night, I could accept an acquittal with total serenity."

The two men go out into the snowy night together.

PART SEVEN
JUDGEMENT

31

As the spectators, journalists and lawyers leave the courtroom on the afternoon of Friday December 5th, there are lights burning in the *Hôtel de Ville*. The journalists walking along the snowy streets stare up at two windows, brightly lit against the falling snow. That is where the tribunal is now, debating the fate of Cyril Belshaw.

By law, the tribunal must meet immediately after the adjournment of the trial and deliberate without stop until they reach a verdict. There are provisions made for them to continue the next day, but according to the *code* the best procedure is for them to render their verdict immediately after the trial.

The manner of their deliberations is set out by the *code de procedure pénale de Vaud*. They will each speak in turn, the president will speak last, and when everyone who wishes to speak has had their say, they will vote. A president such as Guignard who has strong views, who has studied the dossier intensively, who has years of experience on the criminal bench, will surely carry weight with the two *juges* and the jurors. But in the end it is assumed that they will, as good Vaudois, conscious of their heavy responsibility, vote according to their consciences.

The tribunal of Aigle finishes its deliberations by 9:30 that night. It is a long and difficult ordeal, but they are able to reach their verdict that day. By Monday the 8th, the president has rendered their decision in writing and has had it typed. They assemble and read over the judgement, to be sure they are in accord.

And so, as scheduled, 5:00 p.m. Monday the 8th, the court reconvenes for the reading of the judgement.

This time the courtroom is really packed. Not only have chairs been placed in the aisles and at the back but people are standing in the rear of the room. Diana, sitting between Adrian and the Scotts clutches her brother's arm; her face is pale, betraying her anxiety. Adrian is expressionless. McLaughlin looks extraordinarily nervous. The jurors sitting at their bench have a sombre air and the atmosphere in the courtroom is unbearably tense. When Belshaw comes in he nods to the jurors, but they do not look at him. There is a long silence, then the president begins to read.

"Deliberating immediately, in secret, the tribunal renders its judgement, then disperses at 21:30 to permit it to be typed.

"The judgement is as follows:

"*1. The facts:*

"1) The accused was born the oldest of a family of two children. His father was a professor of political economy in New Zealand and his mother was a nurse. The accused was born in 1921 and carried out his studies in his native country, finishing them in London with a doctorate in social anthropology. He went to Canberra, Australia to live in 1949; after 1953 he carried on his career as *professeur* in Vancouver. He travelled to Switzerland in 1966, 1972 and 1973 for the purpose of research and established himself in Montana for one year. He is intelligent, ambitious, proud, calm and reserved at the social level, not without humour and imagination, a poet at times, but very conventional in the conduct of his private and professional life.

"His wife Betty, also a teacher at the University of British Columbia, at Vancouver, was of a lively nature, expansive, warm and sensitive in all her personal relations, very attached to principles, rather dependent, and particularly faithful to her husband.

"The Belshaws were a united couple and, leaving aside some unimportant incidents, showed to others a united front. It is true that at times the accused had affairs, notably a liaison which he carried on with a professional acquaintance and neighbour, Mrs. Wilson, the wife of a professional man.

"2) The couple took a sabbatical holiday in 1978. The accused first left Canada, by plane, at the end of May 1978, taking possession of his Citroën-Maserati at La Haye, and driving from there to Montana. He reserved an apartment in the Chalet "Mischabels" and he stayed there in June 1978. It was there that Mrs. Wilson, who was staying in Denmark at the time, telephoned to relate an incident, and the accused invited her to spend a week with him at Montana, where she lived as his companion and mistress. On June 22nd, 1978, in the company of Mrs. Wilson, he reserved an apartment in the Jolilac apartment building which he rented for six months thus providing for the arrival of his wife. The same day the accused, in the company of Mrs. Wilson, travelled to Paris. The couple stayed the 22nd at Ferney-Voltaire, then the 23rd to the 26th at Paris, whence Mrs. Wilson took an airplane to return to Vancouver.

"Betty Belshaw arrived in Europe at the end of September and the couple first spent some time in England with friends, the Firths, who gave them the use of their cottage in Dorset from the 1st to the 4th of October, and then on the 19th to the 20th of November. The Belshaws seem also to have spent several days in London where the Firths resided.

"Towards the 20th of November the accused had a slight car accident in the English countryside, which seemed to trigger a bizarre state in Mrs. Belshaw, who slept practically a whole weekend, waking only once for breakfast.

"3) The couple arrived by road on November 29th, 1978 in Montana. The accused was to attend a conference in New Delhi, and left for this destination on December 8th, returning on the 20th. On December 22nd Adrian Belshaw, accompanied by a girlfriend, came and stayed with his parents until the 31st, when he left by train for Paris. The Belshaws made plans, at this time, to make a short stay in Paris in mid-January 1979; Betty Belshaw wished to obtain certain information from the Bibliothèque Nationale about the writer Katherine Mansfield with a view to writing a book on this subject. For his part, the accused was working on a comparative study of Swiss and Canadian political systems. The family atmosphere was gay and warm during the holiday, but Betty Belshaw was sad to part from her son on the evening of December 31st.

"4) On the 11th January, 1979 the accused was obliged to have his car looked after. It had been snowed in and would not start; and he was not able to take possession of it until the morning of the

12th. According to the accused, the couple left Montana on January 13th in the morning, and stopped at Geneva to dine at the Möwenpick restaurant. They stayed the night of the 13th at the Relais du PLM in Beaune, where the accused wrote on the registration form of the hotel the first name of his wife, although later no one could remember seeing her. The next day they set out for Paris, according to the accused, and checked in to the Novotel Bagnolet the same evening. There again the accused wrote down his wife's first name on the registration form, but no one was able to remember her. Belshaw explained that they took the Métro the next morning, January 15th, and that they separated at the Bourse station, the accused continuing by Métro while Betty was to traverse some 200 metres in order to reach the principal entrance of the Bibliothèque Nationale. They had arranged to meet for an aperitif at the pub of the Galleries Lafayette and the accused was on his way directly to that neighbourhood. Mrs. Belshaw never arrived at the rendezvous, and not a trace of her could be found at the Bibliothèque Nationale, where she had not signed in. The accused would have then gone there, and would have discovered this troubling fact and returned to the hotel by Métro. There, no one had seen Mrs. Belshaw. The accused then went to the *Commissariat de Police*, and very calmly told his story, giving a detailed description of Betty's clothes and personal effects. He returned to his hotel, and early the next morning went to the Canadian Embassy, where he was received by the Canadian Consul, Mr. Nasrallah. It is striking to note that the accused revealed neither at the *Commissariat* on the 15th and 16th of January, nor when he visited Consul Nasrallah on the 16th, that the couple was staying for six months in Montana from November 29th, 1978. The same day the accused telephoned his children to tell them the news.''

The courtroom is hushed as they hear Belshaw's side of the story treated so harshly.

''On the 17th, the accused brought a letter of thanks to the consulate. In it he gave his address in Montana after the 18th of January. He left that day for Montana, stopping the night at the Motel St.-Christophe at Bex. Having arrived in Switzerland on January 19th, the accused did not notify the police of our country of Betty's disappearance.''

As the president reads out this fact, the mood in the courtroom, which has been growing increasingly tense, darkens. The defence had certainly thought that they had explained this fact, yet here it reappears in the judgement. An ominous note.

The president continues. "It is only later that the accused will propose to Consul Nasrallah that he ask the Swiss and English police to intervene in the affair, and it is thanks to a favour of a high-level federal civil servant that Betty's disappearance will be communicated to Switzerland by telex on February 19th and March 22nd, 1979. The accused did not even contact the Valaisian police to enquire about the nature and the result of the searches undertaken, although he constantly affirmed that he believed at that time that Nasrallah had done what was necessary.

"5) The accused was interested in the Swiss press, for professional reasons according to himself. It is known that he was a subscriber to the Valaisian *Nouveliiste* until February 28th, 1979. It is not impossible that he received this daily after this expiry date, as is the general rule when a subscriber does not renew his subscription, but this fact has not been proven." A small note for the defence here but the points on the other side are beginning to mount up.

"On March 29th, 1979, the *Nouvelliste* published a notice announcing the discovery, on the 28th, of the body of a woman on a slope below a lay-by on the Les Ormonts road, just past the Larrevoin bridge. The notice stated that the body was naked, wrapped in dark grey plastic garbage bags, that identification was difficult, and that the corpse appeared to be that of a woman of between thirty and forty years of age, about 167 centimetres in height, with lightish hair, well-cared for teeth, four gold crowns and a slight overlap of the incisors. The accused affirms that he never saw this notice."

The jurors have become flushed. They still do not look at Belshaw.

"He left the next day, March 30th, for London, with the intention of giving a lecture at York in the beginning of April. On the 31st he met the Firths, but did not speak with them of the accident and Betty's subsequent sleep.

"On April 2nd, he went to the Salvation Army, and thinking to profit from the enormous experience of this organization in finding missing persons, told Major Smith about Betty's disappearance in

Paris, again without mentioning the stay of the couple at Montana, which he did, however, indicate as his address.

"6) On March 28th, the body of a woman in a state of decomposition was discovered by chance several metres down the slope from the lay-by described above, among the refuse thrown into the forest by drivers. It was wrapped in three dark grey plastic bags, of the 65-litre size, held in place by twine knotted like shoelaces. The body was entirely undressed and stripped of all identifying jewelry. These plastic bags, made in Switzerland, were on the market from December 1978 on, and the accused admitted to having bought some, but of a smaller size, in several large department stores. The police undertook an investigation and established a possible relationship between this body and Mrs. Belshaw, whose disappearance had been announced by two telex messages, on February 19th and March 22nd, 1979. On April 13th Inspector Reichen of the Valaisian *police de sûreté,* accompanied by a Vaudois inspector, paid a visit to the accused at Montana, where they learned the circumstances of the disappearance. They asked the accused to provide them with Betty's dental chart, or to give them the name and address of the dentist. The inspectors in no way suspected the accused, who could not have considered himself threatened. Belshaw told them that he would provide this dental chart for them, and gave them a photograph of Betty.

"The same day, the accused wrote a letter, which he mailed on April 14th, to his wife's dentist in Vancouver, Dr. Nishiguchi, in which he said that large-scale searches were being made, but without success, by several police forces and other agencies, and that one of these thought that a copy of a dental schema would help in their enquiries. Therefore he was writing to see if one, or if possible, two, of the dental charts of his wife could be provided. "As the usefulness of this is highly speculative," he added, "and the implications rather disturbing, I would be grateful if this could be handled personally and confidentially." On the 14th the accused also wrote to his daughter Diana: "Two fellows from the *sûreté* at Sierre came here yesterday afternoon. They had telephoned the morning of Good Friday. They spoke as if they were asking questions for the first time, in a very pleasant way. But I found out that they were informed since January 27th and they have taken this initiative only now. They insisted upon Mommy's dental chart to 'complete the dossier'. Naturally I have written for it (but not tele-graphed as that would have made too much talk). In my opinion, they were trying to verify something, and didn't want to tell me without being certain about it. I think they must be reasonably certain, or they wouldn't have gone so far. So, I try to take courage, to have patience, and to occupy myself with the identification, the requests, and all the official complications. Naturally it could be nothing but a false alarm, but the system seems finally to be getting going on its own.''

"On May 2nd Dr. Nishiguchi wrote to the accused a typewritten letter which was in the form of a certificate stating that Betty had been his patient for thirteen years, and giving a precise list of the work which had been done on her teeth. A postscript stated that a copy of all the x-rays taken of the mouth would follow shortly. The letter was accompanied by a small dental chart dated and signed by the dentist, Nishiguchi, which he had made out in ball-point pen on a blank printed form.

"As the accused was to leave in mid-May for London, he wired Nishiguchi, asking him to mail the x-rays after May 3rd to him care of the Institute of Anthropology in London. He also telephoned the dentist to inform him that he could expect this request. He wrote, finally, on May 3rd, a letter to Diana where he revealed that he had telephoned Nishiguchi at 8:30, asking him to send the charts im-mediately, the x-rays could follow, and stating that Nishiguchi had promised him to mail the first 'today'. The letter added 'They are going to arrive just before I leave. If necessary I will wait a day or two. If I hadn't called ... I felt much better afterwards ....'

"Having meanwhile received the dental charts, the accused de-posed a falsified copy on May 9th at Sierre police station. He disposed of the accompanying certificate.

"7) The accused proceeded as follows. First he covered up a certain number of indications of real work with white ink, then drew in marks of imaginary work on certain teeth, then made five photo-copies of the falsified dental record; he sent one to the Swiss police, another to Paris, and the third to London. The two last were put into a file which the accused began on January 19th in Montana, on his return from Paris.

"When the falsification was discovered, and this fact was re-vealed to him, the accused made a declaration to the Canadian police on August 14th wherein he admitted the falsification. Throughout the entire inquiry and trial, the accused explained this operation by his incapacity to bear the psychological trauma which would arise from an identification when he was far from the presence of family and friends. He expressed, moreover, his inner refusal to accept the idea of Betty's death.

"8) Dr. Imobersteg, the legal dentist consulted by the investigators upon the discovery of the corpse, entertained the first suspicions. He was uneasy over the falsified dental charts and the police asked the Canadian police to procure them more precise data directly from Dr. Nishiguchi via Interpol. Constable Smith then telephoned the accused, who was at that time in Vancouver, to obtain the name and address of the dentist. He then made contact with the latter, obtained the original material and so informed the accused, who then avowed his falsification on the following day.

"Under a *commission rogatoire* of the magistrate charged with the inquiry, two agents of the Swiss *sûreté* went to Canada, obtained the assistance of the Vancouver police, and were able to meet with the accused at his home. Conforming to a technique which is customary under the Canadian judicial system, the Canadian police taped the conversation with Belshaw, the Swiss police not having raised any objection. The material from this tape has been removed from the dossier of the tribunal at the request of the defence.

"In Vancouver, the accused refused under various pretexts to explain himself, although he was unaware that the interview had been taped.

"On July 19th, 1979 the accused was surprised in Mrs. Wilson's car, in a dark secluded spot, by a police officer who recorded the observations he made by the light of his headlights and flashlight. He discovered the couple in an equivocal position and dress. Interrogated separately, but after having talked with one another, the two partners denied that they maintained a liaison, but finally admitted it, complete with precise details.

"Now in possession of authentic documents Dr. Imobersteg was able to formally identify the corpse of March 28th as Mrs. Betty Belshaw, in a report of September 20th, 1979.

"9) The investigators learned that the accused intended to participate in an anthropology conference on the 11th of November, in Paris. An international order of arrest was issued on the 7th, and carried out on the 11th when the accused left the airplane. He was extradited on the 1st of February 1980. He has been in preventive detention for 394 days. "The accused was regularly interrogated twenty times. He steadfastly denied any participation whatsoever in the death of his wife and her transport to Larrevoin. From the beginning to the end he has declared to everyone that his wife suffered from depression and amnesia, in the years preceding her death, which has not been verified. The accused advanced no hypothesis, either reasonable or irrational, for Betty's disappearance. Nor has he explained why he suppressed the certificate which Dr. Nishiguchi sent to accompany the dental record."

The president has been reading the judgement in the same rapid-fire delivery he had used at the beginning of the case for the reading of the *pièces*. Now his voice slows, and his words weigh more heavily. The atmosphere in the courtroom, already dark, becomes increasingly ominous as he reads on.

"*2. Discussion and law*.

"The accused explains his falsification of the dental record by his inability to bear the psychological trauma of an identification procedure. This thesis is absolutely contradicted by the following arguments:

"*One*. In Paris on January 15th, 16th, then later elsewhere, the accused gave a detailed description of the clothes and underclothes which Betty was wearing at the time her disappearance was announced, the 15th of January. He gave the investigators a recent photograph of the victim. Such comportment would lead, in the case of a discovery of a body which was still clothed and wearing jewelry, to an almost certain identification.

"*Two*. The accused was not asked to personally identify a body in a morgue but to provide a way of decisively and scientifically identifying a body, according to a procedure which would be well known to a man of science such as the accused.

"*Three*. Any man endowed with a normal sensitivity and the elementary moral level of a palaeolithic man would not accept that a being dear to him, thrown down a slope among garbage, be deprived of a decent resting place and remain forever anonymous.

"The contradictory attitude of the accused, logically inexplicable and morally shocking, incurred upon him an enormous presumption of guilt which justified the opening of the inquiry and its being remitted to the tribunal. Certainly, the system of the freedom of conviction of the magistrate imposed on the cantons by article 249 of the PPF does not require that the accusation prove all the material circumstances of the infraction; the conviction of the tribunal can be based on the exterior circumstances of fact of the act itself, on the objective or subjective level. In criminal law, as in the civil law, when from all the evidence neither a positive or negative proof can be advanced by the accused or the defence, the latter must accept the legitimate obligation to contribute to establishing the facts, and to collaborate in the advancing of the necessary evidence.''

The courtroom, following the argument which seems to be leading inexorably, ominously towards Belshaw's guilt now, suddenly, hears it shift.

"In this case, an analysis of the facts and their interpretation is confronted with the obstacle of the foreign nature—to our mentality—of the character of the accused and his conceptions of justice, founded on the Anglo-Saxon law. So, an absolute conviction of guilt, with the severe consequences which would flow from it, in the presence of the constant and firm denials—however suspect these may be à propos of major and immediate facts—is confronted by a very light doubt. In consequence, the tribunal refuses to find the accused guilty of murder, although it is convinced of disloyal and morally shocking manoeuvres.''

There is an exhalation of withheld breath in the courtroom. It is as if a balloon, blown up larger and larger, its skin stretched to its limit by the force of the air, seems about to burst with an unbearable explosion. Suddenly, the air is let out instead and the balloon deflates.

The judge continues.

"3. Cyril Belshaw is further accused of faux dans les titres, falsification of evidence.''

He goes on to recapitulate the argument made by Stoudmann on this point and concludes:

"The false dental chart created and utilized by the accused therefore does not constitute a title, a piece of evidence, in the sense of article 110, chapter 5 and article 251 of the penal code. It is of little importance that this dental chart was sufficient to identify the victim with all the juridical consequences of such a proof.

"4. Court costs come to 34,791.75 francs. At the end of a proceeding conducted with means proportionate to the accusation weighing upon Belshaw, conducted with diligence, founded essentially on the methods which conform to our law, carried out at its first stage in a perfectly correct way by the police, the accused is freed by the benefit of a very light doubt on the accusation of murder and acquitted for evident juridical reasons on the charge of *faux dans les titres.*" At this Belshaw nods his head slightly. His face is immobile. "For this last reason, alone, a part of the costs will be left to the State. On the other hand, the accused provoked the opening of the inquiry by his comportment from his first contact with the police. He alone must take the responsibility for a relatively short detention, considering the extreme complexity imposed by his attitude and his refusal to come before Swiss justice. It is thus equitable that he pay the major part of the costs, which the tribunal sets at 30,000 francs.

"5. The presumption of innocence from which every accused benefits until judgement is reinforced by the decision of the tribunal, even if it is not yet final and executed. In the absence of a specific request from the *Ministère-Public,* it appears thus in conformance with the basic principles of modern law to order the release of the accused, his detention being no longer justified by any legal cause.

"For these reasons the tribunal, applying articles 157 and 158 of the *code de procedure pénale:*

"*One:* frees the accused Cyril Shirley Belshaw from further penal pursuit;

"*Two:* orders him to pay the court costs to the sum of 30,000 francs, the balance to be borne by the State;

"*Three:* orders the immediate release of Cyril Shirley Belshaw."

The president rises and leaves the bench. There is a stunned silence. Belshaw stands, looking bewildered. From the audience, Mrs. Scott's small, well-bred voice can be heard asking desperately in English, "What does it mean? What does it mean?"

32

After the first silence, there is a babble of voices in the courtroom. Diana is gasping, as if she cannot catch her breath; racked with dry sobs, she clutches Adrian's arm. Someone is patiently explaining the verdict to the Burridges and the Scotts, who look more and more bewildered. Mrs. Scott says, "Does it mean we won?" Finally understanding that Cyril is free, she hugs Diana with joy. McLaughlin is ebullient. "Maybe I was wrong. It's not like our system, but it works for them."

Reporters and spectators hurry out of the courtroom. Now, from the small waiting-room where Belshaw is being reunited with family and friends they can hear happy laughter, and cries of congratulations. Outside, the photographers cluster.

Paschoud is furious when he sees them. Perhaps he is feeling a let-down, for he had surely hoped for a pure not-guilty verdict, and he must be finding not-guilty-by-reason-of-doubt a bitter victory indeed. He stands between the photographers and the door to the little room where Belshaw and his family are having their reunion. "Don't take his picture," he cries out to him. "Let him go. He is a man like you, you know! He is a free man!" But the photographers ignore him. Their eyes are concentrated on the door, and they seem not to hear. Finally Belshaw emerges into a flurry of flashbulbs and hurries from the courtroom, stopping briefly to say to reporters that he is too emotional to talk.

Diana, detained by friends and well-wishers, tells the reporters that she is very happy and that they will all be going away somewhere together, right away.

Reporters are rushing around trying to talk to everyone at once. Heim is explaining the verdict to confused reporters. He agrees it is peculiar that the judgement did not go into some of the reasons which contributed to the tribunal's doubt. He cites the long drive between Montana and Le Sépey, the difficulty of moving the body from the apartment to the car, the used lingerie Diana had found as being, most likely, the things which created the doubt. "His behaviour," Heim explains, "would have been cause for suspicion in a Swiss, but it was proper behaviour for an Anglo-Saxon. If he had been Swiss, he would have been condemned.'' In response to a question about the significance of the verdict, Heim explains, ''He got off by the skin of his teeth. But the verdict will leave a stain forever.'' Heim is happy with the verdict. ''It gives a good idea of Swiss justice,'' he says.

A written version of the judgement is now given to the reporters. As they read it over, they see that the preponderance of evidence of apparent guilt in the judgement makes the verdict all the more unexpected.

A reasoned argument in print over the Belshaw judgement is impossible. The laws of libel prevent an observer from postulating a case for Belshaw as guilty, or putting up a case for his innocence. And even the right of fair comment, which is interpreted so broadly in the United States, must be considered in the light of the procedures of the Swiss court, where the press hears evidence which is hearsay, or totally unsubstantiated. There is a delicate balance between the proper consideration of truth in a matter of public interest, and the protection of the rights of a man who has been acquitted, who is now, as Paschoud so passionately said, a free man.

But the Belshaw case raises profound questions, questions which go beyond the sensational interest of the moment, and reach into the fundamental concepts of justice, and of truth itself.

As Inspector Margot and the *procureur-générale* Willy Heim said, the Belshaw case was tried primarily on ''psychological evidence''. The tribunal considered the actions of a man after the mysterious death of his wife, judged them, and considered their significance. The judgement stated that in view of Belshaw's behaviour there was an enormous presumption of guilt. Faced with this, according to the Swiss idea, it would have been a miscarriage of justice *not* to try the Belshaw case simply because the material evidence was weak. But because the Belshaw case was tried on *immaterial* evidence, it became a question of human nature. It became a matter, as the Swiss press asked so dramatically, of *Who was Betty Belshaw? Who is Cyril Belshaw?* Those questions had to be answered first before the tribunal could evaluate the significance of the actions before them and judge their import.

So in the Belshaw case the stark drama of the law stood out, unencumbered. Truth and Justice, the abstractions that provide play for philosophers and substance for the casual manipulations of politicians, were the central issues which, in the real world, in the courtroom in Vaud, had to be considered, analysed and decided upon while a man's future hung in the balance.

Further, in that courtroom in Switzerland, the drama of justice was played out in a very pure form. For so often in the real world the sides are uneven, the players are handicapped by ineptitude or corruption; or vested interests bend the rules and spoil the purity of the contest.

But in the Belshaw trial this did not happen. Belshaw himself was a man of extraordinary intelligence and strength of will. His defenders, Paschoud and Stoudmann were of the same class as his prosecutors, and they showed, in their defence, the highest standards both human and forensic.

As for the state of Vaud, it too conducted itself according to the rules. Although the defence attacked the behaviour of Fischlin and Wyss, in the end their conduct was outside the main battle. Margot's investigation was impeccable, and the summing up of the prosecutor, Willy Heim, will certainly be remembered as one of the great moments of Swiss trial law. From many fragments he created a plausible, conceivable reality to put in the balance against the presumption of innocence.

Is the Belshaw case really the enigma that Stoudmann so ably characterized in his *plaidoirie*? Or is it not possible, by putting together all the small pieces of the investigation, to build a logical chain, link by link, and come, inexorably, to a conclusion about the guilt or innocence of Belshaw?

It must be remembered that whoever murdered Betty Belshaw did more than commit a crime, perhaps involuntarily, or on a sudden uncontrollable impulse. They committed a cruel and horrible desecration upon the body of a woman to whom appearance and propriety were everything. And however it began, the last act of Betty Belshaw's murder was carried out with cold-blooded planning and calculation.

No observer of the trial can now fairly or legally speculate about the correctness of the verdict in print, even if their conclusion were to be that Belshaw was absolutely innocent. But readers, apprised of the facts, can weigh the information put before the criminal tribunal of Aigle and draw their own conclusions. As in a classic murder mystery, you, the reader, have reached the last chapter. You have the threads in your hands. You have, as the prosecutor told the tribunal, your experience of life and your own understanding of human psychology. You will come to your own verdict.

And when you consider the conclusion of the tribunal of Aigle, that self-characterized group of petit-bourgeois from the small agricultural community in the Suisse Romande, a community of men whose ancestors had fought hard for their liberties, and who prize them now, you will see a subtlety, a compassion, a breadth of understanding that speaks very well for the human condition.

These men judged Belshaw and they tried mightily to understand him. They pondered where the truth lay. They considered the requirements of justice. They gave him the benefit of the doubt.